ROUGH ROAD HOME

Also by Melissa Mather
Damian (novel), New York, 1986.
Emelie, New York, 1982.
One Summer In Between, New York, 1967.

ROUGH ROAD HOME

MELISSA MATHER

Paul S. Eriksson, *Publisher*
Middlebury,   Vermont

Manufactured in the United States of America

Library of Congress Cataloging-in-Publication Data

Mather, Melissa.
   Rough road home.

   Reprint. Originally published: 1st ed. Philadelphia :
Lippincott, 1958.
   1. Vermont--Social life and customs. 2. Mather,
Melissa. 3. Vermont--Biography. I. Title.
F54.M38 1986   974.3   86-19774
ISBN 0-8397-7236-X

To Longin

who kept us going

ROUGH ROAD HOME

CHAPTER I

We live in Vermont, and thereby hangs this tale.

Sometimes I'm asked when we're going to move back to the United States. I couldn't be more there right now, I say. Well, then, what are you doing here in Vermont? I'm asked. Not, of course, by native Vermonters. It's only folks so unfortunate as not to have been born here who wonder.

I drive down to meet them in Four Corners and I advise them to leave their car in the Woodruffs' lane and let me take them up in the jeep. The jeep has nearly nine inches' clearance, which is none too high to get over the ledges, and it has a number of extra gears with enormous power at low speeds, and four-wheel drive for mud, ice, snow, or fresh gravel, which can act almost like quicksand when it's several inches deep.

"Melissa," my friends gasp as they clutch their elegant handbags and brace themselves when the jeep lurches over the naked rock of the mountain and throbs up the washboard of the steepest hill, "how did you ever find this place? Why did you ever choose Vermont?"

I find the first question vaguely flattering, implying that I must have set out into the wilderness with gun, compass and Bible. "Real estate agent," I replied briefly, putting a Vermont twang to my words. "I told him what I wanted, and he figgered I meant what I said. So he showed me the farm and I bought it."

"Yes, but what did you want?"

What I didn't have, I think. But I don't say so, because it would sound too flip. Nevertheless, it is true. I chose Vermont because, at the time of choosing, which was 1950, I was living in Virginia: Fort Monroe, Virginia.

If you have ever lived on an Army post, especially in the thank-you-Tommy-Atkins-and-the-hell-with-you-now period after World War II, you may know what I mean. Although Bob, my husband, was expecting at any time to be promoted to full colonel, he had been assigned quarters in one-half of a converted mess hall in a group of temporary barracks (temporary after World War I) down by the swamp at the edge of the post. I daresay these quarters might have seemed roomy enough if we had had no children, or a conservative one or two. With four, we were jam-packed in.

There was a kind of living-dining room curled around the furnace room which separated us from the family quartered in the other half of the building. (Bang on the wall. Shout, "Dodie! Dodie Dunn! Come over for coffee!" After we had seen *Born Yesterday*, Dodie and I had a marvelous time standing in our living rooms and braying invitations at each other.) The three bedrooms were excellent for the posture, the narrow passageways between bureaus and beds demanding tummy-tucked-in and seat-sucked-under. Into the largest, the nine-by-twelve, or possibly it was ten-by-thirteen (let's be fair), we crammed two bunk beds and a spare, three inadequate chests of drawers, a bulletin board, and our three boys, the twins, Pat and Mike, age eight, and Chris, bright red hair, age six. Three-year-old Kitty had the smallest bedroom to herself, except when my family visited, and Bob and I stepped over each other's feet in the third. The bathroom literally didn't have floor space to spare for a bathroom scale, and I felt crowded in the kitchen when I was in there alone.

That was it. No storage space, three afterthought closets without doors, and a warning from the fire department to lose no delay in evacuating, in case of fire, because these structures had been known to burn to the ground in six minutes flat.

It would have been easier to accept all this with good grace and sportsmanship if Bob's pay hadn't had deducted precisely the same rental allowance ($125 a month, which was a good deal more money then than it is now) as was deducted from the pay of other officers, no higher ranking than Bob, who had quarters more suitable for their years of service. Fifty dollars would have been high rent for our cracker-box quarters, and we could have used the difference for Mike.

Mike, you see, though eight years old, was unable to talk, and could not, of course, go to school. I tried to keep track of him at all times, but he could vanish, in less than a minute, like a tumbleweed, now here, now gone. As soon as he had slipped from sight, he would get into trouble. He took delight in smashing the glass of the furnace-room doors. When I had swept up the glass, I would call the Post Engineers and ask them to replace it, and to charge it to my husband, and I was invariably treated with kindness and a quiet courtesy, as if it were the most normal thing in the world to have a child smashing glass over and over again. (Post Engineers, I love you.)

Nor could Mike resist bending the extended aerials of car radios, and once he scratched the shiny chrome on the rear-view mirror of a Cadillac. Bob had the aerials repaired, and he replaced the mirror. The time that Mike tossed pebbles into a baby's playpen, had I been the mother of the baby, I too would have been upset and a little frightened. I tried to soothe the mother, and I repeated for the hundred-thousandth time, "Mikey, you must stay in your own yard." And again I resolved, desperately, that somehow I would have to keep a closer watch over him, no matter how the housework piled up, no matter how I neglected the other children.

Some people were human beings, and treated us as if we were, too. But there were others, who couldn't understand why people like us "were allowed . . . you know . . . to live on the post. Wouldn't you think . . . I mean, after *all*—" We knew that for these folk conversation need never drag at Kaffeeklatsch or cocktail party. There was always "the Coughlins' kid" to talk about. We reminded ourselves that these people were the way they were

[11]

because, so far, Life had handled them gently; they didn't know, as those who were kind to us knew, what it was to have a grief without end, for which one was not responsible and before which one was helpless. We reminded ourselves of all this, but it didn't help. We were still agonizingly sensitive—and ashamed of ourselves, when we listened to Pat tell how he had "beat up that kid in the next area who was laughing at Mike. *Laughing* at him, Mother! If he does it again, I'll *kill* him!"

We were even more ashamed of our self-pity when we looked at Mike, such a beautiful child, so apparently perfect, his features delicate, his movements graceful, his eyes, large and dark, so full of loneliness. Unpredictable, moody, subject to fits of violent despair, Mike was the one who suffered, day after empty day.

Of course we looked for help. Whenever we had any money, we took him to another specialist, another clinic, hoping that somewhere, some time, we might find a doctor willing and able to tell us what ailed him. We had been told that he was not cerebral-palsied; that he was, and that he was not, schizophrenic; that he had a very high IQ, that he had a very low IQ, that he had a borderline IQ; that he might be deaf, that he was not deaf; and that he was emotionally ill and must be allowed all possible freedom from restraint. (On an army post!)

Bob and I had reached the point where all we wanted was for two doctors to agree. We got through each day as best we could, and allowed Mike as much freedom as we dared, and rescued him from danger and repaired what damage he did in spite of our vigilance. Each day we looked for any signs of improvement and each day our hearts broke all over again.

And then war broke out in Korea. Officers began leaving for overseas with the suddenness of dry leaves sucked up by an autumn wind. Bob and I agreed I had to find a place of our own to hole up in for the duration. I couldn't go back to my parents this time, as I had in '44, not with Mike as big as he was now, as difficult to handle. I shuddered at the thought of how Mike would disrupt that peaceful suburb, how impossible it would be to keep him from driving the sheltered inhabitants of that modestly elegant neighborhood simply wild.

"It has to be somewhere with no neighbors near by," I said. "I don't want my skin crawling at the thought of strangers gaping at him playing in the mud or with his beloved pebbles."

"Nor any cars," Bob said. "Lord, I wish he would quit wandering blithely out in front of cars."

"It would be nice," I said, "if there were some help, somewhere near. Something that might somehow help him."

"And, of course," Bob added grimly, "it has to be something we can afford."

We knew precisely how much, or how little, we could spend. We had exactly two thousand dollars' worth of war bonds, saved from the money Bob had sent home during World War II. These bonds were supposed to be Mike's grubstake. We had agreed not to touch them until somebody came up with something which would *really* help Mike. No guessing, no experimenting, no more tentative-diagnosis stuff. We didn't see anything unfair in this for the other children, either. They had spunk, health and brains. Furthermore, if we should be able to rescue Mike from his imprisonment of silence, he would then never be a burden to them, later on.

But this looked like one of those emergencies you can't dodge. We decided, reluctantly, that we'd have to use the bonds for a down payment on a house. If something ever did turn up that might cure Mike, we'd figure how to finance it then.

"Money you can always manage somehow," I said, "as long as you have spunk, health and brains."

"God will provide," said Bob cheerfully, and sat down to write an advertisement in the Richmond *Times-Dispatch*.

Army officer seeks modest country home or small farm in Virginia.

He mentioned Virginia because we thought it a good idea to be within driving distance of the University in Charlottesville, where there was one of the best speech clinics in the country. The phrases "Army officer," "modest," and "small," we thought would

[13]

eliminate a lot of offerings which would be way beyond our two-thousand-dollar down payment and our top of a hundred dollars a month for payments on the mortgage, plus all the other et ceteras so destructive of a home owner's budget.

If you are ever dissatisfied with the amount of your mail, put a little ad in the paper—don't worry how obscure it may be—that you want to buy a place in the country. Stand by for a snowstorm of replies.

We got enormous, slick-paper, four-color advertisements for brick mansions, genuine early Georgian style, two hundred acres of land, a gift at $125,000, taxes sixty-three dollars a year (a clue to the condition of Virginia's public schools, though I didn't recognize the symptom then), fully modernized, a staff of four could keep the colonel comfortable. We got quite a stack of these. Everybody in Virginia seemed to be trying to sell Great-grand-pappy's home.

Were we interested in a ten-thousand-acre hunting preserve? No price mentioned—come down to Georgia and hunt for a week or two, then make an offer. Practically virgin forest, no buildings marring the peace. . . .

"How can anything be *practically* virgin?" Bob growled, pitching it in the wastebasket.

How about an interesting property on the James River? Brick factory . . . slight modernizing needed . . . sound investment.

"What's the matter with these people?" I snarled. "Can't they read?"

"We should have made things plainer," Bob said. "Something like 'Poverty-stricken soldier with large family wants place to dump them for the duration, no near neighbors.'"

The idea enchanted me. "Oh, let's! Imagine what we'd be offered!"

"Here's a fellow near Charlottesville who sounds businesslike," Bob said, shoving a letter across to me. "And here's another, from Appomattox. Why don't you scout around and see what the possibilities are? You'll have to take Mikey, of course—too bad Longin can't get leave."

[14]

Longin was an honorary member of our family. He was a Polish DP whom Bob had befriended after the war and whom he had helped get a visa and passage to the States. At the moment Longin was "paying us back" by serving with the paratroops at Fort Bragg.

"Would Dad go with you?" Bob went on. "Then if you find something you like, maybe I could grab a day off and take a look at it."

So I wrote my father in New Jersey did he want to come house-hunting in Virginia, and Dad being Dad, he replied of course he did, so off we went.

We looked at houses forty feet from railway tracks, and we looked at houses smack on U.S. Highway 29. "Away from traffic," I reminded the agent gently. So we looked at houses two miles in the pine woods (road to be maintained by home owner). "Small farms" started at twenty thousand. When I finally convinced the agents—and they wouldn't believe me until I had turned down everything else—that I really could not spend over ten thousand and it had to be away from traffic, we were shown a number of ghastly shacks, unpainted, windowless, partially roofless, sagging-porched, rusty-iron-sinked. It is true these were away from traffic ("—no running water, but the power line's only half a mile away—"). It is also true that Mikey, being easier to please than I, found something attractive about each place, a charming piece of loose drainpipe, or an agreeable doorknob that fell off as he approached. I thought them the most expensive firewood I had ever seen.

The agent would say, as he patted the remaining clapboards gently, lest he knock the hovel down, "Now, this is quite a buy at eight thousand!" He would say this enthusiastically.

"Oh, that's ridiculous!"

"Yes, isn't it?" Suavely. "Not many buys like this left in country property."

My father merely cleared his throat, but in an eloquent, my-Scotch-blood-is-boiling, sir! way. The agent would shrug, and lead us to another miserable, abandoned dump.

All of which was why I thought the modest little farm tucked in the bottom of its own saucer-shaped valley much more attractive than it really was. We wouldn't be able to see very far—not more than a hundred yards or so—in any direction, but then, all the land we saw would be ours. The house had been built by the present owner and had some strange construction features, but it also had what seemed to me a simply enormous kitchen, ten feet by fifteen. The house wasn't very large, nor very high off the ground, which was damp, nor very sunny, with all those locust trees peering in the windows, but it would give us a roof over our heads, I pointed out to Bob, and furthermore, though it wasn't exactly under ten thousand, as he had specified, nor was it over.

Bob drove up, inspected the place, and agreed with Dad that we were being robbed but obviously the place was unique, seclusion in the country in Virginia being, everywhere else, either for the very poor or the very rich. So he signed the purchase agreement, into which he had prudently had the clause inserted, "if mortgage arrangements can be made through a bank," and consoled himself with the thought that he could, after all, sell the place as soon as he got back from Korea.

That was in September, 1950. Three weeks later we received word from the agent that no bank would assume a mortgage on the place at the agreed purchase price, and the owner refused to come down. We were not, after all, property owners.

"Maybe it's all for the best," I said bravely. "Maybe I wouldn't have liked living at the bottom of a well."

"Don't waste more time looking in Virginia," Bob said. "Where else are there speech clinics?"

"There's one in Connecticut—"

"We can't afford the country in Connecticut."

"Well, there's sort of a speech clinic in Rutland, Vermont. Children's Rehabilitation Center, I think it's called. Making rather a name for itself, too."

"There's certainly plenty of seclusion in Vermont," Bob remarked, "and probably not too expensive, either. But you've never spent a winter in the North—"

"I have, too," I said. "I spent four winters in Ohio, where the wind comes in off Lake Erie so cold you can't believe it. I never heard of any winter resorts in Ohio but there are lots in Vermont. If people pay good money to go there it can't be too bad."

Using logic like this, Bob and I decided I should go up North and take a look. I got the names of some agents from the Strout Realty catalog and I wrote to them, stating what we wanted as plainly as I could. I sorted through the replies, drew up a loose schedule, wrote back making tentative appointments, wrote Dad to get our bonds out of his safe-deposit box and mail them to us, cashed one for expenses and put the rest optimistically in my purse against the hoped-for down payment, accepted with gratitude Dodie's offer to look after the rest of the family while I was gone, put Mikey in the Chevy, and kissed Bob, Pat, Chris and Kitty good-bye.

My parents—bless them!—thought I'd accomplish more without Mike to look after, so I left him with them in New Jersey and headed north alone.

It was the last week of October. The rolling hills of Virginia had been just beginning to show color, and in New Jersey the oaks flamed red over the neat suburban lawns. As I crossed into Vermont and followed Route 7 northward along the valley floor, I saw I had left autumn far behind. The mountains swelled up on either side, their slopes blackish green where the evergreens grew, and gray where the deciduous trees clung, leafless, motionless, waiting for winter. I began to have a peculiar sensation for which I could not account. I've been here before, I thought, though I knew I hadn't. I feel as if I'm coming home.

I decided I must be drunk on scenery. This intoxication is a definite driving hazard for anyone coming from the flat lowlands, especially those near the sea, where too often the crossroads have a cardboard-and-tin look, and the natural beauty has been eroded by gas pumps, soft-drink and shaving-soap signs. Vermont looked clean, uncluttered, in some indefinable way unfettered, and, though not precisely hospitable, not hostile, either. Here we are, the mountains seemed to say. Remember us? Strangely, I did remember them.

When I reached Rutland, I located the Children's Rehabilitation Center and introduced myself to Harriet Dunn, its director. I explained to Miss Dunn about Mike, and why I was looking for a place to live somewhere near. With the candor of true kindness, Miss Dunn told me that she could not promise that the Center could help Mike until she had seen him, but that she thought it an excellent idea for us to settle in the country. Country people, she went on, are more tolerant, more understanding.

And this, I have found out, is true. I have no way of knowing if it is true of country people everywhere, but it certainly is true of country people in Vermont. I needed, as I have found, people who accept physical differences with an instinctive serenity, based, perhaps, on a belief that we are as God made us and we are not personally to be held responsible if the results sometimes look as if God has a puckish sense of humor and delights in the charm of imperfections. If the difference is so striking as to be tragic, as in Mike's case, why that is the way it happens sometimes, they seem to say, nobody's fault, a shame, though, hard on a family. Perhaps this impersonal acceptance is the result of the generations of farmers' blood in their veins, of knowing how sometimes things go wrong with the calf, no need to blame the cow.

I had been checking with real estate agents as I traveled, and, although I had been shown no $125,000 mansions, and the hovels were priced closer to eight hundred than eight thousand, there was still the same misunderstanding about what I meant when I said no traffic. A blacktop road running right by the front door is an advantage, they said. (Now I know what they mean but I still don't want a blacktop road running right by the front door.) This place is only a tenth of a mile from Route 7, they said. You don't want to live out, a village home is much better. Not to me, I said. I don't want neighbors. They looked puzzled. You always have neighbors, they said. Especially in the country.

So when I happened to see Harold Potwin's sign in Taftsville, and on an impulse stopped, and explained that I wanted a place away from traffic, and he rubbed the stubble on his chin thoughtfully and said how far away from traffic did I have in mind, did I mean to get in and out by dog sled, I had a hunch that I was nearing the end of my quest. I said no, that wouldn't be practical, I had a large family, and he said how large, and I said four children, and he cackled in delight and called to Mrs. Potwin who was sprinkling clothes on the dining-room table, "You hear that, Mama? She says she's got a large family and all she's got is four! Why, we've got fifteen!" To this Mrs. Potwin replied that my four probably seemed as many to me, living where I did, as her fifteen seemed in the country.

"I pity city kids," said Mr. Potwin, shaking his head.

"Why don't you show her that place over in Hartland, Pa? The Ferncliffe place. It's set back nice from the road."

This struck Mr. Potwin as a sound suggestion. We went in Mr. Potwin's Ford, because, he said, it knew the roads better than my Chevy. We came into Hartland Four Corners from the north, along Route 12, which at that time was a dirt road blacktopped only near the villages. From the north I could see the white blur of a church and its spire framed by the curve of the hill beyond, and the birches on the hill and the church in the valley and the meadows stretching to meet us haunt me still. There are places which demand no talent of the painter, only a seeing eye. The composition is already faultless, the symphony of line and color is already there. The scene is so lovely in itself, your fingers ache for a brush and your nostrils long for the reek of turpentine and oil, and in your mind's eye you can see the seductive tiara of paint blobs set out on the palette. Such a scene is the village of Hartland Four Corners from the north, and it haunts me because I still haven't painted it, and probably never shall. By the time I have time, it will be lost, lost behind yet another billboard, or a new line of telephone poles, or a gas station, or a motel. (If you haven't seen Vermont—do hurry.)

Mr. Potwin and I turned west from Four Corners on another unpaved road, and we drove up a narrow valley three or four miles, with the hills on either side crowding closer and closer in, and the road scarcely wide enough for two cars to pass. And then we plunged into a woods, where the hemlocks leaned over the road and the ferns drifted down the steep banks on one side, and the land sheered away on the other so that one little skid would have landed us in the brook that foamed and twisted between the rocks. And then we were at a crossroads and I thought I saw a house on a ridge, and then we went sharp left across a plank bridge with no railing and back up a steep hill and still in the woods, only now there were birches gleaming in the shadows, and oaks with rusty, raggedy leaves clinging. And suddenly there we were, out in the open and nearly to the top. The land fell away in bronze and sulphur curves toward the north, and in a wide sweep there were the hills, ancient and everlasting.

I felt a swelling of emotion. Joy, exulting joy! Lost in the valley are worries and cares, here on the hilltop is only joy, joy to be alive—alive and breathing—

"Isn't it beautiful!" I cried.

Mr. Potwin drove on as if it were nothing at all. I suppose he was used to it.

"Deer up there," he said, pointing across a field towards the south.

I saw the deer browsing along the edge of the woods, and then I caught an impression of a saltbox house, and we passed more fields, and an empty house, and then the road dipped down again, and Mr. Potwin turned off into a lane.

And there it was.

It was a haphazard house painted a tired lemon yellow with windows scattered casually wherever needed or convenient. It had the comfortable, settled-down look of old Vermont farmhouses, no line exactly horizontal or exactly vertical, but "more or less." There were no shutters or vines to soften its plainness, and the skinny chimney poked up not quite in the center of the roof. From the straggling stone wall to the lawn which swallowed up the driveway (or the driveway which simply dwindled away into lawn), from the front doorstep to which there was no proper walk, only grass, to the enormous maples which dwarfed lawn, drive, and house, it was everything an army barracks is not, and I wanted to buy it at once.

It was friendly. You can be yourself and I don't give a damn, it said. Paint me blue or paint me pink, I don't care. Holler and shout and sing at the top of your lungs. Nobody will tack up a notice in the kitchen on how to clean the stove. Nobody will instruct you just where you may hang your washing. Do your housework in your bare feet if you like. I don't care what you do, as long as you're happy.

"Do you suppose no one is home?" I worried, peering at the silent house.

"Dunno if she's up," Mr. Potwin said. He added by way of explanation, "She writes poetry."

Mrs. Ferncliffe was, nevertheless, up, and she appeared in the doorway, a short, stocky figure well wrapped in an enormous woolen shawl. She reminded me of those little apple-cheeked wooden dolls which will rock but not topple over.

"Welcome!" she called to Mr. Potwin. "And who, pray tell, is this?" She beamed at me.

"Wants to see the place," Mr. Potwin said.

"Come in, come in, dear child!" Mrs. Ferncliffe cried. "Look around to your heart's content!"

I tried to assume a poker face as I followed Mr. Potwin down the narrow cellar stairs and prodded the birch log beams with his penknife. (Hmm . . . sound.) It isn't proper to buy a house the moment you clap eyes on it, I reminded myself. "That wall, there," I said in a businesslike voice. "What makes its stones sag in like that?"

"Frost," Mr. Potwin said. "Shovin' from the outside."

"Is it likely to collapse?"

"Dunno. Probably will, some day. Been standing for more'n a hunderd years now, though."

I nodded, satisfied. I prowled around a strange brick structure, something like a kiln, in the center of the cellar, being careful to duck under the low beams and nearly tripping over a pipe on the dirt floor near the narrow chimney.

"That furnace burns either coal or wood," Mr. Potwin informed me. "See that big tank? Holds eight hunderd gallons of water. Come in handy in case of fire."

"Where does the water come from?"

"Spring, down at the foot of the hill. Want to see it?"

I said I did, and Mr. Potwin, treating his Ford as nonchalantly as if it had been a cow pony, drove across the field and over the hill down towards the woods, the Ford bucking and prancing over the uneven ground. I looked and saw there was indeed a spring, and a pump, and a house over all. The springhouse was not much more than a shack about six feet square, and on the inside of the door was penciled, "In the big snow of 1937 Dad went to town and was gone four days."

Then Mr. Potwin drove back up over the hill, and waved his hand at the woods skirting the meadows. "Dunno where the line is," he said. "Down in there somewheres. You got sixty-five acres, more or less."

I looked at the woods, and then across at the line of hills to the north, and then up past the orchard to the hill to the west. I couldn't see another roof from where I stood. The field towards the south belonged to the farm just up over the hill, and the field towards the east to the farm just down over the hill. All around lay raw-siena fields and burnt-umber woods, and the air was so still and transparent that the trees in the hedgerows stood with every twig clearly defined, their intricate patterns giving the eye something to look at, to trace and decipher while the mind occupied itself with peaceful thoughts. We'd all be here, together, safe, cradled by the hills, all together. Bob would not have to worry about us, anyway.

"You got a barn here," said Mr. Potwin, indicating a picturesque structure of weathered boards, well ventilated by the loss of windows and doors. "Couple of old car wrecks out behind, good for the kids to play in. Lots of good manure here—" pointing to a heap that sprawled half in, half out of the barn. "School bus goes by the gate. Fields run down, of course. Nobuddy farmed here

[22]

for years." Mr. Potwin was an expert salesman. What did I care if the fields were run down?

We went back into the house and I took a second look around. The rooms were strung together in a line, like beads on a string. Living room, hall, kitchen, with a chunk out for the bath. Woodshed. Garage. Upstairs, three bedrooms were cramped down under the slant of the roof. I didn't see a single room as it actually was, smoke-smudged and water-stained. I had transformed them as I walked through with fresh paint in clear colors and with bright curtains and lots and lots of books and pitchers of wildflowers and toys all over the place underfoot.

"I'll have to think it over," I said to Mr. Potwin and Mrs. Ferncliffe, though I knew I didn't have to, at all. But, I thought, you're *supposed* to have to think it over.

"Any time," said Mr. Potwin genially.

"You'll be back, my dear," said Mrs. Ferncliffe.

I drove around for one day. I looked at a house in a swamp and one next to a body-repair shop and another next to a chicken slaughterhouse, and I thought, this is silly, and I drove back to Woodstock and phoned Bob.

"I found exactly what we need," I told him. "There isn't any traffic and we can get it for five thousand and taxes are only thirty-three dollars a year and there's a telephone already in, and electricity, running water, and inside plumbing—"

Bob said, "If you think you can be happy there, buy it."

I called Mr. Potwin and in the morning we drove out once again. It wasn't particularly early for either of us, but Mrs. Ferncliffe hadn't had breakfast and we ate cinnamon rolls and drank coffee and discussed why this was such an astute purchase on my part. Mrs. Ferncliffe reminisced about how close she had come to selling to the wrong kind of person—"She wore bracelets that *jangled*, my dear!"—but Fate, obviously, had intervened, because now I had bought the farm, as she called it out of deference to the barn and manure pile.

"And you, my dear, were *destined* to buy it. You are the kind who can appreciate it. Now my heart is at peace and I can leave

[23]

without regrets." She waved her hand towards the orchard. "It's best not to keep a dog. The deer love to eat the apples during the winter. Always leave plenty of apples on the trees for the deer. And cherries—leave plenty of cherries. I always did, and the birds were *so* grateful."

But cherries ought to be for children, I thought. "What an unusual idea!" I said, proud of my unaccustomed tact.

"And Beethoven," Mrs. Ferncliffe went on. "For the deer, you know." She gestured towards the old-fashioned phonograph that occupied one corner of the room. "Something gentle, rather thoughtful and profound—the Fourth Symphony, perhaps. When I played Beethoven, the deer would come and stand out there—" she waved towards the front lawn—"and listen, sometimes for hours. Strange, they didn't care for Debussy," she added reflectively.

What an amazing old woman, I thought. Why is she moving? What is she looking for that she didn't find here?

"And another thing, my dear." She leaned towards me earnestly and laid her hand on my arm. "There are times during the year when the sun does not come up too desperately early. You must see the sunrise. It is an experience you'll never forget. The eastern sky is a glory, and the colors spread and spread—I can't convey to you in mere words what a sight it is. Too, too magnificent! You must make a point of getting up early enough, at lease *once*, to see the sunrise. Promise me you will!"

I promised her I would.

She gave me an autographed copy of her poems, and assured me that I could assure my husband the children and I would be safe and happy here. "After all, my dear, I've lived here two years and I don't even drive. The neighbors—the *soul* of kindness, my dear! Shopped for my groceries and met the trains and fetched my guests. And in the winter, when it was icy, the telephone operator would call me and ask if I'd been out for the mail yet—the box is at the end of the lane—and if I hadn't, she'd say, 'Now, Mrs. Ferncliffe, when you get back in the house, just give me a ring so I'll know you didn't slip and fall.'"

[24]

This sort of conversation went on for some time, and then, after Mrs. Ferncliffe agreed to move out as soon as she conveniently could, since there was no telling how soon we would want to be moving in, and after I signed an agreement to purchase and gave her as down payment a check for five hundred dollars, which, she assured me graciously, would be more than ample, I ran around outside taking snapshots to show Bob, and then Mr. Potwin and I went off to arrange for the mortgage. This was very easily arranged because I was careful to follow his advice and always refer to the object of my purchase as "a country home" and not a farm. Farms, it seemed, were not good risks.

In a state of high elation I headed south. It seems incredibly callous, when I look back on it now, or perhaps it was just that head-in-the-sand attitude which protects the nervous system against unnecessary abrasion, but I was ignoring completely *why* we were buying a place in the country: because Bob was going to Korea. All I felt was a bubbly sensation of tremendous achievement. We were landowners! After years and years of living like rootless nomads, we had sixty-five acres to call our own, and a house, a shed, a barn, and a springhouse. Wonderful, wonderful!

I stopped in Schenectady to see my brother Ted and Myra, his wife, and to tell them the great news. We spent the evening pouring over road maps, inspecting penciled diagrams—"Now the front entrance is here, facing east—" and talking non-stop for hours. It was nearly midnight when I said good night, shoved maps and sketches back into my purse, and retired to the guest room.

Myra and Ted's apartment occupied the first floor of a middle-aged house on a quiet side street near a very large cemetery. There was no traffic and the night was still and quite warm for the second of November. I decided not to open the window until I was ready for bed, and, putting my purse on the bureau next to the window, I pulled the shade, took off my blouse, and, toothbrush in hand, disappeared into the bathroom across the hall. About three minutes later, I was back.

Something was wrong. I stood in the doorway, trying to discover what it was that had caused that cold finger up and down the back of my neck.

The window shade billowed out . . . the room looked too empty . . . my purse! That was it—my purse was gone!

I ran to the window and jerked up the shade. I leaned out the open window and strained my eyes into the darkness. There was a narrow alleyway between the houses, and it was utterly silent, empty except for the screen leaning against the house just below me . . .

"*Ted!*" I screamed. I ran towards their bedroom. "My purse— my purse has been stolen—right out the window—*my God, all our war bonds are in it!*"

I raced back to the bedroom and grabbed my jacket and swung through the window, jumping to the alleyway below, and I began to run about in the darkness, crying as I did so, "Somebody stole my purse! Damn you, where are you? *Where are you?*"

And if I had caught the thief, I think I would have tried to kill him. I was consumed with terror and rage.

"Come in here, sis." Ted's voice was calming. "You'll never find him in these alleys. I've phoned the police. Come on in the house."

I came in, and sat on the sofa beside a white-faced Myra, and began to shake and sob. "I've got to find those bonds!" I said, shuddering with reaction. "We've got to have the farm!"

Myra put her arm around me. "Listen honey, honey," she said soothingly. "You will. Don't worry. You will have your farm."

The folks upstairs were coming down. I heard them in the hall asking Ted, "What's the matter? Was that your sister we heard outside, carrying on something fierce?"

I calmed down at once. "Did I?" I asked Myra in a low voice. "Carry on awfully, I mean?"

"It's just a local idiom," she assured me.

Ted came back in. He'd been checking around outside, but couldn't see a thing. He poured Myra and me a thimbleful of brandy apiece, and the only sign of agitation he showed was to keep looking at his watch. After half an hour had passed, he called the police again, requesting in a calm, executives-are-never-rattled manner any information on the call for police he had put in. It had been acted upon, he was told. Fifteen minutes later a car drove silently up and a couple of policemen came to the door.

They listened with impassive faces as Ted explained what had happened, but one of them could not keep himself from throwing me a look of disgust. "On the bureau?" he said. "You left your purse on the bureau next to a window? My gawd, lady, you ought to know better!"

"I do, now," I said, adding spitefully, "I don't know much about safe, peaceful cities. I've only lived on army posts and in postwar Germany—"

Ted interrupted me quietly, "As I say, that was forty-five minutes ago."

"We got a call right after yours that there was a Peeping Tom about a block away from here," the policeman explained. "We figured that's who your thief probably was, and we've been cruising around trying to spot him."

They went on to say that the thief would probably get rid of my purse as soon as he had a chance to empty it, and he'd probably get rid of the bonds, too, since he couldn't cash them, and he wouldn't want them on him if caught.

"He can't?" I said, grasping at a straw. "He really can't cash them?"

"Well, he might if he belonged to some highly organized crime ring, but I doubt very much if he does," the other policeman said. "These Peeping Toms are almost always just some local yokel. Cheer up. It may take some time but you can get your bonds back. You'll have to report the loss and give the numbers, of course."

They left, and after a few minutes, we all went back to bed. But not to sleep, at least not I. I lay staring into the darkness and arguing with God.

"I have to have the farm, You know that. And I can't get the bonds back because I haven't got the numbers. I can't tell Bob I lost them and don't know the numbers—I simply can't! I have to find them, that's all, and You have to help me!"

At five o'clock it was still dark, but I couldn't lie there any longer, doing nothing but praying. I rose, dressed, and sneaked out of the house.

There was no one else about. The sounds of the awakening city came to me faintly, hushed by distance. I started searching the alleys, peering down drains and lifting the lids of rubbish cans. There was no sign of my purse. Then I thought perhaps the thief had gone into the near-by cemetery to empty my purse undisturbed; perhaps he had tossed it behind a gravestone. In the growing light, the cemetery looked enormous, stretching for several blocks, gravestones pebbling the ground as far as I could see. The thief, I reasoned, would throw my bag away as soon as possible. In the eerie silence, I began to search behind the stones nearest the entrance.

About an hour and a half later, very tired and sick with discouragement, I returned to Myra and Ted's. Ted had just phoned GE that he'd be somewhat late, and Myra was watching the clock, waiting until the bank opened, to phone and say she wouldn't be in. "I couldn't count five dimes accurately," she said. "But I'll give them the numbers of the bonds, honey, just in case the thief isn't as bright as given credit for, and does try to cash them."

I swallowed. "I don't have the numbers, Myra," I said. "It—it never occurred to me to write them down."

She and Ted exchanged a quick glance.

"I bought them at the Caldwell National Bank," I said. At least I knew that much. "Maybe the bank has a record?"

"It won't hurt to ask," Ted said, so gently I knew it wouldn't do much good, either. "Phone Dad and ask him to go over to the bank right away."

So I put in a call to New Jersey and when I heard my father's voice I had to steel myself to sound calm and as if I had more than two brain cells clicking. I told him the bonds were stolen and I needed the numbers and would he please go over—

"I have a list of the numbers," my father said, generations of

[28]

prudent Scottish ancestors in his voice. "I listed them before I mailed them to you. *I expected you'd lose them.*" (Italics mine.)

After that it seemed almost like an anticlimax to learn that the bonds had been found. Ted, strengthened by the knowledge that his father, at least, had some sense, thought he might just give the police a ring to see how they were progressing, and it turned out that they were just going to give him a ring. The bonds had been found by a wholesale florist, scattered on the ground behind a greenhouse out beyond the city limits, and the police would appreciate it if I would stay put long enough for them to bring me my bonds and have me sign for them. Ted said never fear, I would be there.

The police were very prompt. By nine thirty they had come, I had counted the bonds and signed for them, everybody had thanked everybody else and shaken hands all around, and they had left. There had been no sign of my purse, and Ted lent me money for gas and food. My driver's license was gone with my purse, but the police said never mind, just get another when I get back to Virginia, and meanwhile if I run into trouble, tell the cops to phone the Schenectady police, where, they said, I was known.

On my way out of town I detoured long enough to thank the florist for reporting my bonds so promptly, and he showed me the exact spot where they had been found. And then I headed south again, this time not quite in such a state of exultation. I felt as if I had been teetering on a high wire and had nearly fallen, and would have, except for God's help.

On an impulse I snatched my cigarettes and chucked the pack out into the ditch.

I'll quit smoking, I vowed. I'll get healthy as a pig and even tempered and I'll stop cussing. And furthermore I'm going to start Using my Brain and Always Taking Due Precautions. It is somewhat late, but I am going to grow up.

Or try to, anyway.

CHAPTER II

Two months later I returned from the January meeting of the Fort Monroe PTA to find Bob stretched out in the big chair in our living room, looking tired and under a strain. I searched his face swiftly. Overseas orders? But he would have told me . . .

"I'm sorry you didn't feel up to going to the meeting," I said brightly. "I wish you could have heard my secretary's report."

Bob grinned. "How did it go?"

"It went," I said with satisfaction, "like this. I quote approximately. 'The monthly meeting of the executive board was scheduled for three thirty P.M. on January umpteen, 1951. It was called to order at three fifty-five. Business transacted: It was decided to purchase ash trays for the use of the executive board when meeting in the school. There being no further business, the meeting was adjourned at four thirty-five.' "

Bob laughed. "How to win friends?"

"Oh, damn and blast," I said. "I *hate* begging Dodie to look after Mike and then wasting time and wasting time."

Bob said, "We have to make other arrangements for Mike, Melissa. We can't keep him here any longer."

I said, "What?"

"I didn't tell you because I knew you had to go to this meeting tonight, and I didn't see how you could go if you knew about the report."

"What report? What are you talking about?"

"The report on Mike." Bob seemed to be choosing his words carefully, as if the information he was trying to convey were so outlandish I might not be able to grasp it. "It seems there has been a lot of complaints about him. Somebody was assigned the job of going around and asking how much damage he has done, how much of a nuisance he's been—things like that."

I stared at him, fighting down a cold nausea. "Asking? Asking whom?"

"Everybody we know," Bob said evenly. "Our friends and neighbors, everybody within the perimeter of Mikey's wanderings."

"Well, that's nice," I said. "What do you suppose they said?"

"Plenty. Enough so it looked as if we never did a damn thing to control him. At first no one wanted to show me the report. I was told it wasn't anything personal and I shouldn't take it that way, but that it appeared best that we find some place for Mike off the Post. I insisted on seeing the report, and my God, they had everything down, everything he's done since we came. And there was a lot of stuff I never heard about. I said we couldn't be expected to make amends when people either didn't bother or preferred not to tell us. Wrong attitude, of course. Showed resentment."

I said painfully, "But what has Mikey done that's so awful?"

"No one thing, sweetheart. It's the total of little things. 'After all, Coughlin,' he said in that clipped, ball-of-fire way he has, 'if you had a dog that barked and made a nuisance of itself, you'd have to get rid of it, too.' "

Bob stared at his right hand, and flexed the fingers.

After a moment I said, "Officer and gentleman."

"Yeah," said Bob softly.

"Did they have down what the Post Engineers once told me?" I said. "Did they put down that the Engineers say Mikey doesn't destroy as much property as some of those so-called normal teen-agers?"

"No, that wasn't included in the scope of the report," Bob said. "But they did say—sorry, darling, you might as well know—they

[31]

did have it down that once when you were told Mikey was throwing stones, you said it was great, you were teaching him to."

"But that's ridiculous!"

"That's what I said. I said I was positive you would never say anything of the kind, that the woman who reported that was either an idiot or a liar or both. I said—"

"Wait a minute." My mouth was dry and it was hard to talk at all. "Listen. I *did*, Bob. I did say something like that, but it wasn't . . ." I tried to remember exactly, and my hands grew clammy. I remembered the phone ringing and it was Mariannalee and she had said did I know Mikey was throwing stones at the school bus and I had said . . . I wet my lips. "I said, 'Oh, great, great.' You know, how you say something's great when you don't mean it's great—" It was like a nightmare, when you explain and explain and nothing really makes sense. I sat there on the sofa and I could feel my face twisting and contorting and the tears running down, and I couldn't stop them, I couldn't stop myself. "My God, she must have known what I meant! And then I said, 'And here I've been teaching him to throw!' Because I was—for weeks and weeks I'd been trying to teach him to throw back the ball, to get him to throw it back— She knew I was, she knew about the throwing—"

I couldn't think clearly. This all seemed worse than the report itself, or the verdict.

"Why, this is awful, Bob, *awful!* I've known her for years—she's my friend!"

"Oh, darling," Bob said, and several tons of weight were lifted from my heart. He believed me. He didn't blame me. "I told you long ago she's constitutionally unable to hold her tongue. Don't be so upset. It doesn't make any difference anyway—they'd have reached the same decision. They were looking for an excuse to boot Mikey off the Post right from the start."

"Give me a cigarette," I said shakily. "I'm glad I gave up giving up smoking—it's such a comfort when the world rises up and kicks you in the face."

I was ashamed to have broken down and cried. I fought for

[32]

self-control, not able to look at Bob's face, staring with a desperate intentness first at the tip of my cigarette, then at Bob's tie, tucked so neatly and precisely into his shirt, his shirt with the row of ribbons just over the left breast pocket. I'd sewn them on for him, the brownish one for the campaign in Europe, crowded with battle stars; the blue, white, and red for the Silver Star . . .

Bob was saying, "I know an army post isn't set up for caring for a child like Mike, and I really don't blame anybody for the decision which was reached. But it's *how* they reached it—there must have been some other way, some decent way."

"Without pillorying you, you mean? Don't be naïve. The Army doesn't give a damn about your feelings, Bob."

"I'm not talking about my feelings," Bob said. "They couldn't matter less. What I mean is, did they have to do it such a dirty way? Going from house to house, behind our backs, gathering gossip. . . ."

It's true your heart can ache for somebody, it's not just a trite remark. I could feel a terrible pain inside me as I looked at him.

"I guess I am naïve, as you say," he went on. "I was thinking how I always wanted to be an army officer. I never wanted to be anything else. 'Duty, honor, country—' it really got me. I always thought there wasn't anything better a man could do. I was always so damn proud."

In the morning I phoned home, and when my mother answered and I tried to tell her what had happened, all I could say was, "Mother, they've said we can't keep Mikey . . . isn't it awful, isn't it awful . . . we can't keep Mikey!" And of course I started crying again.

"He'll be better off here," my mother said. "He'll be happier. We'll take good care of him—it will be a blessing for your father to have something to do, he's nearly beside himself since he retired. You bring Mike, Melissa—can you hear me?—bring Mike, and plan to stay a while and rest."

As I hung up, the phone rang. It was Mary Buechler.

"Hi, Melisse!" she said gaily. "What are you doing?"

"Bawling," I said, starting in again. "C-crying my eyes out. Mary, they've booted Mikey off the Post!"

"*What?*" Silence. "Let me come over—I'm coming right over!"

"Please do," I said.

I was thankful she was coming. I needed her. Colonel Buechler had been Bob's regimental commander in the Army of Occupation, and I had known Mary in Germany in '46 and '7. She was my ideal of a C.O.'s wife, charming, full of fun, and never a shell around her so the younger wives couldn't reach her. We felt she took on our problems as if they were her own. Mary is sympatico, and I love her.

She came right over, and Dodie, too, and Dodie and I cried and Mary sat there white-faced, and after a bit I felt better. I wiped my face and put the coffeepot on the stove.

"I was crying," I said, "because I am so mad and so helpless."

"This is the first I've heard of this—survey," Mary said, looking fastidiously revolted. "Teddy didn't mention it. Perhaps he was away during the actual inquiry."

"I knew about it," Dodie said. "I couldn't bring myself to tell you. They asked Joe and me. In case you're wondering, we said Mikey had never bothered us."

"Weren't you under oath? Thanks for lying, anyway."

Dodie looked as if she'd like to cry again. "For heaven's sake, Melisse, I wasn't lying! Mikey has never *bothered* us!"

I stared at her, thinking of the times without number Mike had wandered into her living room, the hours he had spent in her kitchen, watching her washing machine sudsing and churning.

"You are a human being," I said huskily, "and not just a reasonable facsimile."

Once again Dodie volunteered to look after my husband and my children, and I packed Mikey's clothes, only this time I packed everything he had, and all his toys, too, those toys so young for his size, his teddy bears and beach bucket and shovel and his bright-colored ball with the bells inside. And we drove to New Jersey, Mike and I, and I thought, This is the last time.

My parents said that, if Bob did not go overseas before then,

Mike should stay with them until June, because in this way Pat and Chris could finish their school year without interruption. "And the children can be with their father that much longer," my father said. And my mother said, "And you can be with your Bob."

"And then I'll take the children and move to Vermont," I said. "I just hope Mike doesn't wear you out before then."

Bob and I had reached the decision of the move to Vermont ourselves, but the timing of the move was to be up to Mother and Dad. Bob and I both felt the enormity of what we were asking of them. We knew Mike would take up their every waking moment. We knew what demands he would make, on their patience, their strength, their quick wits, their sense of humor. We knew we were asking too much, but we couldn't *not* ask, because we were asking for time, priceless time.

We felt a closeness, during the next two months, that we had not felt since the days before Bob went overseas in '44. Again, there was the feeling of impending separation. But this time it was more painful to contemplate, because this time each of us knew, from experience, how agonizing it is to be apart. This time, too, it was Mikey and not the Army who was separating us, and this would make it all the harder.

Late in March Bob flew to California on an inspection trip of the Pacific Coast. Three other officers from the Post accompanied him, and they were to start back on Friday, April 6, traveling by civilian plane.

At noon on Saturday a colonel from Bob's office, and his wife, came to tell me officially that the plane was late. I didn't seem able to grasp any of the details. Bob's plane was down somewhere, I had no idea where, or when it had gone down. Someone would let me know as soon as there was any word. . . . I thanked them, formally, for coming.

I told the children that Daddy would probably be late, and not get home in time for supper after all. Pat wanted to know why not, and I said the plane was down somewhere, and Daddy probably had a long walk to go get help, that's why he hadn't phoned. Sure, Pat said, and he and Chris went out to play.

The afternoon, which could have been an endless test of endurance, passed very quickly. Directly after the children went out, a priest, who knew Bob but whom I did not know, as I am not Catholic, came to call, and engaged me in conversation. He was charming, he was witty, he was well read. We discussed current books, plays, and movies, theories of philosophy, and the significance of various personal experiences. As the hours passed, I felt as if I had become two people, the one, who was visible, who sat and talked and laughed and behaved as if nothing in the world were wrong, and the other, invisible, who watched the first with astonishment and disapproval.

When the priest left, it was nearly five o'clock. Dodie came in, and then Mary Buechler. A reporter from the Associated Press phoned, wanting to know my father's address. I gave it, and then I put through a call to Dad. I hadn't wanted to phone him until there was some definite news, but I thought that if the reporters were going to be bothering him, perhaps he ought to know that Bob was on that plane that was down. "In California," I said clearly, so there would be no mistake. "Somewhere in the mountains. There are about twenty-five people aboard, besides Bob."

"I see," my father said. "Yes. Well, thanks for calling."

As I hung up I saw an olive-drab sedan stop outside, and General Lawton and the Protestant chaplain get out.

I opened the door.

"Mrs. Coughlin?"

I nodded.

The general's face looked pinched and gray. "There were no survivors."

Because I had to know, I said, "Was it quick?"

"Yes," the general said. He cleared his throat. "Instantly."

Thank God. It was the first I had spoken to Him all day.

"Would you like me to pray?" the chaplain asked.

"Why, yes, if you like," I said courteously.

The living room was empty. We sat down and the chaplain

knelt stiffly on one knee and I bowed my head and listened to him saying something about fortitude and God's ways are inscrutable, and nothing seemed to make any sense. And then Dodie and Mary came back in, and the others left.

Dodie threw her arms around me, and burst out, "Oh, Melissa! Melissa!" and I patted her on the shoulder and said, "It's all right, Dodie. It's all right."

I couldn't imagine what I meant.

Someone gave the children supper, and Joe said he'd phone Fort Bragg and tell Longin, and I went over to the Buechlers, who lived on the main post, inside the moat. On the way over, Mary, who was driving, said, "What about the farm, Melisse? If you need money, I've got some. Tell me what you need."

I thought about Bob's few uniforms, kept presentable only by constant care, and our shabby Chevrolet, and how for years I had protested at Bob for being so "insurance poor." "I've got money," I said. "Thanks just the same."

And my second self watched my first self eating, talking of the future, coming back to our quarters and, finding a number of people there, talking and offering everybody something to drink, and my second self said, "What's the matter with you? Don't you know Bob's dead?"

Dodie slept beside me that night, and in the morning, when I first woke, I turned to see if Bob was awake yet, and in that instant my two selves fused, and I knew.

I heard the boys stirring, and I went in to tell them. "Your father's plane was found," I said. "He is dead. Everybody on the plane is dead."

Pat and Chris stared up at me, sleep driven from their faces. Neither made a sound. Chris's face twisted, but he did not cry.

Pat said, "I'll quit school and go to work."

"Don't be silly," I said harshly, because I could feel my insides begin to crumple and go to pieces. "You haven't even finished third grade. Besides, it won't be necessary. Your father has taken care of us."

There is, I understand now, always something of the dead—

[37]

some little thing, like a book left open and unfinished, or a meal prepared and not eaten—which holds in itself the whole of the abruptness, the senselessness, the crippling finality; and this small thing seems harder to bear than the enormity of the loss, which is too enormous to understand. It was the thought of Bob's uniforms, rubbed thin along the edge of the sleeve, while he had put enough into life insurance to buy a new uniform every month, it was the thought of these which began to sabotage my self-control. And I felt again the merciful splintering, one self standing aside to hold on to the unbearable knowledge that Bob was dead, to hang on to this knowledge until I could look at it, and the other self going on about my daily tasks, behaving as if nothing had happened, nothing at all.

I was getting breakfast when Longin walked in.

"Hello," I said. "How long can you stay?"

It was precisely the question we always asked whenever Longin got a pass to come home.

"Three days. Children haven't eaten?"

We fed them, and then my sister, Mary, walked in. "Dad and Mother can't come," she said, dumping down her suitcase, "because of Mike. I came to help you pack."

"Well, that's very nice of you, I think," I said. "What about your job?"

Mary gave me a penetrating look. "Phooey," she said briefly, and started clearing the table.

And then began a constant procession of visitors. Everyone on the Post who had known Bob, his friends, his superiors in rank, his juniors, WACs who had worked in his office, neighbors and former neighbors, cars kept coming and going, footsteps to the door constantly, and never time to stop and think. Gifts poured in, mute evidence of people's sorrow and sympathy and helplessness to help, but they had to do something, they couldn't bear not to do something, and they brought cakes and fruit and a roasted turkey and bottles of wine. And the women looked at me with eyes from far away, eyes bright with unshed tears and burning with the prayer, *O God don't let me have to follow her, don't let it happen to me.*

Somewhere in the midst of the first day's callers came the priest who had been there the day before. "I want to talk to you alone," he said, and I took him back to the bedroom, which seemed the only place in the house with any privacy.

"First of all," he said, "let me explain the Church's stand on sudden death. The Church holds that there need be only a split-second awareness of impending death, that is long enough to achieve a state of Grace. For the salvation of the soul, it is every bit as good as a complete Act of Contrition."

This was something to which I had literally given no thought whatsoever. I realized he was explaining not so much to me, a Protestant, as to Bob's children, who might one day ask about this.

"I understand," I said. And then because I didn't feel as if I had answered everything he had said, "Bob was a very fine man," I said, and the inadequacy of my words kept me from trying to say any more. It's useless to try to put one's feelings into words, I thought. Words change and distort and blur and muffle one's thoughts. . . .

"Secondly," the priest said, "you must realize that your marriage is now over." He stressed each word slightly to emphasize the importance of what he was saying. "Your marriage no longer exists. It is ended."

"I know," I said.

"So there must be no vows, none at all," he went on, "no vows that you will not remarry, no vows to remain true to your dead husband. It is all over."

"I know."

"What about yourself? What are you going to do now?"

I told him we had a place in the country, that I thought I'd make out all right, I could raise the children there—

"That isn't precisely what I meant," he said. "I want you to remember that although your marriage is over, your life is not. You have a tremendous task ahead of you, and it is not a task

[39]

you are supposed to do alone. Children, especially boys, need more than a mother, they need the companionship of men. You must see to it that they see a lot of their grandfather and their uncles, men teachers, young priests. You have a big job, an enormous job, but, you know, I think you can do it alone better than Bob could. You've been in training for this, haven't you? How many times Bob had to go away, leaving you in charge, to carry on alone until he got back, and you did it. This time it is for good, but you will do it, with God's help."

He rose to leave.

"Thank you, Father," I said, and I wasn't thanking him as much for what he had said as for the rock he offered me as consolation, the rock of reality which he had made me see so clearly was still there, it was there any time I wanted to stand on it.

That was Sunday. On Tuesday the visitors were still streaming in and out, and no word had come when Bob's body would be shipped east, no word of what plans we should make. I couldn't imagine what was causing the delay. Could some bumptious local official, swollen with importance, be playing with red tape?

I felt wound up tighter and tighter, and finally I asked to see the priest. We went into the empty church to talk.

"Father," I said, "I can't stand it. I'm not let alone a minute. Somebody is always trooping in."

"You can always come down here," he said with a smile. "They'll never think of looking for you in the church."

"What's the matter, Father?" I burst out. "Why doesn't anybody tell me when Bob's body will be coming, when we'll have the funeral—you know, all the formalities which have to be got over with? Why does everything have to be all drawn out this way?"

He said, "You mean no one's told you they can't identify Bob?"

"So that's it," I said. "Why didn't they say so?"

"Perhaps," he said gently, "they don't know, as you know, it is only the soul that counts. I think it would be a good idea if we held a memorial mass. I think you would feel better."

So it was arranged. And then I could see no reason for remaining any longer at Fort Monroe. My sister had had to go back to work, but Longin's three-day pass had been extended to a month's emergency leave, and he thus would be able to supervise the packers and moving men, drive us to New Jersey, and help get us settled in Vermont.

It was raining when we left the Post. Pat, Chris, Kitty and I arranged ourselves as best we could in whatever space we could find in our five-passenger Chevy not already occupied by suitcases, very pregnant cat, and a basket of fried chicken which someone had shoved into my hand at the last moment. Longin drove. By the time we reached the Maryland line, the rain was so intense that other drivers, unable to see or to hold the road, had pulled over to the side. We drove steadily on, cloudbursts and flooded roads seeming like very minor perils to us.

We reached New Jersey safely, and as I crawled stiffly out of the car, my mother kissed me on the cheek. We are not a particularly demonstrative family, and I knew, by this gesture, how overwhelming she was finding her sorrow and compassion. "They didn't have to be in such a hurry to be rid of Michael, did they," she murmured.

I shook my head. I knew, too, that mine is not a forgiving nature, and that I would never forgive the unnecessary grief and humiliation which Bob had suffered over Mike, the wholly pointless disillusionment he had had to endure, seeing at last with blinding clarity what a pitiless, egocentric juggernaut is the peacetime Army.

I waited to be told what to do. Joe Dunn phoned to say there were four others, besides Bob, for whom special plans must be made. The problem seemed to be a technical one. All were servicemen, and entitled to burial in a national cemetery, but since no one knew for sure who was who, how to label the graves correctly?

"My God," I said, "what does it matter?"

"I know, Melisse," Joe said. "It strikes me just as idiotic as it

[41]

does you. But you know the Army, Melisse. Got to go by the book."

I knew the Army, all right. "Oh, sure," I said.

"Present plans are for a common grave, one headstone, in the national cemetery in St. Louis. The Army will fly you out."

I thought that over for one split second. "*Fly?*" I said hotly. "What the hell do they think I'm made of? I've got four children to raise—I certainly will not fly!"

"Okay, Melisse, so go by train."

I was feeling stubborn now. "And why, may I ask, St. Louis?"

"Because three of the men are from the West Coast, and two from the East."

I almost laughed. Naturally the Army, faced with a problem of this kind, would get out its slide rule and come up with an answer that suits nobody.

"Listen, Joe," I said, "tell them to try to realize this problem isn't something on paper, it concerns *people*. And why not Arlington? Bob once said he thought it a great honor to be buried in Arlington. Maybe the other families will think so too." And if his body isn't there, I thought, what does it matter. Let his name be there. . . .

"I can't promise anything," Joe said, "but I'll see what I can do."

In a day or so he called to say Arlington suited the other families just fine. It would still have to be one casket, though, and one headstone.

"Listen, Joe," I said firmly, "I'm bringing Pat and Chris. I feel they have a right to be at their father's funeral. And they already know there will be four of his comrades buried at the same time. I'm not explaining to them about one casket. I don't feel equal to it. They're not old enough to know that the body doesn't matter. But they're old enough to count. Five caskets, Joe."

Damn it, I thought, the Army can use four empty ones. And the hell with the damn taxpayers' money.

Joe said he'd see what he could do, but he didn't sound hopeful, just tired out, and I remembered suddenly this was his friend he was burying, and I thought vaguely, poor Joe. As he hung up, I glanced at the clock. Seven P.M. Okay, let's get busy. I picked up the phone again, and asked the operator to locate the Senator from New Jersey. Which one? Plucking the name from midair, I said, "The Honorable H. Alexander Smith." No, I didn't know where he was. No, I didn't know his home address. No, I had no reason to know whether or not he was home.

"Operator, I have to talk to him," I said. "You may consider this a matter of life and death."

Twenty minutes later she had located him at a cocktail party in a Washington hotel. I explained why I was calling.

"Senator, I'm going to bring my sons," I said. "And I'm not going to burden them with any explanations of precisely what happens when a plane smashes into a mountainside. Will you please call the Pentagon and urge them to cut out this letter-of-the-regulations stuff. If the Air Force can use empty caskets when necessary, why can't the Army?"

"I don't know about that," he said cautiously. I could hear voices, pitched high, and a burst of laughter somewhere. "Put the facts as you've told them to me in a letter. What I want are names, dates, places, serial number, that sort of thing. Send it to my office. You understand I can't promise anything, but I assure you," the Senator said in a very human voice, "that I will do everything I can to help."

I thanked him and hung up. I was shivering with a chill that set my teeth to chattering. When I could control myself, I went into the kitchen where Mother and Longin were sharing a pot of coffee.

"Let's get out of here," I said abruptly. "Let's go up to Vermont tomorrow and get settled. We've got an awful lot to do before you go back to Bragg, and God knows when they will get this straightened out. I can't stand this doing nothing."

I got the letter off to Senator Smith that evening, and we left all the children and the cat with Mother and Dad, and drove to Vermont the next day. The further north we drove, the colder it grew. By the time we turned east at Manchester and headed up

[43]

over Bromley Mountain, it was dark and the air was thick with snow. Everything seemed unreal, the darkness, the cold, the snow, the car moving into strange roads, Longin driving, who should have been a thousand miles south getting ready for maneuvers with the paratroops, I sitting there, no child near, I who should have been busy getting supper in my crowded kitchen, and calling the children in off the warm sand where they had been excavating roads for their fleets of toy jeeps and tanks, calling them in to clean up before their father got home. . . .

"I can't believe it," I said. "Snow! Imagine, snow in April!"

We had hoped to eat dinner in Chester, but it was five after eight, and the inn stopped serving supper at eight o'clock, we were told. We drove on several miles in a state of numb, hungry depression. The muscles in the sides of my cheeks were straining and stretching, and I was desperately afraid I would begin to cry.

Longin pulled up in front of a building which looked as if it had sat down for a moment by the crossroads. There was a vaguely Hawaiian air about its entrance, above which flickered in cerise neon tubing, Trade Winds Café.

"If they won't feed us, I threaten to die on their doorstep," Longin said, and disappeared into the entrance. He was back almost at once. "We are welcome," he said. "The lady said—she's a handsome blonde, by the way—she said, 'Soldier, you can eat here *any*time.'"

It was a delicious meal, well cooked, served piping hot, and with servings just as huge as those which had stunned me on my trip north in the fall. Where the climate is cold, I decided, you can't toy with a salad and a piece of fruit.

I felt my courage had returned. "Isn't it humiliating," I said, "the way you—you know, the real *you*—depends for its existence on eating regularly and well. Actually I am nothing but a walking three-meals-a-day."

"Subtract one and you are a snarling, primitive beast," Longin said.

"You may be, but *I* am then a whining craven."

We drove north on 106, the snow coming in brief flurries, the

[44]

mountains unseen in the darkness but making their presence felt anyway, closing in on us. I felt as if we were speeding through a tunnel, a tunnel of white dots dashing towards us. The effect was hypnotic, the light from our headlights and the speed of the car making each flake rush towards us as if we were its particular target.

I was nearly asleep when we reached Woodstock. There were heaps of unmelted snow two to three feet deep along the northern side of the houses. In Fort Monroe my daffodils had finished blooming, and the women had begun to sun themselves on beach towels, and the children ran barefoot along the shore. . . .

The guest house where I had stayed before was full, and we were directed to another house that took tourists, across the street. It wasn't actually open for business, but since it was so late, and if we didn't mind that they weren't serving breakfasts yet, why they would be glad to fix us up with a couple of rooms. Come in, come in, it's cold out, spring sure is late this year. Will three blankets be enough? Sure, now?

Comforted by the kindness of complete strangers, I fell asleep.

In the morning we went off to locate our household goods. They had been shipped care of Mr. Potwin. When I went up to knock on the door of his house, Mrs. Potwin flung open the door and swept me into her arms.

"Oh, you poor baby!" she cried. "Good gracious, this is awful, just awful!" She wiped her eyes on the corner of her apron. "All your stuff is in our barn. This truck the size of a house come up here, and Harold says to him, 'You're not plannin' to take that up our back roads, are you?' he says. 'It's mud season now and you'll be stuck till summer.' So this fellow says he'll take the stuff to Bellow Falls and put it in storage there, and Harold says, 'Well, what's the widow supposed to do then? Put it in our barn,' he says. And that's where it is."

"Well, thanks very much," I said. "But how—"

"Harold's gone off to get our boy who's got a loggin' truck," she said. "They'll take your stuff up on that. Good thing the mud is mostly gone, though," she said, setting out some coffee

[45]

cups and heading for the kitchen. "Else you never would get in, not now, not on Hartland roads."

"What does she mean?" I muttered. "What's all this about mud?"

Longin smiled. "In Poland, in the spring, no one tries to go anywhere, not on the roads. The frost goes down three or four feet into the ground, and when it thaws, the roads are like chocolate pudding."

I stared at him in dismay. "How long does this go on?"

"Two weeks, maybe three."

It was a very eventful day. Mr. Potwin located three of his sons, who quit their logging and came and loaded our household goods on the truck, and we drove up the unpaved roads, which, Mr. Potwin said, weren't so bad after all. At first glance I would have called them impassable, but obviously they weren't because first the Chevy made it, and then the truck. I noticed a sign saying nothing heavier than 16,000 pounds was supposed to go on the road, and I asked if that was put up because of the mud season, and Mr. Potwin said oh, no, that was for year round because of the bridges. And I said well then, the moving van couldn't have come anyway, and he said, oh, he could have made a try for it. Lots of heavier vehicles do actually make it, lime trucks and logging trucks and the like.

"But what about the bridges?" I persisted.

"Oh, if they go through a bridge, the town isn't liable, they've been warned," he said casually.

Mrs. Ferncliffe had left everything very neat, you'd have thought she'd had army-wife training. Cupboards and woodwork and all looked clean and scrubbed. But there wasn't time for any proper unpacking. The men worked like Trojans, and by the time it was getting dark, the truck had made three round trips and all our furniture and other gear were inside, under cover at least. Mr. Potwin and his boys swung up on the logging truck for the last time, and then Mr. Potwin leaned out and handed Longin a lantern. "Say," he said, "my wife thought you might need this, in case the electricity isn't on."

[46]

We thanked him, and the truck squashed down the drive and over the hill and out of sight. After a few minutes we couldn't hear it any longer, and it was very quiet.

We went back into the house. I flipped a light switch and nothing happened. Longin lit the lamp, and then, in the gloom, with the lamplight unable to do more than make a small pool of light, we both became aware of how cold it was, a bone-biting cold.

"I better start a fire," Longin said, his breath visible even in the feeble light from the lamp. "You stay here."

He took the lamp and went down to the cellar, and after ten minutes or so he came back up, announcing success in building a wood fire in the furnace. "Not much firewood, though. I better get some."

To the cozy sound of an axe in the woodshed, I got supper on the old wood stove which Mrs. Ferncliffe had offered to leave, and which I, with admirable foresight, had accepted. I could feel the cold gradually recede, become less knifelike, and the room grew warmer until it was actually almost pleasant. I took off my coat.

Longin came in from the woodshed with an armload of split lengths of firewood. He sniffed.

"Where's the smoke coming from?"

"Smoke?" I looked at him, and I could see it too, drifting in layers across the room. It was filling the room, and it wasn't cigarette smoke, either.

Longin dropped his wood and jerked open the door to the cellar. Billows of smoke swept past him, filling the room, filling the house. He grabbed the lamp and rushed down, the smoke closing behind him like a curtain. I stood at the head of the stairs coughing and choking and asking stupid questions. "Can I help?" I gasped, my eyes streaming. "Where's the fire?"

Longin came back up. "In the furnace," he said briefly. "Some fine furnace. Smoke is pouring out the back."

"What shall we do?" I was holding a wet handkerchief over my nose. It came to me dimly that you are supposed to crawl on

[47]

the floor, but that seemed extreme. "Shall we put the fire out? Pour water on it, maybe?"

"It would just smoke worse," Longin said. "We'll have to let it burn out."

"But we can't breathe!" I said, coughing to demonstrate.

Longin opened the front door, but the smoke refused to blow out. "I'll have to open windows upstairs," he said, and went up, and shortly came down. "They won't open. They've all got second windows on the outside, nailed shut."

He went up on the shed roof and, in the dark, removed two of the upstairs storm windows, opened the inside windows, climbed in and came downstairs and propped open the front door, to create a draft, he said. The smoke began to drift sullenly upstairs, and soon it was gone, accompanied by all the warmth in the house.

In the morning Longin went down to see whatever had been the matter. He diagnosed that the hole at the back of the furnace was where the pipe to the chimney should be. The furnace hadn't been connected to the chimney at all. We had been like a couple of hams in a smokehouse.

"Funny thing," Longin said. "There was the pipe lying on the ground, right there. Looked like it had rusted through and fallen off. How did that old woman manage to heat her house?"

"She had little stoves set up in the living room and hall," I said. I decided not to mention stumbling over a pipe behind the furnace, when I was buying the house.

"You better buy yourself an oil burner, if you have money," Longin said. "You cannot manage that furnace even if it is fixed. You will be going up and down, up and down, crying over a dead fire, and freezing."

I'm not one to argue when told to spend money to make myself comfortable. "Okay," I said agreeably, and went to get the coffeepot off the stove. We had set up the table by the window which looked out on the orchard, and as I turned back from the stove, Longin jumped up.

"Look!" he exclaimed in delight.

There, near the top of the orchard, was a deer. She was almost the color of the dead grass across which she moved, as gracefully and effortlessly as water flowing, now lifting her head to stare at the house, then lowering it again to graze on the fallen apples.

We watched, enchanted.

"Right here!" I breathed, half unbelieving. "A deer, in our own orchard, the very first day. It's some kind of an omen, don't you think? A good omen . . ."

Suddenly something startled her, and she sailed over the hedgerow, the white of her tail flashing.

A car was turning into the drive. It was the plumbers promised by Mr. Potwin, who were to remove the small iron sink lurking in the corner, and to install the new one shipped from Virginia.

Everything needed doing, and at once. It was hard to know where to start. The wood stove, though useful in an emergency, was really too picturesque for every day, but when it went, the tiny hot-water heater attached to it would also go; we would need, therefore, not only a furnace subservient to the whims of a lone woman, but also a hot-water heater willing and able to anticipate our needs. As for cooking, I was advised that bottled gas was the most reliable and least expensive, after wood, but I knew this meant some kind of containers resembling small, sleek bombs which would be outside, in plain view of Mike, and I shook my head when the plumbers said these containers were quite safe. They didn't know Mike. I would have to cook by electricity.

Mr. Potwin sent an electrician, who put wires in for a stove, and an outlet for the washing machine in the woodshed. Water must be piped in to it, and water must go out again. . . . We worked like the proverbial beavers for several days.

"Unless you need me very much," Longin said, "I am not going to Bob's funeral. There is still so much to do before you can bring the children here, and soon I have to go back to Bragg."

"Well, all right, if you don't want to," I said awkwardly. I didn't know what to think. Was he not going out of a sense of duty to Bob's family, or couldn't he bear to go, having seen too much of death already?

[49]

"I want to go," Longin said, "but there is one thing you cannot hire a man to do for you. I have to get rid of all those tin cans and broken bottles that are heaped up behind the barn, they cannot be here when Mikey comes. I never saw so many junks lying around, on land somebody called his own. Did you see? A space as big as this kitchen, and heaped six feet high."

You cannot hire a man to do it. . . . My eyes burned. "Okay," I said. "You stay here. I'll manage."

The Bests had come up, from their farm just over the hill to the east, and had said I was to use their phone any time I needed, whether or not they were home, just walk in, don't mind the dog. And they had come a second time, to say they had a message from my father to phone him that afternoon about three, and I had walked over the hill in the clear spring sunlight, and had gone on in, and sure enough, no one was home but Teddy, the dog. I had rung Central on the old-fashioned wall phone, and had looked out of the window as I waited, looking past the huge trunks of the maple trees and over across the barns and the pasture just below, past the evergreens on the rise beyond, and then away in the distance to the mountains of New Hampshire, blue and gray-lavender, their snowy peaks white against the sky. And then I could hear my father's voice, sounding very far away coming over the country phone system, telling me that everything was arranged now, five coffins, as I had wanted, but one headstone, so there would be no errors.

"Thanks," I said. I stared at the peaks, white, white with snow and it was nearly May. "That's all right, Dad," I said, and I wanted to say it didn't matter, but I didn't think I could make him understand, long distance and all.

"What's that?" Dad said.

"I said it's all right," I said, more loudly. "I have a better perspective on things here. . . . There's still snow on the mountain tops, can you believe it?"

"Good," my father said. "I'm very glad."

The following morning I left Longin digging a huge pit for the trash, and started the drive to New Jersey. From there we went

[50]

to Washington by train. Pat and Chris went along, as planned, and my brothers Ted and Bruce. My father and mother remained behind to take care of Mike, and my sister, Mary, was unable to wrest any more time from teaching school.

We were met at Union Station by Joe and Dodie Dunn, and by old and good friends from Fort Leavenworth and Fort Knox. To see them all there stirred up memory, that saboteur, that treacherous saboteur. As we drove through Washington, the soft southern wind blowing through the cherry trees and stirring the pink bouquets of the magnolias, I knew that pride and pride alone would see me through this day. *Pride in your outfit,* Bob had said once, *will give you courage when nothing else will.* I looked at Pat and Chris. They were my outfit—I must not fail them.

We drove to the chapel at Fort Meyer and my brothers and my sons and I sat in the front pew on the left, and we listened to the sounds of life all around us, the scufflings and creakings as the chapel filled, and the stirring and flapping of the battle flags overhead, the past and the present breathing together, life still in us all. The five flag-draped coffins rolled in almost silently, each accompanied by a guard of honor.

Chris leaned over to me. "Which one is Daddy?"

"The first one."

And why not?

There were to be three ceremonies, Catholic, Protestant, and Christian Scientist, those three strands of the rope of Christianity being represented by the silent coffins before us. The Catholic service was first, and it rolled over me, the unfamiliar Latin being without power to hurt, though I knew it was for Bob, these prayers. It was the sweet majesty of the words I knew so well, *I am the resurrection and the life, saith the Lord: he that believeth in Me . . .* —these were the words with power to reach in and drain my strength, to test the fiber of my resolution not to yield to weakness.

I was staring straight before me, summoning all my flagging self-control, when I heard Chris's urgent whisper, "Mother, I have to go to the bathroom!"

[51]

I glanced at Bruce. "Please take him," I whispered.

Bruce, bachelor-like, looked both appalled and baffled.
"Where?"

"I don't know . . . try the side door."

I watched them leave, Bruce looking as dignified as possible and obviously wishing they were both invisible, and I was shaken with inner laughter. Not even here, Bob, darling, I thought. How provoked you always were at Mass! He never made it, did he? Dear Chris . . .

And then I was safely past the Protestant service, and the Christian Science speaker was saying there is no death, and I thought, Now, Bob, don't start to argue, though you hold all the cards now, though you know all about it. I listened to the speaker, and I thought, How you would love to take him on. You always said there's nothing better to argue than politics and religion. And if there is no death, Bob, what in heaven's name are we all doing here?

And then we were following the coffins out into the warm sweet spring sunshine, and we got into a car and started down through Arlington cemetery, moving as slowly as the guard walked, the drums keeping time with the slow labored pounding of my heart, beat . . . beat, dull . . . dull, death . . . death. How Bob hates those drums, I thought. He always hates those drums.

"Why are we going so slow?" Pat asked, and I couldn't answer him, and his uncles kept silent.

And after a bit, Chris looked up at Pat and said, "Do you think Daddy is a skeleton yet?"

"*Shut up!*" Bruce said savagely.

Amen, I thought, my eyes shut.

And then we were at the graveside, and while we listened to the chaplains again saying three assortments of prayers, Joe Dunn leaned over and said softly, "They'll fire three volleys, Melisse, don't let it startle you." I nodded, and Chris and Pat asked me what he had said, and I explained to them in a whisper. And all around us the world was so beautiful and soft and lovely with the promise of life beginning all over again, and the pure, clear notes of the bugle sang Taps, and I seemed to be feeling no grief at all, only the most intense pride, pride to have been Bob's wife, to stand here, his sons beside me, on this hillside stony with heroes' names.

Crack! went the first volley, and scarcely had its echoes faded when Chris whirled and demanded sharply, "Were those real bullets?"

However does a woman see it through, who has no children beside her, no flying buttresses to brace her against the future?

CHAPTER III

In Vermont it was still cold. The snow was nearly gone except for a few patches in the deep woods, but the fields were still brown, the bushes in the hedgerows still bare, no sign of new green anywhere. And the cold crept out of the rocks and down from the mountains and into our blood and bones.

"I haven't been this cold since Germany," I said, eating again. Longin and I were hungry all the time. I assumed my hunger was my body's reaction to my thin blood, and Longin's to the immensity of his self-imposed work program. "I swore then I would never be cold again if I could help it. What if the electricity goes off in a blizzard? What then? The oil burner will be absolutely useless."

"Better leave the wood stove set up in the kitchen," Longin advised. "You can always cook on it, and it will heat this room, anyway."

"Then there won't be room for chairs around our table," I objected. "And where will I have work spaces for cooking?"

There was a cluster of old-fashioned cupboards from floor to ceiling along the wall next to the bathroom. "I take out the lower ones," Longin said, as if no more work were involved than rearranging some cardboard boxes, "and I make work spaces of them, facing the sink and stove. Next I remove the bottom shelf of the upper cupboards, shorten the doors to match, and table and chairs will fit under."

"You have to leave in five days," I said faintly.

"So I will just have time to match these windows over here, this one over the sink is too long, sill goes down too far, and this one over the stove—" he broke off, shaking his head. "I don't think there are two windows in this entire house that are the same size, or even on the same level. They look like they were located by somebody seasick."

"Now wait a minute," I said. "There's no point in knocking yourself out. What does it matter how those windows look?"

"They have to be on same level," Longin explained patiently, "or how to make the shelf across the back of the stove, work spaces, and sink?"

I gave it up. I went off to discuss with Mr. Potwin about a mason to put a fireplace in the living room. "And one in the new bedroom, too," I said recklessly. I was planning to give the three bedrooms upstairs to the children, and convert the garage into a bedroom for myself. "I suppose it will cost a lot of money, but money won't keep you warm. Not me, anyway. Not if it's just jingling in my pocket."

I sounded reckless, but I wasn't, really. I knew, because I'd had lots of experience at scrimping, that we could get by in the country on our Regular Army pensions. It would take scrimping, because at that time it had not yet been decided that the Korean conflict was a war, and then, too, pensions for widows of the Regular Army were about a third as much as for the Reserves. Nevertheless, I had more cash in hand than I'd ever had before in my life—there was Bob's G.I. insurance, his civilian policies had had double-indemnity clauses, and before he'd got on that plane he'd dropped some coins in a flight-insurance machine. Bob had told me that such money was not intended to be saved, it was to be spent so that I would not lack for comfort nor the children for opportunity. Even so, to spend so much of it so quickly frightened me. But it had to be done.

Mr. Potwin located a mason and I showed him where he was to

[55]

put the fireplaces, and he said he would be back as soon as the foundations were ready. Be sure to sink them six feet down, he said, the frost line is four feet down, but with a chimney it is best to play very safe because it won't do to have the frost ever move the chimney even a fraction of an inch. I said I would see to this being done properly, and how much did he charge? Three fifty an hour, he said, and two fifty for his helper. I heard a faint cry of pain from my checkbook, but I stoically ignored it. "Very well," I said.

The sink and the stove were in, and the plumbers were now in the process of ripping out the old furnace, and the electrician was putting in a few scattered floor plugs, of which the house so far was innocent, and some wall switches. This turned out to be trickier than expected, because the studs, we were impressed to find, were slabs of logs often as wide as fourteen inches, with only a couple of inches separating their rough edges, to which the bark still clung. Finding a passageway for the wires, and persuading the wires to proceed along the passageway, consumed a lot of very expensive time. But it's necessary, I kept telling myself. It's capital investment—isn't it?

Then came the telephone man to connect up the phone again, and he was aghast to learn that I had been paying full amount since November through April, the entire $2.75 required monthly from subscribers to our ten-party line. I should have paid only half, he said, since the phone was disconnected though not removed. I must be sure to ask for a refund. He repeated this several times, and seemed so concerned at this unnecessary extravagance on my part that I was simply charmed.

"People up here are so *honest!*" I exclaimed enthusiastically. "Don't you think it's wonderful how honest people up here are?"

Longin didn't say anything. He rarely shared my enthusiasms about people, and I put this down to his bitter experiences with the Germans. Naturally such experiences would sour anybody, I thought, but some time he ought to get over it. The rest of the human race isn't like that. Not all of it, anyway. Not all the time.

Perhaps it would be in order at this point to explain how Longin came to be an honorary member of our family. He had seen his family wiped out, one by one, as Russia and Germany grappled with each other across his native Poland, and finally, in 1941, he was one of the many thousands of his countrymen who were seized by the Germans, packed ruthlessly into cattle cars, and shipped to Germany as slave laborers. "They took away our leather shoes," he told me once, "and our woolen coats, if we had any, and gave us wooden shoes to wear, and rags, and marched us through the streets, and the Germans stood on either side and laughed at us as we passed. 'Clomp! Clomp! Clomp! like horses!' they shouted. 'Look—Poles are like animals!' they said. They say now it was all Hitler. I never saw Hitler. But those Germans lining the streets, they threw things at us, and laughed at us, and some of them spat."

That was just the beginning. It must have seemed several lifetimes to him before it was, at last, 1945 and the American troops swept in. Longin managed to avoid the stagnation of a DP camp, and attached himself informally to the unit which had liberated him, and in due time he found himself a member of Bob's household, in a luxurious house requisitioned, according to the rough justice of the times, from the family of the leading Nazi of the community. By the time the boys and I joined Bob overseas in '46, Bob regarded Longin fondly as a younger brother, and when we were all to return to the States in '47, it was unthinkable to leave him behind. So we wrote a few letters to Senators, and urged all our New Jersey friends to do the same; Bob jogged the memory of the State Department; and, when at last the visa came through, he bought Longin a third-class ticket on the *Ernie Pyle*. Longin stayed with us and helped take care of Mike the year we were at Fort Knox. When we moved to Fort Leavenworth, and Mike could not come too, but spent the year commuting between my parents' home and various centers of diagnosis and treatment (improving not in the least), Longin felt it was time to strike out on his own, and he enlisted in the paratroops. By now he was a sergeant with some forty-two jumps to his credit, and I suppose juggling cupboards and windows around in our little house in the peaceful Vermont countryside seemed to him a far simpler project than it did to me.

What with carpenters, plumbers, masons, Mr. Potwin and a fire-insurance man, one day there were seventeen people, besides ourselves, churning through the place, and I wondered if we had lost forever the peace and quiet of the country. And the next day it was absolutely quiet. Not a soul showed up. About ten in the morning, when were were finally convinced that nobody was coming, we sat down to fix coffee and a snack of several sandwiches and to warm up our hands because we had started to paint the outside of the house and it was so cold we had to wear gloves.

"It's funny nobody came," I said. "Is it some kind of local holiday, do you suppose?"

"First of May," Longin said. "In communist countries it's a holiday."

"That hardly includes Vermont." I was really puzzled. "I remember once when Bob was stationed at Camp Polk and I went into Leesville to go to the bank and it was closed and all the stores too. And I said for heavensake why is everything closed? And you know how Northern you sound down in Louisiana? Well, this man absolutely glared at me and said, 'Ma'am, it's Gen'l Robuht E. Lee's *buht*day, ma'am!' "

So when the plumbers and carpenters and masons turned up the next day, I tried to be tactful. "What happened yesterday?" I said casually.

"Nothing much. Too cold." Then, seeing my puzzled look, they said, "You didn't expect us, did you? Gosh, it was May first! You know, first day of fishing season!"

Whoever had painted the house yellow had been very extravagant and had given it a lavish one-coat job on all four sides. But whoever had painted the house previous to that had done a typical Vermont frugality job, three sides only, no paint wasted on the fourth side, the one away from the road. This, then, was the side needing paint the most urgently, and this was where we started, covering the thin, tired yellow with bright new white. But not

[58]

even Longin, mighty worker that he was, could finish the house in the few days remaining to him, and inevitably it was the last day of his leave.

I drove him to White River Junction and he caught one of those convenient trains on the Boston and Maine that leave about one in the morning. He said he was very sorry that he had not had time to finish painting all the high parts, especially the undersides of the eaves, very difficult for me. Maybe he could get another leave. And if he couldn't his three-year enlistment would be up in November. And in the meantime if the pump should break I was to ask the plumber to look at the packing. And the instruction sheet for the hot-water heater was pinned to the post next to it. And . . .

"Will you quit worrying about us?" I said. "After all, *you* are jumping out of airplanes. Good-bye, good luck, and thanks for everything."

I had left the lights on in the kitchen, and my little house looked warm and welcoming as I drove up over the hill. It was only the light that had made it look warm. Inside it was cold, a mutinous cold that mocked me, taunting me with the emptiness of my house, and the enormous number of tasks still to be done before the children came at the end of the school year, tasks which it was confident it could prevent me from finishing.

I turned on a burner and extended my hands over its reddening coils. There must be some way to shut off the living room from the rest of the house, I thought, otherwise even with the fireplace there it will be cold. Board up that open archway, and put a door in, over near the wall at the foot of the stairs, otherwise there would be no wall space in either room, no place for a sofa in the living room or for our dining table in the hall. Better keep our big dining table, maybe we'll have company some time. I better paint the ceilings, too, they look frightful from all the smoke from those stoves. They look like storm clouds, no wonder I have this uneasy feeling of a calamity threatening. And the hall, what a dirty beige . . . maybe a cool, sophisticated gray? A good, strong, alive-looking green would do for the living room. Not too much yellow in it, use what Longin calls a green green. The bathroom, though, that's worst of all. How can anybody paint a bathroom lavender and black? Makes you almost cower under the bedclothes and refuse to get up. Can't do anything about that floor, though. Longin says to leave it alone, any time it's going to fall through to the cellar and have to be replaced, so don't go putting down new linoleum. . . .

Comforted by the thought that I had a mountain of work to do, and so would have very little time to think, I went to bed and fell asleep. I was awakened almost at once, or so it seemed, by thunder in the wall. No, it couldn't have been thunder. It was some kind of abrupt, blasting, drumming noise. There it went again. . . . I got up. The sky was turning gray. The day, I supposed, had started for some damn early bird.

I put on my coat and shoes and stomped sullenly outside. I was right. It was a bird. A robin, female, no doubt—who else would be so anxious to get the nest done?—was already hard at it, dragging bits of dry grass and twigs and other junk through a hole under the eaves. She didn't have to be so noisy. Even out here, her take-offs created a nerve-rasping racket. I glared at her, and I was tired and cross and I wished I could bop her with a rock, or at least figure some way to get up there and nail something over that hole, at least before she got any eggs laid.

Or maybe she already had laid them. I didn't know much about birds. Maybe she was like me, family started and still fixing up the nest. And wasn't there supposed to be a father bird somewhere around? Singing to her to keep her entertained while she worked, flashing his feathers around so she'll think it's all worth while? Well, where was he?

I went back to bed, and plopped the pillow over my head to shut out the noise of the robin forlorn, slaving away in the early morn. But it was no use. I was in such a froth of pity, first for the bird and then for myself that I couldn't sleep.

I spent most of my time that day feeding wood to the little black stove and fixing coffee and drinking it. It seemed rude to sit down in a clammy old house and drink coffee when men were

[60]

working in the damp, cold, cramped basement. I asked the plumbers if they didn't want coffee, and, looking rather startled, they accepted. And then, by the time they had left and I fixed my supper, I realized I was running out of wood small enough to get into the stove.

I picked up the axe which apparently had been included in the purchase of the woodshed, and I began making ineffective swipes at a chunk of wood. The shed door creaked open and a tall, lean boy of about fourteen walked in.

"Mother thought maybe you need some kindling," he announced, and removed the axe from my astonished hand.

Half an hour later he had created an impressive heap of wood. Then he leaned against the wall in the kitchen and chatted for a while, and I learned that he was Lloyd, the older Best boy, and he was going to high school, and there was a younger sister and a still younger brother, and I was very happy to learn this, because I had been afraid there would be no children near for mine to play with.

Oh, there were lots of children in this neighborhood, he assured me. There were two in the house half a mile up this way, and there were six in the house half a mile down the other way.

And then he made motions to go, and I wondered if I ought not . . . after all, it was a lot of work . . . but how much?

I said awkwardly, because I wasn't sure I was doing the right thing, "Thanks an awful lot. Please take this—" and I groped in my pocket for my wallet.

"Oh, no, no thanks!" And he bolted out the door as if mortally offended.

Obviously, I ought not.

The next time I saw Vivian Best, I thanked her for sending her son, because I had needed that wood very much, I said.

She gave me her serene, clear-eyed look, a direct-in-the-eyes look which was a new experience for me. "Melissa," she said without further preamble, "don't offer my children money for being neighborly."

I flushed. "I'm sorry. I just didn't know what was expected. I'm not used to neighborliness."

It was something I had to get used to, like the climate. It was new to me, this neighborliness from strangers. I didn't know if all country folk were like this, or if I was just incredibly lucky. It seemed to me then—and it still does—that I was dropped down between two of the nicest families that existed anywhere.

I met Ellison Alfonse one afternoon not long after Longin left. It was my intention to put some flowers along the west side of the house, toward the orchard, and Longin had somehow found the time to spade up a strip about six feet wide, and I had planted there some iris and peonies I had brought from Mother's garden on my return from Washington. Of course the weeds found all this delightfully amusing and were showing me what weeds can do, given twenty years' head start. I was walking along with my head down by my ankles and was pulling at something fiendish called witch-grass when a slender, dark-eyed woman and two of the prettiest little girls I had ever seen came around the corner of the house.

Ellison introduced herself and her daughters and she excused her visit (as if it needed any excuse) on the grounds that she was the local correspondent for the weekly paper in Windsor, and she wondered if I minded her putting it in her column that I had moved there? And we talked for some time, and all the while I continued to weed, and Ellison weeded right along with me. By the time she left we had won a round against the weeds, and I had a crick in my back and I presume she did, too, and I could only think that this was one of the loveliest women I had ever met.

As for the Bests, I had scarcely recovered from the wood-chopping incident when I was overwhelmed by lesson No. 2, neighborliness, country-style. I had ordered a bureau from Altman's (we didn't own any storage units of this kind, having always used quartermaster issue), and it had arrived in Windsor via Railway Express, but that was as far as Railway Express cared to be responsible for it. We lived, it seemed, beyond the delivery zone. Come get it yourself if you want it.

I asked the carpenter if he would mind picking it up for me in his truck, and he had brought it. And that evening the Bests, all of them, came up over the hill, and it took only one glance for me, trained to such nuances by years of receiving Mike-offended neighbors, to know I had done something wrong. What, I couldn't imagine, but I had offended them somehow.

After Clifford commented that it was a nice spring evening and I agreed that it was, and Vivian said it was time we had some warm weather and I agreed it certainly was time, Clifford came to the point.

"Melissa," he said bluntly, "I understand that you had something down to the village that you needed brought up."

"A bureau," I said, groping in the dark.

"And you had that fellow that works here bring it in his truck."

"Why, yes—"

"I got a truck," Clifford said. "And I could just as well have brought that bureau for you. You might just as well know right off what kind of neighbors you got. When I got something that you need, and you don't have, and if you don't borrow it, *I'm going to be offended.*"

Such neighbors did take getting used to, but you can get used to almost anything, if you put your mind to it, and we rapidly got used to the Bests. In fact, we got used to them so thoroughly that we have borrowed constantly and continually and almost without shame, ever since. A can of gasoline for the tractor, a sack of grain for the cows. Mower, tedder, rake, hay-baler. The harrow that works better than ours on wet soil, because you can change the angle of the disks. Corn planter, binder, chopper and blower. Meat grinder when making sausage, knives and saws and how-to-do-it diagrams when cutting up the pig. Once we even borrowed their barn.

Christopher was soon to have his first Communion, and I must be there. I drove to New Jersey to attend the ceremony, and Pat and Chris wanted very much to go back to Vermont with me. "Not yet," I told them. "It's only three weeks, and school will be over. Then your Uncle Bruce will bring you up."

"But Kitty is going!" they cried. "How come Kitty can go?"

"Because she's only three years old and doesn't go to school," I answered, stating the obvious. I certainly wasn't going to tell them the real reason, that long hours of the companionship of Kitty were exhausting her grandmother. My mother found Mike easier to take care of than Kitty. Mike, at least, did not make conversation every waking minute. You could, so long as you kept an eye on him, sometimes even relax.

But Kitty was a little girl born grown up. As soon as she could talk she had begun to give me directions, and although I had become used to it, my mother, schooled to the behavior of a previous generation, was unprepared for the erosion of the mind which this produced. "Don't you think it's time to clear the table?" Kitty would say, when the grownups tarried over coffee and dessert. "Do you really prefer making cakes this way?" as my mother gathered shortening and sugar, flour and baking powder. "*My mother always uses a mix.*" This sort of thing went on from morning until night, and when her grandmother sought refuge in another room, there would come through the wall the sound of Kitty's voice, conversing with her imaginary friends. "Sally, don't take all the cookies! Do you want to be a gimme pig? You'll get a gilded conscience if you're greedy!" Wherever Kitty was, it sounded like a crowd.

"Nature," my mother explained apologetically, "didn't intend a woman of my age to look after a child of three."

"I know," I assured her.

As we drove off, Kitty's suitcases on the back seat of the Chevy carefully hemming in the box containing our pregnant cat, now very close to her time, Kitty asked, a little wistfully, I thought, "Mama, how soon will I get over being three?"

We made it back to Vermont, where the cat with commendable promptness had kittens on Kitty's bed. Kitty named them Bootsie, Popco, Tico, Loco, and Calico; and then, because I believed Every Child Should Have a Dog, I went out and acquired a pup, a collie in a casual sort of way, and Kitty named him Butch. And it seemed as if my life must have reached the apex of its complications.

But not quite. As the days passed, I realized I was not suffering from shock, as I had thought, but I was pregnant. And with the realization came understanding, of why I had been unable to accept the finality, the *it's all over* of which the priest had spoken, of why everyone else's grief had seemed to me almost theatrical, of why I had felt, so often and so strangely, Bob's presence. Of course I had never felt alone. How could I feel alone, still to bear his child?

It would not be truthful to pretend I was completely delighted. There were times when I could not see how I could ever manage, times when my physical strength failed me, and with it my courage. I had to get the vegetable garden planted, and it was so difficult to stoop, I felt weak and dizzy, and angry to be weak when I *had* to be strong. I could not force myself to accomplish a fraction of what I had planned, and barely managed to finish painting the hall when Bruce brought the boys.

"Count yourself lucky," Bruce said. "You should think of this as a gift from Heaven."

"I keep telling myself that," I said. "Give me time. After a bit, I'll believe it."

When I told the children, they screamed with joy. They danced about on the lawn like wild Indians, and whooped and hollered.

"You realize you'll have to help," I said to my sons. "I'll need you to help in the garden. I won't be able to do everything by myself."

They promised seriously that they would help in every way possible. I said, well then, start by stopping the crows from eating the corn sprouts. It was maddening and disheartening to look at the rows of corn, where I had toiled so painfully to plant the kernels, and to see that as fast as the green shoots showed, the crows had come along for hors d'oeuvres, tugged up the shoots and eaten the sprouted kernel. I suppose they were delicious, something like soybean sprouts.

"Didn't you use crow repellent?" little David Best asked me.

"You put it on the seed before you plant. The crows don't like the corn, then."

"Too late," I said gloomily. "I'll remember to do it next year."

Every morning I would be awakened by the thunderous take-off of Mother Robin, about four A.M., and then, after wrestling for an hour or so with my problem of How to Get Through the Winter With New Baby (a topic of worry arising logically from stimulus of the yapping and squabbling of the baby robins in the nest in the wall), I would be just about to drop off to sleep again, when the impudent *caw! caw!* of the crows would sound from the corn patch, and the boys would get up and rush out of the house, hurling threats and stones.

And every day the rows of corn looked more and more ragged. We were nearly in despair, and I had about decided not to count on any corn in the freezer at all, when Lloyd Best, one pleasant evening, came strolling up over the hill, gun over his shoulder and a dead crow dangling from his hand.

We all gathered around to admire the crow. It was a large bird, seen close up, and with a powerful beak, a triumph of functional design.

"I brought him for you," Lloyd said shyly. "I'll put him up, if you like."

He took a pole about six feet long and planted it firmly in the middle of our corn patch. Then he tied the crow to the pole, using a generous length of string, so the corpse would flap and swing and look very, very dead.

"You'll not have trouble with crows now," David said.

He was right. The crows avoided our garden like sudden death, and the boys and I agreed, as we gazed fondly on the crow from well to windward, that never had we received a nicer housewarming present.

The weeds, however, could not be discouraged. They loved everything about the garden, its location, its soil, the rain (the rain came every other day, as regular as a metronome, sun rain sun rain), but especially the weeds were enchanted by our inexperience. We didn't know anything whatsoever about hexing them away. We waited until they were of good pulling size, and then we pulled, scattering ripened seeds as we worked. It was a ghastly summer, and the weeds were almost the worst thing about it. I would have let them grow, finally, but they threatened to choke the peas and lettuce right out of existence, and some of the more mighty ones were even shading the tomato plants, cutting off what little sunshine there was.

I weeded as long as my strength held out, and I forced the children to labor along with me, and often they were in tears, and I would tongue-lash them to further efforts, and it was frightful. Whether or not this kind of scene developed their characters, I don't know. I'm sure it rotted mine.

David and Marilyn often came to play, and they would find us out in the vegetable garden, one big, unhappy, snarling family.

"Don't you want to eat this winter?" I'd demand savagely. "Then keep at it—work!"

"We *are* working!" the boys would bawl.

David and Marilyn would weed right along with us. "Some day, Patrick," Marilyn would observe, "you'll be grateful to your mother for teaching you how to do a decent day's work."

Speechless with rage, Patrick would yank up another four-foot-high weed and hurl it towards the hedgerow.

Once in a while my maternal heart would melt, and I'd think, poor fatherless children, to have to work so hard, I'll go easy on them when they get home. Unfortunately, whenever I felt these attacks of leniency, it always happened that the children would come bounding zestfully up over the hill from Bests, bursting to report on their good times. "Gee, Mother, did we have fun! David was weeding corn and we helped. Gee, I bet we worked two hours!"

Work, I discovered, becomes toil or drudgery only when performed at home.

I sent off to Sears, Roebuck for a gadget called a wheel hoe. In the catalog it looked like a marvelous idea, just what we needed. All we would have to do is shove it along, and there would be our garden, soil all crumbly, plants joyously freed from weeds. That was the trouble. We had to shove it along. Whatever was needed for this, shoulders or muscles or red blood, I didn't have. I couldn't get the darned thing to move more than a foot or two when I felt as if I were committing infanticide.

"Let me!" Pat said, his manhood challenged. *Whang!* he hung up on a rock, and impaled himself on a handle.

"Let me!" Chris said, and *whang!* he hung up on another rock and rapped his teeth on the crossbrace.

"Never mind," I said, bright and cheerful as all get-out. "This wheel hoe is probably a marvelous idea, but not yet. For us, I mean. Our soil has to have several million tons of rocks chucked out first. Then it will work fine."

"Never—" Pat was still fighting for breath. "I mean—David— every spring David—rocks in his garden—"

"He means more rocks keep coming," Chris explained. "David says they clear them all out and plant their garden and the next year there they are again, not the sames ones, of course, but more anyway. He says you have to get the rocks out every year. I *think*," Chris added vaguely, testing his mouth for blood, "they come from the middle of the earth."

"What a comforting thought," I said. "Listen. Here's a picture of a gadget that runs with a motor. Garden tractor, it says. All you have to do is steer it. The motor is as strong as two and three quarters horses."

So we sent off for a garden tractor, and some extras, such as a harrow and a cultivator, and this cost us not much more than groceries for two months, but what-ho, I thought, with several qualms in the budget, penny wise let us by all means be. Anyway, what we sow we must reap.

The garden tractor came, via freight. A postcard announced its arrival in Windsor, and I breezed around in the Chevy to see what weight vehicle would bring this purchase, and the man said I could easily· fit my shipment into my car, and so I could. The garden tractor arrived in fourteen separate pieces. All I needed now was several years' apprenticeship to a capable auto mechanic, and I would be all set.

[68]

I dumped the smaller of the pieces out on the grass, and the boys and I stared dolefully at our purchase.

"I know what those things are," Kitty said helpfully. "Those are tires for the wheels."

"A genius," sneered Pat.

"Hush," I said. "Let's not be bitter. We have been misled, that's all. The catalog didn't say a word, I could swear, about this do-it-yourself assembly job."

David Best had appeared at Chris's side, cocked a bright eye at our fragmented tractor, and disappeared. Shortly he reappeared, accompanied by his father, mother, brother and sister. We womenfolk had a most pleasant social time, sitting about on the lawn, exchanging items of local news, and admiring the menfolk reconstructing the garden tractor.

"Let me know how it works out," Vivian said. "I've always thought I'd like one for my vegetable garden."

We tried it out the next day. Two and three quarters horses, we found, were too much for either a pregnant woman or an eight-year-old boy. I couldn't steer the contraption, and demolished a row of spinach, and Patrick couldn't stop it, and went screeching on out of the garden, hanging onto the monster for dear life, with Chris and me shrieking directions how to turn off the power.

We decided we would park the goldurned thing in the garage until the boys were older, unless, of course, the Bests cared to borrow it—be sure to mention we have something for them to borrow—and meanwhile, back to coolie labor.

The rare June days became the peas-are-ripe July days, and life became more grim and earnest than ever. I had thought to spare myself the work of providing support for the peas—stakes and strings and wire, all energy-consuming to erect—and so I had planted dwarf varieties. It said right in the seed catalog that dwarf varieties would not need support. Maybe not in a normal year, but this was not a normal year. Rain sun rain sun produced unusually long vines, and these grew very tired as they grew very long, and they lay down on the ground. In order to pick the ripe pods (and every day there were more pods ripe), I had to lift

[69]

each vine, strip it of its plump solid-feeling pods, and lay it down again, gently, lest the vine somehow be broken and all the pods-that-would-have-been doomed to wither away. By the time I reached the end of a row, I would be unable to straighten my back, and I would hobble out of the pea patch, crouched over, bellowing at the children to *come down here and help pick peas, do you want them to rot on the vine?*

I think they did, but they didn't dare say so.

By now the plumbers had finished their tasks, and presented their bill. It took only one shocked glance at the total, which was precisely double the estimate, to convince me that something was drastically wrong somewhere. I thought I could now pinpoint the trouble: my brain. I had been most sympathetic, I recalled, and had nodded my head just like a donkey, when the boss plumber had said, good heavens no, he wouldn't want to sign a contract for such and such an amount—you never knew what you would run into in these old houses. In order to protect himself he'd have to set the amount awfully high. . . . Ah, well, they say an education is expensive. It certainly is, particularly when that topnotch teacher, experience, is assigning the lessons. The trouble with experience is, you're never sure you've had all the fundamentals, and you don't get a diploma guaranteeing you won't be a sitting duck next time.

For the benefit of other unwilling and inexperienced scholars, let me list the highlights of my brief course in House Repairs, How Not to Lose Your Shirt in Process Thereof:

1. There is no truth whatsoever in the statement, "You never know what you'll run into in these old houses." Brother, there is one thing the plumber/mason/carpenter knows he'll find: you. A juicy plum, ripe for the picking.

2. Get a contract, no matter how staggering the total thereon. You might as well know ahead of time how much of a jolt this is going to be. You'll find out sooner or later, and it might as well be sooner, when you still have the strength to scream. Also, a workman unable to figure ahead what his materials will come to, and to estimate how much time the job will probably take, knows

so little about his job you would be better off doing the work yourself. Furthermore, any job can be dragged out almost indefinitely, if you are paying by the hour. This is not to accuse anyone of deliberate cozenage, whether by bogus delay or counterfeit complication. Nevertheless, nasty suspicions will creep into your mind, should, for example, the pump break, as ours did, and required some ninety cents' worth of replacement parts, an exact description of which was given over the phone by my clever engineer-brother, Bruce, and yet the fixing of the pump took three trips from town, one, to see what was the matter, two, to bring the wrong part, three, to bring what Bruce had ordered in the first place—all three trips of twenty miles each at our expense. Unconvinced? Typical traditional behavior of plumbers, you say? Then what about the time our thermostat for the furnace broke down and we sent for a man to fix it and he came in sub-zero weather and froze the new one, repeated his trip and this time managed to install another, and it was worse after he left than the old one had been, and finally Longin took things apart and found two wires neatly crossed, so that the furnace and the thermostat were simply not *en rapport*, as the psychologists say? Didn't the repairman know any better, or couldn't he bear to say good-bye?

3. To return to our course, and following on the observations under (2), above, it is obvious that you should not serve coffee, no matter how cold the day, when you are paying the workmen by the hour. It is especially bad if you are not aware, as I was not, that you are paying them by the hour. Naturally they think money means nothing to you, and naturally (and who can blame them?) they feel money is better off where it is appreciated, i.e., in their pockets. Never waste a workman's time, and be most particular not to allow your sons to ask the carpenters to make arrows for them, not even for the purpose of shooting crows in the corn. It gives, as I say, a most unfortunate tone to the whole thing.

4. Do not pay the bill until the work is finished. It is five years later as I write this, and the ink well-nigh faded on the check, but there is still no grill over the cold-air intake in the floor of our bedroom, and every now and then a child or a kitten or something

[71]

else small falls into it. We try to keep it covered with the waste-basket or a floor lamp, but such things have a way of being moved, and *thunk!*—screams—"Band Aids!"

5. In all matters try to put yourself in the other fellow's shoes. It's a case of, if I were a fox, how would I run? The fox is the carpenter/plumber/mason/painter, and he is firmly convinced, and nothing but bankruptcy proceedings on your part will unconvince him, that nobody moves to the country but millionaires in disguise. (Perhaps nobody else ought to. . . .) Remember his every action will be based on that belief. So— You Have Been Warned.

By the middle of the summer I no longer was convinced everyone was as honest as the day is long, and the days were very, very long. The tomato vines, sprawling on the wet ground because I had not had energy to prop them up on anything, were bearing tomatoes that rotted before they ripened, and the only way to prevent this was to pick them green and ripen them up on boards. That damn robin was apparently raising a second brood, because she still took off with a deafening roar before sunrise, and I don't care if she was dragging back twice her weight in food every day, so was I. And the beans took over where the peas left off, the cat and her kittens refused to become house-trained, and all through the house, things were collapsing.

I suppose it was because the roof was becoming water-logged with all the rain. The frugality of the previous owners had resulted not only in the three-sided paint job, but also in a two-faced roofing job, several years back, in which asphalt shingles had been used only on the surface visible from the road, the surface facing the orchard, and therefore likely to be seen only by the owners of the house, being covered with rolled roofing, which, expanding under the summer sun and contracting from the winter cold, had sprung innumerable leaks. And through these leaks in every rain water had seeped, staining the bedroom ceilings and adding what must have been the last few tons of weight too much for the foundation, which sagged. Not much, but a foundation doesn't have to sag very much. A fraction of an inch will make it impossible to close the front door. An inch or so will do strange things to the line of the eaves, springing leaks in the gutters, from which the rain pours down to streak the paint on the siding, until the water finds another route to the ground, inside the walls, and you may have no warning of this until a favorite painting shows flaking paint or bulging canvas.

The floor of Kitty's bedroom developed a lurch it had not had before, and as a result the bed was not properly supported. One by one the legs, screwed to the frame of the box spring, loosened and came off. We would laugh merrily as if this were all ever so jolly, and prop the bed up on bricks. And with every really heavy rain, the waters came through the ceiling and ran in under the windows and blew in through the cracks around the front door, and we built dikes under the windows with bath towels and put our cooking pans around on the floors, upstairs and down. There was a big drip coming through a hole in the center of the living-room ceiling, this hole being a new and informal drain for the water pouring in the leak in the west wall, the one which had caused all that mildew and mold on the clothes, books and suitcases stored in the closet adjacent to the wall. There was a stream pouring down the wall above the door between the kitchen and workroom, this wall being the one where the shed roof joined the main house, and where, later, Longin discovered that our "skilled workmen" had put the flashing *over* the shingles. Here we used the turkey roaster, being of appropriate size, and we placed it strategically in the doorway. Pong, ping! ting, poing! went the water. "Listen to the music!" Kitty cried. "It sounds just like crookets singing!"

When the news of my pregnancy reached Fort Monroe, Mary Buechler had sent word from the Red Cross that if I wanted Longin home, they'd do all they could to help. If I wanted Longin home! I'm drowning, would I care to catch a lifeline?

I didn't know how Longin would feel about it. It didn't seem fair to be such a clinging vine I'd choke off his future. If he had ever owed Bob and me anything, he had already more than paid it back taking care of Mike. But when the pump broke and the roof leaked and the children wept as they weeded the vegetables and the house sagged so I couldn't close the front door, the instinct of self-preservation stifled any qualms and I wrote him that the situation, more complicated than anticipated, was getting out of control.

Longin phoned at once to say he was applying for a discharge, and this news I relayed to Fort Monroe, which put the energies and resources of the Red Cross at his disposal; and in due time Longin obtained a "compassionate discharge." On the second Sunday in August, he phoned from Windsor to say there he was, would we mind to come and get him? And the children leaped screaming with joy into the Chevy and I drove the ten miles in twenty minutes, which is very good time considering the roads, and all the way into Windsor all I could feel was relief.

But this was one time I couldn't ask, "How long can you stay?" I could see no end to our need of him. Yet he had a right to his own life, and someday we'd have to talk about it. But not yet. Not soon. Now, nothing mattered but that he was here.

As soon as we got home, Longin inspected the work on garage and woodshed, now known as my bedroom and the workroom, and on the new garage, strung out beyond my bedroom.

"How do they work, these men? You have to keep them until they finish?"

"Oh, no, they're just working by the day," I said. "But I already told them I can't use them any more. Nothing is finished, but it's already cost so much money, I thought we'd just have to finish things ourselves."

"Good," Longin said. He sounded angry. "Look at that. Tell me, please, why did they make such a useless construction?"

I stared up at the boards crossing overhead in the garage. "I don't know what you mean."

"Those boards, there." Longin jabbed savagely with his finger. "The purpose of those boards is to keep the roof from spreading. They are supposed to tie the rafters together. Then why nail them in that fashion? They are toe-nailed into the girder, see? They should be fastened *this* way—" he slapped his palms together as if they were two boards overlapping at the ends. "How can they hold, toe-nailed in? What will happen when there is the weight of snow on that roof?"

Even I could see the construction principle involved. With a sinking heart I followed him as he paced about, looking first at the lack of bracing here, then at the inadequate thickness of a board there. By the time he was ready to go down into the cellar and look at the new furnace, I couldn't bear to go along.

I sat nervously in the kitchen preparing a half bushel of beans for the freezer. When at last he returned from the cellar, I said brightly, "Isn't that a lovely oil burner?"

Silence.

"What's the matter?"

"Melissa," Longin said seriously, "this house is going to fall down."

I wet my lips. "Soon?" I croaked.

"I don't know how soon. Maybe this year, maybe three, four years from now."

I repressed an hysterical impulse to giggle. "Why? What makes you think so?"

"The beams. They will give way."

"Oh, *no*, Longin," I said, greatly relieved. "You must be mistaken. I tested those beams myself. They are nice and solid."

"How do you mean, you tested them?"

It's his Slavic blood, I thought impatiently. He has to have something to worry about, or he isn't happy. "What I could reach," I said. "I rammed them underneath with a penknife, and it didn't go in. Not more than half an inch at the most."

"Yes," he said patiently. "Out in the center of the cellar, the beams are solid. But the sills are all rotted away. You can see daylight right past where the sills are supposed to be, didn't you see? And the beams were whittled away like this—" swooping with his hand in an upward curve—"in order to fit over the sills, which once were logs. Now they are nothing. Naturally this rot spread onto the tips of the beams. Those beams had been cut out," he repeated, "so that the whole weight of the floor was rest-

[75]

ing not on a nice solid beam but on two inches of wood. *Two
inches.*" Apparently he couldn't believe it. "Now rotted, those
two inches." He picked up his axe. "I go to cut some poles. I
shall prop up the beams but it is only temporary. Please ask the
children not to run or jump."

He went out.

I snipped away at the beans mechanically, feeling very philosophical. I might have known, I thought. Just like my life. Paint
the surface, fix it up all pretty to look at, and *whoom* . . . the
foundation gives way.

My brother Bruce drove the 150 miles from Schenectady every
week end, and climbed into jeans and an old shirt, and from early
Saturday until late Sunday he was carpenter's helper—plumber's
apprentice—painter's aide, donning goggles and mask and spraying
paint on the shingles of the bedroom wing, crawling in the space
dug out beneath the bathroom to measure the give of the floor
boards when the tub was filled with water, handing shingles and
nails and level and shingle-liner-upper to Longin as they both
drove themselves without mercy to finish the siding on the new
garage. This was the most unpleasant task of all. It rained every
day they worked on it, and the shingles grew soggy with water, and
the final slam of the hammer to drive home a nail would send
water squishing out into their faces.

Bruce spent Friday and Saturday nights on a collapsible army
cot, canvas type, somewhat too short for his six feet three, and he
stood in line to use the bathroom, and he helped wipe the dishes,
and he ate at our informally served (*there's* an understatement for
you!) meals, flanked by his nephews who fought for the privilege
of sitting next, but whose elbows were like wings, whose glasses of
milk toppled. *He loves me like a brother*, I thought, misty-eyed
with gratitude, *mine not to wonder why.* And as he left, showered
and shaved and back in his elegant tweeds, we all trooped out to
say good-bye, and, "Thank you very much," we'd say, "for all
you did," and the phrase never sounded so inadequate.

Although I hardly dared hope for such luck, we began to have
a stream of visitors. Friends from New York, on their way to

Maine, naturally found Vermont right on route. Friends from Michigan drove over in an effort to keep up morale while waiting for mail from Korea. My mother spent a week or two. And then came Marjorie Coffey, an old Army friend. We had first met when her husband and Bob were attending Command and General Staff College at Fort Leavenworth; I had not seen her since she stood beside me at Bob's grave. And now she was here, just a little too soon for her own good.

Although the leaves were turning russet and gold, the tomatoes, defying the frost, continued to ripen as they rotted, or rot as they ripened—really it was about fifty-fifty—and Marjorie spent the ten days of her visit standing in front of the kitchen sink, carving blackened spots from the tomatoes, hurling the gushy parts into the pail on the floor by her feet, and developing a callus on her thumb.

"Next time I'm going to bring my own paring knife," she said. "Yours doesn't seem to have the right balance."

"Oh, is there going to be a next time?" I felt cheered. "I was afraid maybe something about your visit, some faint nuance of sordid living, might put you off us for years."

"If you are referring to your cats," she said, "I daresay you'll have them housebroken by the time I get here next year. Or strangled. Though I don't see why you have such trouble. Cats are easy to housebreak."

"Not these," I said with a snarl. "It runs in their family. The mother was a streetwalker from Phoebus, Virginia. Strictly a pickup."

"Kitty says she brought her home," Marjorie said. "Over your frenzied protests, I suppose. Is she responsible for the name, too? Lucky, the Acquired Cat."

"You don't have to do that sort of thing, you know," I said. "Scooping me off the wall and rushing me into the open air, and then cleaning the cat's mess yourself. Not even Em Post includes that in the duties of the Perfect Guest."

"It would bollox up my whole visit if you expired of nausea,"

[77]

Marjorie said. "But wasn't Lucky enough? Did she have to have kittens, too?"

"How should I know? You can't psychoanalyze a cat," I said. "Judging by their inability to adapt themselves to civilization, I should say their father was no better than their mother. Probably some old roué from a back alley."

The screen door slammed and Kitty came in, Tico and Loco darting about her feet.

"It's all this in and out, in and out," Marjorie sighed, putting down her paring knife and cornering the kittens under the black stove. "No wonder you can't keep them out of the house." She went to the door and tossed them gently out into the pale golden sunshine.

While we slaved in the kitchen, the hills and valleys all around were singing the glories of the Lord. It was pure torment to stay inside, forcing ourselves from a sense of duty to work, work, work for the winter cometh, when all the while a Bach chorale of color was lifting towards the sky.

Luckily we had to make frequent trips to town for groceries. One good thing about a kitchen with not enough storage space, it gives you an excuse to get out in the fresh air. We would bring home two or three huge cartons of groceries, as much as the kitchen could hold and still leave room to prepare the meals, and these supplies we would stash away as best we could, and within three days at the most everything would be all eaten up, and back to town we would have to go.

The boys were gone to school in the village, so Kitty, Marjorie and I would pile lightheartedly into the Chevy and swoop up over Bests' hill. The line of hills to the north glowed saffron and ochre blurred and softened by the air between, and nearer the sumacs smeared alizarin crimson across the deserted pastures and along the edges of the hedgerows. And then we would plunge down over the hill and no time to look now, there's a curve halfway down that's a memorial to the rock-ledge-hard stubbornness of some road commissioner, so it's touch the brake, not too hard or we'll skid, watch it, hug the inside ditch that's a nasty drop down to Clifford's mowing—made it! And isn't it a *glorious* day?

"Why didn't they leave the road where it was?" Marjorie asked once. "You can see where it was, over there between those rows of maples and the stone walls. It doesn't look so steep over there, and the road would be straighter, without any need for this suicidal curve."

"Don't talk like a consarned furrinner," I told her. "They moved the road because there's a ledge near the top that used to give a little trouble. It would have taken maybe half a day's work to get rid of it, plus a touch of blasting powder. So they moved the road instead, and now there's a turn that any time you're tired of living, all you have to do is be in a hurry. Clifford says also they found they were running into precisely the same ledge where they put the road now. So what did they do? Scooped soil from the road beyond, on the top of the hill, and packed this over the ledge. That's what makes the last ha!-you-thought-you-made-it,-didn't-you,-slide-back,-baby,-slide-back-to-Bests'-dooryard hump at the top."

"That's quite a name for a hump," Marjorie said.

"That's its winter name," I said. "It has other, more melodic, Indian-sounding names which are used during haying season when you can't haul your haying equipment up, too steep, dad blast it, and you have to take to the fields."

We were across the flat by now, and passing through the old pastures of Red Gates' place, where the hemlock in the hedgerows brush their sooty branches at us, and then we were climbing, the road a golden tunnel under the maples, the trees meeting overhead, their branches banks of gold, through which the sunlight filtered warm and golden, and the road was covered with golden leaves.

And then we were at the crest of the hill, and to our right the line of Belisles' sugar maples marched in shouting colors beyond the gray stone wall and to our left the fields fell away steeply to the valley below. On the near hills the birches and poplars distilled the sunshine, and farther away, beyond the hills of Hartland and the Connecticut River, the mountains of New Hampshire faded into the distance, a descending chord of blue and lavender and violet and gray-purple.

So who cares, I thought, who cares about the consarned road commissioner?

"I could eat it," I said.

"Sometimes you can see what the poets are talking about," Marjorie said. " 'Oh world, I cannot hold thee close enough.' "

And after a while we would be in town, and there would be the whole long beautiful drive back home again.

All of a sudden, everything was gone. Our guests ceased coming. The birds, which had been assembling in the hedgerows in great chattering battalions, got their orders to move out. The leaves vanished from the trees and the world looked larger, swept bare, like a house someone has moved out of.

Clifford put his milking cows in his barn to stay. "I don't like 'em left outside during hunting season anyway," he said. "Somebody might take 'em for a deer."

We laughed, the uninformed laugh of newcomers.

"You think nobody would shoot 'em for a deer?" Clifford puffed comfortably on his pipe, and warmed to his story. "Why, a feller in New Hampshire painted his, last year. C-O-W he painted on their sides. Big letters, a couple of feet high. He'd got tired, he said, of having his cows shot." Puff, puff. "Jerseys, most likely."

"They don't even have to look like a deer," Vivian said. "Remember the time your brother had that old Ford car in his dooryard, and he'd draped that bearskin rug over the motor, and a car drove up and two men got out and blazed away?"

"Maybe they were hunting bear," Clifford said with the air of a man who is fair-minded and doesn't care who knows it. "It sure ruined the radiator of that Ford." Puff, puff. "My father says he can swear to this one. He says a couple of city fellers come up to him and asked him where they could find any deer. 'Not very easy to find any, around here,' my father says. 'There's plenty around in the spring, but come hunting season, they all go back in the hills,' he says. Well, these fellers drove off and pretty soon they come back. 'What do you mean,' they says, 'telling us it's not easy to find any deer around here? Why, we drove over the hill, and there was a whole herd of 'em, friendly and quiet as you please. We shot us one apiece,' they says." Puff, puff. " 'Spike-horns,' they says. And there they were, slung over the fenders of the car, two of the prettiest little Jersey heifers you ever hope to see."

Longin and I walked back up the hill, warmed and delighted to have been offered a joke about "city fellers."

"You know something?" I said. "Cows are really amazing creatures."

"Sure they are."

"No, but they really are," I insisted. "You know what Vivian told me? She told me that those cows they are milking now, those same cows are growing calves. At the *same* time."

Longin stared at me in astonishment. "Well, naturally," he said.

"Naturally, nothing," I said. "That's more than a woman can do. Carry a baby and nurse one, I mean."

"You mean you really never knew this before, about cows?"

"No, I didn't," I said, "and I'm tremendously impressed."

"You would be even more impressed by German cows," Longin said. "There they make calves, give milk, and pull the plow, too."

"Oh," I said uneasily, "that's too much."

"The cows agree with you," Longin said. "It ruins them for milking, and serves those Germans right."

We turned in at our own lane.

"How much did you pay for that field?" He pointed to the wedge-shaped field which lay between the road and the stone wall under the maples.

"Two hundred dollars." I went on hurriedly, "I know it's too much, it's frightfully high, but the man who owned the place at the top of the hill was selling and I didn't know what sort of people would be buying and gosh, otherwise the line would still run right under our living-room windows. What if they decided to keep pigs there, or something?"

[81]

"Two hundred dollars," he muttered, staring at the hardhack and ferns that betrayed the sourness of the soil. "We better get some use out of it, then. Up there, where it's too steep to plow, we plant apple trees, and down here, we grow vegetables. We fix up the soil, it's a better place for vegetables than there below the house. If I plow now, the winter will help kill the weeds."

We, I thought. What a good, permanent sound the word has. . . .

Longin borrowed Clifford's tractor and plow, which Clifford had kindly offered to us in case we wanted to do any fall plowing, and on the thirty-first of October he plowed all that was level enough, nearly an acre. And the next day, which was Chris's birthday, it snowed.

I don't know why it is, but birthdays in our house start out with a deceptive air of peace, and we think this time it's going to be just a quiet, festive day devoted to sentiment and family solidarity, but before the day has got well under way, some pixie puts it on roller skates and soon we are tooling along helplessly, buffeted by one ludicrous or frightening incident after another.

The snow started about nine o'clock, big flakes coming a few at a time at first, and lazily, and then gradually more and more, and the wind increasing, until about ten o'clock the snow was coming so thick and fast it was hard to see, it blew in your face and stuck to your eyelashes and the best way to proceed was with your back to the wind.

About eleven o'clock Vivian rang us up and asked could Longin come down, she was trying to get their heifers into the barn, Clifford wasn't home and she was having trouble, the snow was frightening the heifers and they were running all about and refusing to go where they were supposed to, because towards the barn was into the wind. . . . "I'll tell him," I said. "He's just coming in now."

I relayed Vivian's message. No sooner had Longin left than I stepped on something—what, I don't know, I couldn't possibly have seen my feet anyway—and I slipped, and fell, and creaked my hip. I lay on the floor for several moments, terrified, but after

[82]

I had calmed down enough to do some careful counting, I felt less frightened. Should worse come to worst, the baby would have a chance to live. Perhaps I ought not to move? What to do? I couldn't lie there indefinitely, it was drafty. I hauled myself painfully to my feet, and then it was I heard my hip creak. And it creaked with every step I took until Mary Lee was born.

I hobbled to the phone to ring Mary Milo and tell her I wouldn't be able to make it to the Women's Home Demonstration meeting and luncheon, and then I hobbled to the bedroom and lay down. You are supposed to keep calm, I told myself, and I lay there sobbing into a piece of Kleenex and keeping calm until Longin got back.

"Don't worry," he said. "If you can ride all over these roads and nothing happens, nothing is going to happen when you fall on your own kitchen floor."

Cheered by this excellent logic, I tried to get up. I had a birthday cake to bake, Happy Birthday to Chris. I couldn't get up. However harmless a fall on one's own kitchen floor may be, something mysterious and obscure had happened so that I could not get to my feet unaided, not out of bed, not out of a chair. Hauling me to my feet was one more chore Longin had to face, day after day and week after week, until Mary Lee was born.

I baked the cake and frosted it, and watched the snow falling steadily, the flakes growing smaller as the day grew colder. By the time the children got home, about quarter to five, it was bitter cold out and the cats were begging to come inside.

Chris scooped up Popco and Calico and brought them in. "Butch was playing with them," he said. "You know, he pretends to eat them. He gets them all wet with his tongue. Gee, Mother, look how cold they are! Can't I put them in the cellar? They won't get upstairs, I promise!"

"Popco opens the cellar door," I said. "He climbs up on those mops and things and bats away at the latch."

"I'll put a chair in front!" Chris said. "Gee, there's Lucky and Loco at the door, listen to them. We don't want to lose any *more* cats."

[83]

This was a dirty dig, and he knew it. Bootsie had long since left this earthly paradise, thanks to an accident in which I, according to the children, was criminally negligent. I had come hurrying out the door, way back in June, and I had clipped the unfortunate Bootsie across the back of the neck with the lower edge of the screen door, and after about ten ghastly minutes which I would rather forget, Bootsie had died. Every now and then, with a natural talent for blackmail, the children brought up the subject, lingering over details.

"Oh, well, since it is your birthday," I said. "And if you make very sure they don't get upstairs."

I limped about, finishing up the traditional birthday dinner of roast chicken and all the et ceteras, and just before we were to sit down, Longin went out to feed Butch. When he came back in, he was carrying another kitten.

"Either we let Butch into the house," he said, and I turned pale at the thought of more housebreaking and shook my head violently, *no, no!*, "or we tie him up. Look what he is doing to the kittens. Poor little fellow, he was frozen into the snow. He could hardly whimper."

"Tico!" Kitty breathed, and put out her hands. "Poor baby, all frozen!"

Tico's fur was plastered to his sides, lacquered with frozen saliva. He was encased in ice, and was too stiff to move.

"I better put him in the bathtub. He can thaw there and the ice melting won't make a mess," Longin said. "He will die, but better he dies in the house."

"Why will he die?" Kitty demanded.

"He will get pneumonia," Longin said with fatalistic calm.

"Poor Tico," Kitty crooned. "Going to die. Poor Tico."

We sat down to the birthday dinner. As we ate, it was evident that Tico was thawing. It must have been a very painful process. As the frostbite receded, his wails grew in strength. By the time we reached dessert, and the candles were lighted on Chris's cake, and we turned out the overhead light so the glow of the candles would shine on our faces, and we made ready to sing Happy Birthday to You, Dear Christopher, the screeching of the thawing Tico gave us the pitch, and, as we sang, a trifle uncertainly, our cordial salute to Chris, the cat's ear-splitting accompaniment nearly drowned us out.

After an hour the ice had melted and we could dry him in a bath towel, and then we put him in a box well padded with more towels, and installed him on top of one of the hot-air ducts in the cellar, where he would be warm, but not too warm, during the night. And in the morning Longin went down to see if he was dead yet of pneumonia. Kitty and I hovered anxiously at the head of the cellar stairs. We could hear a scrambling and a racing about, and then Longin came back up, somewhat like the Pied Piper, a cluster of cats about his feet, four small ones and one big. Tico was feeling fine. In this unkind world, he seemed to say, the tip of his tail twitching belligerently, it's better to skip the aristocratic ancestry and keep one's veins coursing with common blood, obstinately indestructible.

November continued as it had begun, with snow, ice, a bit of a thaw, more snow, more ice, and a garnish of sleet. Our Chevy could not cope with the hills nearest home. To attempt to come up the short way, past Bests', was to invite sure disaster, an inevitable moment when the car could go no further, in spite of chains, prayers and voodoo chants. Then came the slipping backwards, the slipping sideways, the lurch into the ditch, the shovel out, the haul by tractor down to Bests' dooryard, the licked turntail and the slow drive back down the hill, turn left at Milo's, and home the long way round.

And then the Bests' hill got so icy we would go the long way when leaving home, too. This meant going up the hill next to our south field, and when the violent struggles of the Chevy gouged the road's curves still more rococo and concave, the ledges took to spanking the car's bottom every time she passed, and we took to parking the Chevy in the driveway of the empty house at the top of the hill, and walking.

And then it was December, and dark by three-thirty, and we had our first blizzard.

It happened on a school day. The school bus did not, after all, come by the gate, as advertised. It never had come by the gate, Ellison told me. No one who had driven our road between October and May would *want* it to come by our gate. On these hills and curves, the children were much safer going on foot. Even in a blizzard, if only school let out in time for them to reach home before dark.

But school did not let out until the usual three-thirty. And it was nearly four o'clock by the time the school bus, following its usual routine, returned from its first trip and picked up the children living up our valley. It would be well after four by the time the young Bests and Coughlins would get off at the foot of the Belisle hill and start their mile-long walk home.

By noon of this day the sky had changed from a sullen overcast to a lowering-in of dull gray clouds that began spitting snow. By two o'clock it was snowing hard. By four o'clock the wind had a nasty whine to it where it cut around the corner of the house, and the snow was streaming past our lighted doorway in horizontal streaks.

At quarter to five Vivian rang on the line to say that David and Marilyn had got home, and Chris was with them. Had Pat come on ahead? Was he home?

"Not yet," I said, glancing out the window and seeing nothing but a wall of snow. "I'll give you a ring when he gets in."

I could hear Vivian talking to the children, and then she said, "They haven't seen him since the hill below Belisles'." Her voice was calm, but there was an undercurrent in it that I couldn't quite believe. I couldn't imagine Vivian ever afraid of anything.

"Maybe he stopped at Belisles' to warm up," I said. "I'll call them and see."

"They don't have a phone," she reminded me. "Clifford says he'll take the tractor and go and meet him."

"That's very nice of him," I said, and hung up. At that moment, Longin came in. He had been outside shoveling drifts away from the door. I briefed him on the situation, and he said, "Ring them back and tell Clifford I'm coming, too."

He got his gun out of the rack, stuffed some shells in his pocket, took up his electric lantern, and left. Almost at once his light was swallowed up by the storm.

About three quarters of an hour later, Vivian phoned again. "They're here," she said, and the relief in her voice was unmistakable. "He was coming along this side of Red Gates'. He's pretty cold, but he's all right."

"I guess," I said, "I don't know much about snowstorms. I didn't realize . . ." My voice trailed off.

"It's just as well you didn't," she said briskly. "I was afraid he'd stop somewhere, get tired and sit down to rest. And I kept thinking about that brook that cuts under the road and crosses our field. If he'd got off the road there, and stumbled into it . . . Well, Clifford is lighting into the children for not all sticking together, so I guess we better eat."

Longin, Pat, and Chris soon came in. Pat looked none the worse for wear. He didn't know just when he fell behind, he said. He'd ridden his sled down to the bus in the morning, and he was bound and determined to bring it home, but the snow had slowed him down, it had been awfully hard to drag the sled along. When he realized he was alone, he said, he couldn't see where he was going because it was dark and the wind was blowing so hard. He'd tried to keep in the road by walking next to the ditch, but those old lumber trails turning off kept getting him all mixed up. A couple of times he had followed one of those trails, he said, but right away it was too hard to walk, so he'd turned back, and each time he'd found the road all right. . . .

By the grace of God, I thought.

"What were you going to do with the gun, Longin?" Pat asked.

"Shoot it off, in case you were lost in the woods."

"Gee, I didn't even hear the tractor motor until you were right there. The wind sure was noisy." He added in genuine concern, "I left my sled by the Red Gates' place, is that okay?"

"Why didn't you go in there and wait?"

"Well, gee, I didn't think anybody would come looking for me," Pat said. "And I knew I better not sit down. I saw a movie

[87]

once where this guy got lost in a blizzard and he stopped to rest and right away he froze to death. I thought of going in there," he added honestly, "but it's all spooky and empty—"

"Let's eat," I said. I felt weak in the knees.

In the morning I called Ellison. "The more I think about yesterday the madder I get," I told her. "Seems to me school should be let out early on such a day. What's the name of the school principal?"

"There isn't any, Melissa."

I digested this. "No school principal? Honest? Well, who has authority, you know, who is responsible for the children's safety?"

"I honestly don't know," she said. "There's the school directors, of course, and the teachers, but as for there being any one person— that's what you mean, isn't it?"

"Yes," I said. "I mean the one who makes decisions in an emergency."

"I don't think there is any one person," she said. "You see, there are five schools, and everybody feels pretty independent— let me think. I guess you had better call the superintendent of schools. He's in Windsor."

"For heaven's sake," I said, "what does he do, phone the schools long distance?"

Ellison laughed. "He can't. There are no phones in the Hartland schools!"

I filed this for future reference, and wrote a letter to the superintendent, and got a very nice reply. In the future, in case of adverse weather, arrangements would be made, etc., etc.

The snow didn't last. The thermometer climbed back from zero and flounced into the upper thirties, and we had a strong hint of what Mud Season would be like. The roads became both sticky and slippery, and our hill road was impassable for cars. Clifford was taking his milk cans out by tractor to meet the milk truck in Jenneville, and Jules Alfonse, who drove his jeep station wagon to his work in Windsor every day, was parking it by the Jenneville bridge and walking the half mile home from there.

Even the mailman gave up, and left the mail for our road down by the bridge.

And then, marooned by the mud as we were, Chris one evening became very ill. He had a dreadful pain in his side, he said. I was sure it was appendicitis and thought we ought to pack his side with ice cubes. Longin leaned over and listened to Chris's chest. "Pneumonia," he said, and directed me to fill bottles with very hot water, and these he packed around Chris, and wrapped him well in blankets, and told me to go to bed, he would sit up with Chris.

"We will call the doctor in the morning," he said. "He would have to walk from the bottom of the hill. In the dark, strange doctor to stranger's house—" He shook his head. "Too much to expect. Chris will be all right until morning."

In the morning Chris was a little better. Nevertheless, we phoned the doctor as soon as it was light, and he came right out from Windsor, and agreed with Longin's diagnosis, and gave Chris a shot of penicillin.

"Next time," he remarked drily, "don't wait till morning to call me. I don't like to come out at midnight in this kind of weather, but on the other hand, I like my patients to live, too."

By late afternoon Chris's temperature was normal and he was demanding food. Longin said he would fix Chris some scrambled eggs, I better go sit down somewhere. I went into my bedroom and sat down by the fire and felt overwhelmed by the exhaustion that so often accompanies relief from worry. I thought I heard the sound of a car, and looking out, I saw an army-style jeep, and a woman, a complete stranger to me, climbing down from it.

I was struggling unsuccessfully to get up when Patrick opened my door and ushered her in.

"Hello," she said. "I'm Ruth Ogden. I live over the hill. I heard your boy is sick, and I thought you wouldn't feel like cooking. Here's something for supper."

She put down the pan she was holding, and lifted out a big pot of home-baked beans and a loaf of Boston brown bread, fresh and hot and wrapped in a towel.

"I can't stay," she said, heading for the door. "My husband is waiting outside. I'm glad your boy is better. Bring the pot back sometime when you're down our way. Good-bye."

And she was gone.

I'll never get used to these people, I thought. Never!

At Christmas time my sister, Mary, came up from New Jersey to be with me when the baby came, and she spent the holidays and was a great help and lots of fun to have around, and then she stayed a couple of days extra, but at last she had to leave. "Must be going to be a girl," she grumbled. "Only a female would keep everybody waiting like this."

"It's just that I'm too tired to have a baby," I apologized.

And perhaps that was why it took me nearly four days, when I did get started. Longin was very good, and ran the house without any help, and came in every day to see me, while Marilyn Best stayed with the children. But he didn't get in the night before the baby finally managed to get born, and I lay there feeling very forlorn and sorry for myself, with the other women all surrounded by visitors and receiving congratulations and their babies down in the nursery where they belonged, hollering lustily for food.

When Longin came in the next day he expressed regrets at having to skip his visit the evening before.

"Butch needed me more than you," he explained. "He tangled with a porcupine, and he was a mess. Splinters—is that what you call them?"

"Quills."

"Quills in his nose and his mouth, way up inside his mouth. I had to pull them out with the pliers. It took us a long time to find the pliers, and then one by one the quills. Whole operation took nearly three hours."

"Poor Butch," I said. And I meant it.

CHAPTER IV

When Mary Lee was four days old, my mother came to look after us and I brought the baby home from the hospital. I felt about ninety-nine years old, and all I could do, it seemed, was sit in the chair in my bedroom and cry, or lie down on the bed and cry. The grief I had been holding at arm's length all those months engulfed me, and it had gained in strength while I had weakened. I felt all the crushing finality of Bob's death, all the aloneness-forever, that I had pretended wasn't there. I was frightened, too, unsure of my ability to handle our affairs, certain I could not be a good mother-father to the children. My head throbbed continually and I quarreled with Longin and snapped at my mother and I could take no comfort even from holding the baby, but would burst into tears when I rocked her in my arms.

My mother was needed to help care for Mike, and after a couple of weeks she went back to New Jersey. And my headaches continued, and I could feel my temples throb even when I woke at night, and finally, when the baby was about three months old, there was a painful lump at the base of my skull, and I thought, this has gone on long enough.

So I went to the doctor, who sent me to some high-ranking specialists, who, in turn, pronounced that nothing whatsoever was the matter with me but I worried and was too tense.

"I've been giving myself a pain in the neck," I told Longin, and found this remark far more witty than it was, and laughed. "Don't let yourself get yourself down," he agreed.

Now I was a firm believer in the behaviorist school of psychology, it having been impressed on me when I was young and impressionable, and I believed, therefore, that it is impossible to worry unless your muscles are worrying, too, that is, unless your muscles are tense, *you* can't be tense. When you force your muscles to let go, you will relax and not worry. I reminded myself of this theory, and whenever I felt my head tightening as in a vise, I would let my face sag and my mouth hang open as if my jaw were unhinged. It worked. (Try it. You *cannot* worry with your jaw hanging open. Obviously, your appearance may cause worry to nibble at your neighbors and kin, and your explanations may give rise to caustic comments. Ignore them.)

Longin decided that there were times when extra efforts were needed to cheer me up. Should I sit at the lunch table and start to add up, again, the amounts paid to plumber, paid to carpenter, my fingers gripping the pencil tightly and my jaw clenched, before I could add in the amounts paid to mason, paid to electrician, paid to insulation fellow, and once more gasp and turn pale at the total, crying futilely once again, "All this and the place is a wreck! It's going to fall down!", Longin would leave the table, disappear into the kitchen, swathe his head in a towel so he looked like Lon Chaney in *The Hunchback of Notre Dame*, and come back into the room all bent over, his hands like greedy claws, one eyelid fluttering dreadfully. Kitty would scream and run behind me for protection, and I would guffaw helplessly, begging him to stop.

"Very well," he said once, drawing himself up as if offended. "You don't like my act." And he withdrew to the kitchen. After a few moments, he reappeared. This time he was wearing one of the children's hats which he had somehow made to assume the general appearance of a boater, the kind of flat straw hat Grampa wore to the World's Fair in 1899, and he came in, Bing Crosby/-Bob Hope, doing a neat Shuffle Off to Buffalo. A ridiculous grin was plastered on his face, and he tipped his hat to his enthralled audience, and sang, "You don't need TV, after all you have *me!*"

"My god," I breathed, "what are you doing wasting your time down on the farm?"

He sat down, once again the withdrawn, self-contained Pole. "Making you laugh," he said. "That's what I'm doing." He poured himself more coffee. "You think Bob Hope is funny?"

"Of course I think Bob Hope is funny."

Longin sighed. "If you have to think Bob Hope is funny before you can get your citizenship, then I never get mine. In the barracks somebody always had the radio on when Bob Hope had his program and everytime he said something, *ha! ha!* all the fellows would go, and I'll be damned if I could ever see why."

"You should have seen his movies," I said. "I remember once he was locked up in a trunk, see, and when he got out, he was all scrunched over, he couldn't straighten up—"

Longin shook his head. "I'll tell you who is funny," he said. "Danny Kaye is funny."

"I agree with you," I said. "But I say Bob Hope—"

"Hope is an Englishman," Longin said. "You know what Danny Kaye is? He's a Polish Jew."

"What have politics got to do with this?" I roared. "Bob Hope did not go to Yalta, damn it! *Churchill* went to Yalta!"

And of course I didn't have a headache any longer, and my neck didn't hurt.

Had I been in Vermont through several winters, I might have realized that these fits of despondency, these Glooms of Winter Dead, were to a large extent purely seasonal, having little or nothing to do with one's personal affairs. The Glooms, I know now, are attacks of melancholy that occur each year about the time that the cows grow restless and detest the barn, the men come down from the hay mow convinced that the hay will give out before turning-out time, and they don't care how the mow bulged in the fall, they don't think they have enough hay. The children announce they will *die* if they don't have a vacation soon, they have been going to school forever and *ever*, but the vacation, which must coincide with the most acute stage of mud, is post-poned from one week to the next, the mud, it seems, not yet being sufficiently frightful, although the womenfolk cannot see how there can be any mud left outside, surely the children have brought it all in the house, on their boots. From the village come rumors of measles and whooping cough and an ache in the middle known only as "that misery folks 're havin'." This is the time to buy in Vermont, if buy you must. Of course, if you are on the other end of the log and are planning to sell, wait—wait until late May or early June, when the roads are dry and scraped smooth, when the orchards are all a-bloom and the birds are courting. But if it's buying a farm you want, come in late winter. That is the time when farmers have to be restrained by their wives from paying you to take the damn place.

In our ignorance, we thought that the Glooms of '52 were something we would experience once, like mumps, and then be immune. We even thought that the Dreadful Plumbing Crisis would be a unique experience, never to recur. Now we know that plumbing troubles in the country are like malaria in the tropics, always there, waiting. . . .

Actually, our plumbing crisis was a long time in growing. Fif-teen to twenty years, I suppose. But the first we knew something was wrong was shortly after Mary Lee came home, and the washing machine shifted into high. One day we noticed that the water, instead of exiting politely into the septic tank, had back-tracked through the pipe whose purpose, bowing to an elementary law of physics, was to allow air to escape from the septic tank as water went in. Unfortunately some unorthodox plumber had installed this pipe on a gentle slant downwards from the septic tank back into the house and across the cellar to the narrow chimney, which was to act as vent. Even I could recognize that there were flaws in this feat of engineering. For one thing, except under the most ideal atmospheric conditions, it didn't work. Finding itself frustrated from its proper course of exit, the air would backtrack up through the house pipes, to the bathtub, the washbasin, the kitchen sink, shouting as it came, let-let-let-let-let-

LET ME OUT! Sometimes it went let . . . . . let . . . . . let . . . . . let . . . . . in a kind of haunted whisper. The air made its way with charming variety in key, rhythm, and mood, and we named its various songs the Lament of the Septic Tank, the Ballad of the Baffled Burp, the Chant of the Choked-up Channel, the Plaint of the Pent-up Pipe. We had lots of opportunity for naming the songs, because we could hear them plainly all over the house. For some reason they seemed to occur most frequently during meals.

But now, as I say, things had taken a turn for the worse. Not only air traveled the pipe back to the chimney, and we began to limit our trips to the cellar to those absolutely necessary and unavoidable, and we felt marvelously immune to almost everything, because why weren't we dead of typhoid, cholera, or dysentery? "As soon as the snow melts," Longin said, rigging up all sorts of temporary expedients in kitchen, bath, and laundry, "I shall dig down to the septic tank and see what can be done."

February dragged into March, and whenever the snow thawed at all, it promptly refroze, so that when Longin could stand it no more, and said he could wait no longer, there were four feet of ice and snow over the spot where the septic tank was rumored to lurk. He got out the pickaxe and started digging. When he reached the ground, it proved to be frozen harder than stone.

"I always knew," Longin puffed, "when I came to the States—" *thwack!*—"sooner or later—" *thwack!*—"I'd be breaking rocks—"

He found the septic tank, and it was in a condition there is no need to describe here other than to say it was utterly unable to function.

"We must replace it," Longin said, "as soon as weather warms up. This one is suitable for a small family that doesn't bathe. We will not buy one, too expensive. I shall make one of cement. Very simple to do. Lots of work, though," he added thoughtfully.

"And in the meantime—" I said.

"In the meantime, I perform like Hercules," he said, and proceeded to do so, with shovel and bucket, lugging the contents of the tank off onto a far field. "Don't worry," he said. "This is all

[95]

very proper. In Germany this is considered the best possible fertilizer." All this was, as he said, only the most temporary of temporary solutions, and we would get through until spring only by continuing to use the garden hose out the workroom door as the drain for the washing machine, a bucket on the shelf under the sink to catch the water there and carry it out to be tossed beyond the drive, plus a drastic change in our bathing habits and a severe rationing of flushings of the toilet.

By late March the Glooms of Winter Dead weighed on us relentlessly. When Vivian said she was going to a cattle auction, wouldn't we like to go? we said we'd love to go to a cattle auction, nothing we would like better. And Clifford said if we felt like buying us a cow, we could always put it in his barn, he had a couple of empty stanchions. So, much in the mood in which an unhappy woman goes window-shopping in hopes of finding an irresistible hat, we packed a lunch and wrapped Mary Lee in several layers of blankets and put her in the clothesbasket, for easy toting, and then we saw to it that Kitty had her mittens, boots and scarf, and we all set off.

The auction was in Weathersfield Bow, a few miles south of Ascutney on the Connecticut River. Vivian parked the car at the end of a long line of cars, we waded through the snow to the drive, and, Longin carrying Mary Lee in the basket and I carrying the lunch, with Vivian holding Kitty by the hand to make sure she returned to earth after each gay leap, we found some seats under the awning by the barn and established ourselves as best we could against the cold. Then we took turns minding the baby while the others strolled through the stable to see the cows.

Afterwards we all agreed that we had spotted Jenny as the best cow there, right from the start. She was down in the catalog as Ascutney Jane, but there was a warmth about her, a maternal glow, that at once persuaded us to the more familiar Jenny. When she was led out to the auction arena, she endured the indignity of the lead rope, the proddings of the herdsman to turn her best side towards the buyers, the comments of the auctioneer on her more personal attributes, all with admirable dignity. She was a noble cow, young and beautiful, and, after some tense moments to see if anyone was going to top our bid, because we had agreed we could absolutely go no higher, "Sold for three hundred!" cried the auctioneer, and she was *ours*.

Longin and I let out our breaths slowly, and Vivian beamed congratulations. "Now you have a cow!" she said, and we agreed that now we did indeed have a cow.

Kitty danced off to follow Jenny back into the barn, and to tell her that she was ours now, and I tried to readjust my thinking to this new circumstance, being the owner of a cow.

"Do you think we paid too much?" I asked Vivian anxiously.

"You couldn't have paid any less and got her."

It was decided that Longin would stay with Jenny and help load her on the trucker's vehicle, and ride with her, to make sure she didn't slip or fall, and also to show the trucker the way.

Kitty shouted the news to Butch where he was tied up under the maple tree, and to Pat and Chris, who burst out the door to meet us, and to the cats, who were under our feet as we tried to come in. "We have a cow, a cow, a beautiful cow!" she sang, as I warmed Mary Lee's bottle and started the supper. "Why doesn't the cow come, Mother?" she demanded, after a while. "What is taking them so long?"

It did seem as if even a truck carrying a cow, and therefore of necessity driving slowly and carefully so as not to jounce or frighten her, need not take as long as this. Maybe something has happened, I was thinking, something nameless and dreadful, when "Here they come!" Kitty shrieked, and we all ran to the windows.

At first we could see nothing, no lights of a truck, nothing at all. And then, moving into the light from the door, Longin, we saw, was coming down the drive, leading the cow. We watched him pause at the maples to introduce Butch, and then they came on. We all ran outside, coatless, and the children admired her and stroked her dark flanks, and I touched her (timidly) on the nose, and told her she was beautiful, and she gazed at me calmly and blew steam from her nostrils and accepted all our compliments as if they were merely her due. Which they were.

"Where's the truck?" I asked.

"Hill looked too icy, he didn't have chains," Longin said. "We unloaded her at the top of the hill."

"Was she frightened?"

"No, not she." He stroked her where the lead rope rubbed her neck. "Come, cow," he said soothingly. "Come, good Jenny. I show you where I shall build you a barn." He led her to the end of the garage, so she could see the old barn to be torn down and a new one to be erected, safer, more worthy of her; and he waved his arm in the direction of her pastures. And then he led her back down the drive and over the hill to Bests'.

"Do you think she'll like it there?" we asked anxiously when Longin returned home.

"I wish you could have seen her," Longin said to me. "I thought she may not want to go in, strange barn and all. She walked into that barn like a great lady or a queen picking her way past her subjects. Arrogant, that's what she is!"

He added that he'd have to borrow my alarm clock. "Bests milk at five," he said. "I have to get down there by then. Jenny would be upset to see the other cows getting milked, and she not."

"I suppose," I said doubtfully, "that a cow is a very practical animal to have, in a large family like ours, all these growing children . . . I mean, it probably costs a lot to feed her, doesn't it?"

"We'll cut our own hay," Longin said, "and raise a little corn for silage. Children drink a lot of milk. She'll pay for herself."

"Mikey cannot stay with Dad and Mother much longer," I said, following a perfectly clear line of thought. "Mary Lee is getting bigger and I could take care of him now."

"He must come home as soon as weather clears up," Longin agreed. "But you cannot take care of him alone, he is getting too big and strong. I must be near. So I think we are in the dairy business."

"I guess we are," I said.

It seemed a casual way to make such a momentous decision.

But we didn't have to spell everything out in words of one syllable. How else could we take care of Mike, and make a living at the same time?

I felt Longin was supplying by far the greater part of our real capital: long hours, hard work, devotion, know-how, and real farming ability—the things that make a farm a success. My contribution of capital scarcely balanced this.

"I'll do the bookkeeping," I said hesitantly, "if you'll handle everything else, okay?"

"Okay," he said. And so we were partners.

March became April, and the snow melted where the sun could reach it, and the air grew warm and pensive, and we went outside and shed jackets and hats, and it was hard to believe, as it always is, but spring had come, as it always had.

I was seized with the urge to clean house. Not only inside, but outside, too. I wanted to sweep the lawn and shake out the hedgerows and get at the clutter against the house, everything all at once. We had banked evergreen boughs along the foundation to keep the frost out of the cellar, and I began hauling these branches off by the armload, and I heaped them beyond the drive, well away from the house. After watering a great circle around them, and leaving the garden hose connected and ready for immediate action, I tried to burn them. All one morning I shoved newspapers under them and lit the newspapers and watched the quick flame flare up, consume the paper, and die, while the stubborn boughs, soaked with frost, refused to catch. Finally, hungry and annoyed, I went in to fix lunch.

I had the sandwiches on the table and was at the stove ladling out soup, and Longin was at the sink washing up, when we heard a tractor buzzing along the road. Any passing vehicle other than the milk truck and mailman was considered an event, and we stared out the window to see who was going by. After a moment the tractor came into view, headed down towards the Bests. Two boys were on it, one driving, one standing on the drawbar. They were staring our way.

"Who's that?" I said. "One is Lloyd Best, isn't it? But who's the other? What are they staring for?"

"We're staring at them," Longin said reasonably.

As he spoke, the tractor came to an abrupt halt and the boys leaped off and ran towards us up the lane.

Longin darted to the door and looked out. "Melissa!" he shouted. "Our place is afire!"

We ran outside. The fire, which so perversely had refused to burn while I watched it, had come to life as soon as I turned my back and had leaped over the circle of wet earth and escaped into the dry grass beyond. By the time Lloyd and his companion discovered it, it had traveled about ten yards and was fleeing in an ever-widening circle.

Longin and the boys grabbed up wet evergreen boughs and raced to try to head it off from the barn. Should the barn catch fire, it would go up like an explosion and only by a miracle would we be able to keep the flames from spreading to the house.

I ran inside to the telephone and rang the operator, and told her we had a grass fire, please send help. I thought she would ring on our line and send our neighbors . . . I didn't know what she would do, there was no time really to think. . . . I grabbed the broom and scrub bucket and told Kitty to come out and keep the bucket filled from the hose, and I sloshed my broom in the water and raced to beat out the flames which were running down the unmown meadow towards the woods . . . towards the woods which went up and down the valley, up and down the valley where all the little homes were, houses and barns which would burn, thanks to me. . . .

A wind had sprung up, or the fire had made its own wind, and it got behind the flames and blew them faster and faster through the grass, higher and higher . . . they were leaping six feet into the air now, and going faster than I could run. I couldn't get around in front of them. I beat futilely at the nearest flames until my broom caught fire, and I threw it into the burned area.

"The woods!" I shrieked at Longin. "The woods will go!"

He and the boys were beating like madmen at the flames that

threatened the barn. I raced over to tell them that *the woods, the woods will go!*

"Snow will stop it," Longin gasped, his arms flailing without stopping.

Why didn't anybody come?

"Phone over to Turners," Lloyd said, stopping for a moment to breathe. "He's got a crawler with a 'dozer blade, it'll turn back the fire from the hedgerow."

I ran to the house, rang on the line, told the young woman who answered who I was, that we had a fire, could her husband come with his crawler?

"He's in the woods," she said. "I'll get him as fast as I can!"

I ran back outside. Kitty stood, calmly keeping the pail full, surveying the whole scene placidly. I picked up another evergreen branch, plunged it in the water, and ran down over the scorched earth, over the brow of the hill, trying to catch up with the flames. My heart was laboring, my chest ached, it hurt to breathe. I lifted my leaden arms and beat futilely at the end of the ribbon of flame, and I listened in anguish for the sound of a motor which would mean help was coming. All I could hear was the sound of the blood thudding in my ears, and an airplane somewhere overhead, a little yellow airplane . . . the sky turned black, and my head swam. It was no use. I could not help it, the woods would go, and all because of me.

Over the brow of the hill roared with throttle wide open a crawler, pocket-sized, and jockeying it with cowboy nonchalance was young Hawthorne Turner, owner of Crag Hill Farm. He roared past me, swung in a wide circle as if heading off a herd of stampeding cattle, and behind him the earth was turned aside in a six-foot-wide swathe of safety. The flames ran up to the furrow, and, baffled, died.

Turner circled around the meadow and came back up the other side, protecting the hedgerow as he came. Finally a rocky ledge barred his path, and he jumped down and helped finish off the fire thus cornered, and, suddenly, the nightmare was over.

Kitty smiled. "We put out the fire," she said happily.

"Yeah," I said, trying to get my insides under control. Everything seemed jumbled about. "I'll go call the operator," I mumbled. "Tell her never mind."

I rang the operator and reported the fire out. "Oh, dear," she said. "The engine just started out of the village. I'll see if I can catch them."

I went out of the house again. The men—for so all four looked to me, young Lloyd and his cousin Roger not fourteen-year-olders at all, but young heroes, and Longin and Turner, too—the men were standing about, joking, rubbing their flushed faces with their sleeves, and staring at the blackened field and the threatened barn as if they, too, couldn't quite believe it.

"How about some cider? We haven't anything else for a thirst," I said. "I think there's some left, though maybe it's turned."

"Bring it," Longin said, "even if it's pure dynamite."

I went down the cellar for the jug and got cups and was about to leave the kitchen when our number rang, and it was the operator. She'd stopped the fire engine on the lower road, she said, they'd been about three miles away when she'd reached them. I thanked her, glanced at the clock, saw to my astonishment it was nearly three-quarters of an hour since I'd rung for help—it couldn't be! but it was—and I went out again into the sunshine.

"We put the fire out, Mama," Kitty said, pleased with herself. "Did you see us put out the fire?"

"Uhuh," I said, pouring cider. I could hear an airplane motor again. The little yellow plane was coming back. It came in low over the hills to the north, and circled over our blackened field.

"Looks like an L-5," Longin said. "Hey! It dropped something!"

Something white fluttered down into the center of the burned area. I ran out and picked up an envelope, smudged and faintly warm. I fished a piece of paper out.

"What does it say, Mama?" Kitty demanded impatiently.

I looked at Longin. "It's from the fire warden," I said. "He says, 'Do you have a permit for this fire?'"

There are always, of course, a number of lessons to be learned

[102]

from disaster, or near-disaster. Aside from the obvious one—beware the fire that refuses to burn—there is another, we have since discovered as our knowledge of country fires has increased, and it is the basic lesson, the fundamental precept, and it is this:

Don't have one.

There will come a long, continuous ring on the phone, and everyone in the house will drop whatever he is doing, and rush to stand by, until the ringing stops; then on every phone, all up and down the line, the receivers are lifted and the operator says where the fire is. The sound of that ringing is a heart-stopping sound, and the waiting until it stops seems agonizingly long. Whose house is it? Whose barn?

Fire-insurance rates are exceedingly high out where we live because the fire-insurance companies are assuming that if we have a fire at all, we'll have a total loss. At the moment I can tick off on my fingers five fires (not counting chimney fires) that have occurred in the past five years, fires involving buildings, that is, located more than a mile from the fire engine's roost. In each case the building burned completely: one barn, two sheds, two houses. When the barn and the sheds went, the near-by houses would have gone, too, except for luck, meaning the direction of the wind. But don't start to heap coals of criticism on the heads of the local fire department. Consider, if you will, what it's up against.

In our end of town, as in most country areas, the fire department is volunteer. That means precious time is lost while the volunteers leave their jobs and race for the fire-fighting equipment. True, the fire chief must first be located and he it is who must call out the volunteers. Local protocol has so decreed. It is a minor unfortunate circumstance that until ten years after World War II the fire chief had no telephone. Nor has our end of town a fire alarm in the form of a widely audible bell or siren. One might reasonably expect the volunteers to plump loudly for one at town meeting, but perhaps not, considering the fire department's difficulty in getting its yearly stipend of five hundred dollars raised to a figure more in line with its needs. Each year the town antes up just about half what is needed, and the department has to raise the rest of its money itself; and so it does, year after year, by the superb efforts of the wives of the volunteer firemen, who, with some outside help, put on firemen's dances, suppers, and the like. What this amounts to is that the fire department is not properly supported by taxes paid by all whom it protects, but by the contributions of time, energy and money from the devoted few.

When I called for help, it was noon, and the firemen rather widely scattered at their several homes. The roads, however, were unusually good, being still frozen, and, furthermore, bare of ice or snow. Consider what might have been the case had we had a house fire, during the December thaw, or during a blizzard, or at any time when the condition of our hill road would force the fire truck to come the long way round. And what is true of us is true of most families living beyond paved roads, water mains, fire-alarm boxes on the corner and fire apparatus ready at a few seconds' notice. So if you live in the country and you must have a fire, be ready to put it out yourself.

Kitty was exceedingly proud of her part in our fire. When the boys got home from school, she couldn't help boasting over and over, "*We* put the fire out. Listen, Chris. Listen to what I'm telling you, Pat. *We*—"

"Oh, shut up," they told her rudely. "We know. We heard you. We knew about the fire, anyway. We saw the engine go by."

"Did you know it was our fire?" I asked curiously.

"Heck, we figured it probably was."

"Weren't you excited?"

Chris looked at me thoughtfully. "What about? I figured you'd get it out okay."

The more I pondered this extraordinary conversation, the less I knew whether to feel flattered—or the opposite.

As April's sun climbed higher and her smile grew warmer, the snowbanks shrank under the hedgerows, the frost came out of the ground and the roads softened. It was Mud Season, and the children had their spring holiday. I was making charts for the vegetable garden and had already ordered raspberry bushes and strawberry plants in reckless disregard of the effort needed to hack out holes in the rocky ground big enough for their roots to spread in without crowding. Spurred on by our disappointment in the quality of the apples our orchard trees had borne the previous fall, we had sent off to Stark Brothers in Missouri for fruit trees. The catalog had displayed intoxicating illustrations of splendidly colored, blemish-free, enormous apples which bore little resemblance to the wizened, gnarled, blotched and spotted fruit which we had been quite willing, after all, to leave on the trees for the deer.

Our order had been most carefully written. How much room is there on the hillside too steep to plow? How many gaps show in the old orchard? Which varieties are the hardiest, which will ripen before our early winter, which will keep well? Do we want tart apples or sweet apples, apples for cooking, apples for eating? Mouths watering, we wrote the order, and at the proper planting time, as promised, the trees came.

In considerable excitement we untied the bundles at once, as instructed, and gave the little trees a long drink in the bathtub, which we half filled with cool water. I started counting, for I am the counting type.

"You know," I said, puzzled, "I could swear we didn't order this many trees." I began to recount.

"We ordered thirty-three," Longin said. "Twelve Stark Redgold, fifteen McIntosh Double Red, six Northwest Greening."

"There are thirty-eight here," I said.

Longin reached over to read one of the tags dangling from a slender branch. " 'Starking Delicious. Our gift for the prosperity of the American family.' " He reached for another tag. " 'Jon-a-red. Our gift for the happiness of the American home.' 'Stark Golden Delicious. Our gift for the prosperity and happiness of our great nation.' Who *are* these Stark brothers, anyway?"

"Santa's helpers," I said. "How long do we have to wait?"

"Three, four years." He was studying the labels again. "Missouri. What's it like in Missouri?"

"Like in Kansas. Awfully flat. Except," I added honestly, "where there are those mountains."

"There are nice people in Missouri."

"There are nice people everywhere," I said shortly. "There are nice people in Vermont."

I bristled with resentment at the slightest implication of any criticism of Vermont, because I felt I was being held personally responsible for whatever was wrong. After all, I had chosen Vermont, hadn't I? Well, how about this broken-down plumbing? How about this damn mud?

The roads were now nothing but stretched-out slithery soup. Clifford was again taking his milk cans down to Jenneville corner by tractor, and no vehicle passed us except the mailman, who had borrowed a tractor from an enterprising dealer in Ascutney and was making the loop up over our hill every day in this invincible vehicle. We were still parking the Chevy at the top of the hill. It's just a boulevard car, we said in fond contempt. Too low-slung for its own good, and likely to lose its entrails if we force it over the ruts. Pampered, too, and wants solid footing for its wheels. How sad it's so civilized.

We hadn't met the people who had bought the place at the top of the hill. Mr. Potwin had stopped by and reassured us that they "seemed mighty nice." They were summer people, he said. Goodness, summer people are city people, I thought, and city people are what I've moved away from. In the country, where you have so few neighbors, it matters even more what kind of neighbors they are. You can't ignore your neighbors in the country, as you can in the city. There is a certain inevitable impact.

So when, one morning, smoke plumed up out of the chimney of the house on top of the hill, and we could hear the sound of a car motor and other, unmistakably human noises such as the ringing of an axe, Longin was dismayed. "What will they think!" he exclaimed. "Our Chevy! Blocking their driveway!" Off he hastened over the fields and up the hill, to move our car and to apologize for pre-empting their drive without leave.

It was nearly three hours before he returned, and in a very mellow mood. "I think," he said, "you will like them very much. They were unpacking a violin when I got there, they were just

[106]

hanging it up on the wall. Father, mother, grandfather, and three sons," he explained. "Roumanians."

"Roumanians?"

"Well, Americans, of course, but Roumanians. Met-ess, their name is, I don't know how it's spelled. And Grandpa is Mew-zat. First thing they did is get out the bottle of wine, and we all drank a toast to the new plantings, and the spring, and the harvest. And so on."

I grinned. "So I see."

"We *had* to," Longin said seriously. "Grandpa, he is going to plant a vegetable garden. Now. I told him, the ground is very cold. I told him, we get frosts for another month. Nothing will live, I said. Time to plant, he said. I like this old man," Longin said, pouring himself some coffee. "He is stubborn, as an old man should be."

"But it will all be for nothing!" I exclaimed in dismay. "It's still April—nobody plants in April!"

"Too bad for an old man, so much work for nothing," Longin agreed. "But worse to have to listen to children's advice and do what they say." He added, "He's going to plant across the road below that old barn foundation. Good soil, faces south, and is protected from north wind. I said I would plow it up for him."

Longin had been in discussion with a tractor dealer in White River Junction, and it looked as if the discussions were going to bear fruit in the form of a Ford tractor, plus accessories: a plow, a harrow, a mower for cutting hay, a manure fork (for loading manure from the manure pile into the manure-spreader—Clifford's manure-spreader, borrowed) and a bucket, a contraption similar to the manure fork but more suited in design for scooping gravel, sand, or snow, and dumping it somewhere else. For the fork and bucket he needed also a mass of metal somewhat like the George Washington Bridge, known as a hydraulic lift. The whole she-bang would set us back not much more than a luxury cruise around the world.

The tractor came, and its extras, and Longin went out and plowed for Grandpa Musat, and harrowed, and Grandpa Musat raked and combed the soil until it looked like a patch of brown velvet, and then he lovingly planted his seeds. He and his clan returned to the city, and the frosts came and shone in brilliant splendor on every naked branch and weed stalk. Grandpa Musat's seeds stirred into life and poked green shoots above ground, and the frosts came again and daubed every weed stalk and naked branch with thick white paint. After the sun had warmed the air, we pulled on our boots and sloshed up the muddy road to see how much damage had been done to Grandpa Musat's seedlings. There they were, as green as ever. We couldn't understand it. There was no sign of fatal black, of shriveled stem, of drooping, dying leaf. And the frosts came again, and again, and every time Grandpa Musat's seedlings, taller now, and thriving, were unscathed.

I have no explanation for this. I simply record it. It happened then. It hasn't happened since.

And then it was May, and the earth itself was warming, the grass turned green, and the flush of green was creeping upwards, into the lowest bushes first, then higher and higher. There was color now in the poplars on the hills, a wash of greenish-rose, not yet of leaves unfurling, but a sign of life stirring, of sap rising. And I brought back five boxes of pansies from Woodstock, to plant on the far side of the driveway, to hide the scar of the fire.

It was early evening. The air was still warm, although the sun was almost down. The whole world smelled good, cool and a little yeasty, a delicious smell to a gardener, and sweet, too, a mysterious sweetness that drifted down from the elms and birches. I was absorbed in selecting the colors that should sit side by side. In the quiet I could hear the children's voices, and the whack of a tool where Longin was doing something to some metal, out of sight behind the old barn. I was vaguely conscious of a feeling of contentment, not happiness, not as strong as that, just a kind of calm tranquillity.

Marilyn Best came cycling into the drive. I called out a hello. With no sign of having heard, or indeed of seeing me at all, she wheeled right on by and went around the corner of the barn. In a moment Longin came in sight.

"Vivian wants me," he said. "Marilyn didn't say why."

I stared after them both. How strangely Marilyn acted, I thought. As if something's wrong. As if Mike . . . but Mike isn't here. *Now* what?

In about fifteen minutes Longin returned. I could tell nothing from his expression.

"Is it serious?"

"Yes, it's serious," he said. "Come in the house."

We went in, and he sat me down on the bed in my room, and sat down beside me.

"Your mother is dead," he said.

I said, "*My* mother?"

"Bests got word from Dad. He didn't want to tell you over the phone. He wanted me to tell you."

I couldn't believe it. It must be true, if Longin said it was, but I still couldn't believe . . . I put out my hand, and it felt good to feel Longin's hand, rough and hard and hot with the blood still flowing where it belonged, the heart pumping it as it should.

"It was her heart," I said.

Longin nodded. She had been hurrying upstairs, and she had collapsed and died, and my father, coming in from outdoors where he and Mike had been putting away storm windows, had found her there.

And the last time I had seen her I had been snapping at her. And she had been alone . . . Poor Mother. Poor Dad, not to have been with her . . .

Patrick came in. "What's the matter, Mother?" He turned to Longin. "Why is Mother crying?"

"Because her mother, your grandmother, is dead, and she won't see her any more."

Patrick accepted this without question. He leaned towards me and said earnestly, "Don't cry, Mother. Grandma died a saint. I bet she's already in Heaven."

My mother had been converted to Catholicism not three

[109]

months earlier. My sister had written how serenely joyous it had made her, how radiant her face when she returned from Mass each morning . . .

She had so little time to be happy, I thought. I wiped my face. "I'll bet you're right," I told Pat.

I packed. "I'll not be gone any longer than I can help," I said. "Can you manage, do you think?"

"Show me how to fix Baby's bottle," Longin said.

"I want to go with you, Mother. I'll keep you company."

Pat and I left the next morning. It seemed to me I was forever driving off on yet another tragic journey. Again and again and again and again . . .

We reached New Jersey late in the evening. My brothers were there, white-faced and tired, and my father. I looked around the kitchen, and it looked achingly familiar, and at the same time strange, changed in some subtle way. "Where's Mary?" Ted gave me an odd look. "At the funeral home." "Now?" I said stupidly. "People may be dropping in," he said patiently. "Some member of the family has to be there."

My God, I thought. How barbaric.

Mikey seemed to realize something was wrong, because his beloved Grandpa was so sad. He stroked Dad's face and crooned softly to him, and whether this was a comfort to Dad or more heartbreak, I don't know. Mikey obviously didn't realize his grandmother was gone.

When everything had been done, and the ceremonies were over, Pat and I gathered up Dad and Mike and headed for the farm. Mary couldn't come. The music department of the school was about to wind up the year in a flourish of concerts, to which her presence at the piano was vital. "I'll look after the house," she said sensibly. But I was glad to leave. Its rooms were full of ghosts. In the living room I could see my brother Ted as he had been in high school, thin and serious, hunched cross-legged on the floor, the innards of the family's first radio scattered all around him on the rug. There on the side porch was the swing where Bruce had been lounging, reading the *Encyclopædia Britannica*, that afternoon so long ago when a car had burned in the neighbors' driveway not thirty feet away, and half of Essex Fells had come to see the fire, and Bruce saw nothing, heard nothing. And the barn at the end of the drive, with its loft where we had put on puppet shows, and its roof where I had climbed, to read unseen from the ground, my feet propped against the chimney to keep me from sliding, this had been my secret place, my retreat, such a high and secret place as every child needs . . . .

As I slammed the kitchen door behind me, and went down the back porch steps for the last time, I knew it *was* for the last time, and I hurried to get away. My childhood was dead behind me, and I didn't dare look back.

In Vermont we found Longin deep in plans for the new barn. The barn which came with the farm would never do for Jenny. It had rotten underpinnings, and its condition was so critical we had not allowed the children to play near, lest it should suddenly collapse. I had had its weathered siding (lovely, silvery gray stuff beautiful to look at but too far gone to keep the rain out) removed, the summer before, and had used it as paneling in my bedroom. With this dubious support gone, the barn threatened to collapse at any moment. Its ability to maintain an erect position seemed to defy the law of gravity. But stand it did, throughout the winter, creaking in the bitter winds and groaning under heavy snows, and throughout the spring, too. It braced itself feebly against the gusty winds of March, and except for an occasional strip of roofing sailing across the yard, the barn itself survived, a monument to Vermont endurance and/or cussed stubbornness.

"Very simple to get rid of it," Longin said. "I'll hitch a rope to it, and haul it down." His eye gleamed.

My father said, "Are you going to rebuild in the same place?"

Longin said he was. "Already there is the excavating done," he explained. "On the west side there is the slope of the ground for a ramp—very practical. But of course," he admitted, "there is the problem of the view."

"No matter where we put the barn, Dad, it will spoil some of our view," I explained. "The best place would be below the house, of course, on account of drainage and convenience to the road and all that. If we had lived here years ago, that's probably where we would have put it, and the heck with its hiding the New Hampshire hills."

"Years ago," said my father, "a view wasn't as precious as it is now. Everywhere you looked was a view, and to country folk there was no prettier sight than a new barn."

"Well, I want to see the hills all around me," I said. "And where the barn is now actually shuts off the least view, in relation to the house, I mean—"

"I told her it would be impractical to suspend the new barn from skyhooks," Longin said gravely.

My father turned the plans around so he could read them easily. He frowned. "This door here—" He pointed with his pencil. "How wide is it?"

"Six feet. It opens into the stable in the lower barn. We're going to keep our cows loose in there, no stanchions. All the time we read about this pen stable method, farm magazines make big thing of it, cows supposed to get fewer injuries, chore time is cut—"

"Imagine having your neck in one of those frames!" I said. "Poor cows!"

"Is it wide enough for you to drive in with your tractor?" my father persisted.

Longin looked puzzled. "It connects with the barnyard," he said. "Only cows go in and out there. For machinery I will build a shed—"

"You will want to bring your tractor in," my father said, "when one of the cows dies. To haul her out, you understand."

I simply do not have Longin's self-control, I admit it. I had to leave the room hurriedly, and I missed his reply. But, as he said later, after all, we were planning our barn for live cows.

"Not even 'if,' " I said, hugging my sides in delight. "No subjunctive mood. Just 'when a cow dies'—simple future—"

"Better to give up now," Longin said, "then to start by making arrangements for dead cows."

"Isn't he a darling," I choked, wiping my eyes. "It's his training, you know. He was a safety engineer, among a dozen other things. He got paid for thinking of all the frightful things that might go wrong, and seeing to it that they didn't happen."

Mikey was now officially home. After a few days, my father, without making too big a point of the fact that he was leaving, gave Mikey an extra hug, eased into his car, and left for New Jersey, to put the house in shape to sell.

The weather and the lull in having company combined to encourage us to finish rebuilding our disposal system. This meant, obviously, that not even the most severely rationed flushings would be permitted; we must rig up a temporary replacement for the bathroom. The year before, when we had first come, there had been an outhouse tucked behind the old garage, but this we had rashly done away with. Longin selected a site beyond the barn over near the hedgerow where there did not appear to be a rock ledge to hamper him, and he constructed a shelter along classic lines, using the old garage doors and another old door which someone, years ago, had stashed away in the cellar. This shelter had three sides and a roof, but no door. The open side faced away from the wind and rain, and we thus could admire the magnificent view towards the east and the New Hampshire hills. And of the road.

I complained. I said we ought to have a door, too.

Longin said, "Whatever for?"

"You can see the road. You can see the mailman's jeep. It isn't decent."

"There is nothing indecent about the mailman's jeep."

I gnashed my teeth, and stalked out to the road and up to the top of the hill, and looked back. Strange, the tall meadow grass which did not screen our view out did obstruct one's view in. I could scarcely see the roof of our little palace. No door went up, then or ever. For the next two months we enjoyed the most modern of architecture, outdoors and indoors blending with no line of demarcation between, a really superb (one cannot quite

[113]

say pure) example of the most advanced principles of domestic design.

Next, Longin dug a disposal hole near the turn of the driveway, this hole to contain the contents of the old septic tank, which, thus lightened, he would be able to haul out and away. The location of the disposal hole was determined by the slope of the land, drainage to be away from the house and vegetable garden yet as far as possible from the spring. Longin had dug the hole, and had the top off the old septic tank, and boards laid between tank and hole to facilitate the passage of the wheelbarrow, and about half the contents of the tank transferred to the hole, when the phone rang.

It was Colonel Buechler. The Buechlers were driving through New England, were calling from Windsor, were wondering if we would care to have them drop in.

My first reaction was one of wild delight.

"We'll be along in about half an hour, then," Ted Buechler said. "Mary wants to shower and freshen up."

"I'll meet you at Four Corners," I said. "I'll lead the way in the Chevy."

So it was agreed, and I hung up. I looked about me.

Mary Buechler . . .

"Emergency!" I shouted. "Everybody come running!"

Kitty, Pat, and Chris came on the double.

"The Buechlers will be here in half an hour," I said crisply. "Pat, you sweep up the kitchen and workroom. Pick up all dirty diapers. Burn the wastepaper, including all those cardboard boxes I've been saving for trash. Chris, stuff the laundry in the washing machine and take the clean clothes upstairs. Hang up all coats and sweaters and put the rubbers and boots out of sight somewhere, I don't care where, just don't forget where you put them. Take the boxes of tin cans down cellar. Kitty, you and I will vacuum-clean the living room and dining room just as soon as we get them straightened—"

"Huh?" Chris and Pat said. "What did you want us to do, Mother?"

"You straighten faster than I can," Kitty said briskly, "so I'll vacuum-clean, Mother. Then while you go after the Buechlers I'll tarnish the furniture."

We began to do the housework on the run. Patrick, going out the door with the paper boxes, nearly collided with Longin, who stared in bewilderment at the scene before him.

"The Buechlers are coming!" I shouted. "Today! Now! I have to meet them in—" I glanced at the clock—"fifteen minutes!"

Without a word Longin turned on his heel and went back outdoors. Oh, well, *men*, I thought.

Fifteen minutes later I shot out the door and started to dog-trot to the Chevy, when I realized what Longin was doing. He had thrown boards over the open septic tank, and was shoveling dirt over them. There was no sign of the enormous hole by the bend of the drive, the hole that he had hacked out at such a staggering cost of time and energy.

I was appalled. "What have you done?" I said. *"What are you doing?"*

He stopped and rubbed an arm across his forehead. "Colonel and Mrs. Buechler are not going to walk into our house past our sewage," he said grimly, and began to shovel again.

By the time I had met the Buechlers and guided them through the woods and up over Alfonses' hill and on home, the yard was neat, Longin had showered, shaved, and changed clothes, Mary Lee lay freshly dressed in her playpen, Kitty had "tarnished" all the furniture, and the household was ready for inspection. None of us looked like fashion plates, and the house itself still looked pretty shabby, the cracks in the walls and the peeling wallpaper and worn linoleum and chipped paint suddenly far more conspicuous to my eyes than they had been for weeks, but at least we no longer looked like candidates for a social worker's call.

"You're all looking simply marvelous!" Mary Buechler cried, and kissed us all around. And Ted Buechler admired the view as extravagantly as if we were personally responsible for it. We showed them the house, as far as the vacuum-cleaner had foraged, and Mary thought my bedroom "breath-taking"—after the rest of the house, it probably was.

"The garage doors used to be there," I said, waving casually at the bay window. "And I always wanted a Dutch door. It opens on the orchard."

And don't you dare pity me. I know the house looks like a dump and you wonder how I can stand it and what do I think I'm doing here on this rocky little hillside working like a field hand, but don't you dare *pity me. Because I love it here. This is my home. I love it.* "Gip mir fünf Jahre," *Longin says mockingly, but it's true. You wait. Come back in five years. . . .*

When the Buechlers had gone, I remarked that it might be a good thing if we could expect folks to drop in unexpectedly at regular intervals. Maybe we'd keep things neater. "Although I like a lived-in look," I added defensively.

"A house is like the Army," Longin said shortly. "You worry all the time how things look, you won't get much done that matters."

"I begin to see why women used to have a parlor," I said, "just for company, and the door kept locked—"

"You mean in the olden days?" Pat said.

I ignored him. "Partly it's because we don't have places to put things," I went on, restlessly. "No attic, and the cellar so damp, and the one big closet leaking like a stall shower. I don't know what it is," I said irritably, "but I keep having this feeling that the house is shrinking."

"Children are growing," Longin said, and went out to undo his work of concealment.

He finished lightening the septic tank, and hauled it out and away to open-air storage beyond the hedgerow behind the barn. "We may need it for something someday," he said, absorbing a point of view from the very air about him.

"Sure," I said, "it would be just the thing in case we want to mine the Connecticut River."

"Very funny," he said briefly, and with pick and shovel and an expenditure of sheer muscle-power too enormous for me to calculate, he dug through rock ledge and flint-hard soil until he had a hole large enough for a thousand-gallon concrete tank. He made forms, he borrowed a large wooden trough from the Bests and mixed cement in this, and then, while the cement cured, he surveyed for the disposal field, a system of pipes which must run in straight lines and at proper slope, no matter what rocky barriers lay in the way, and he dug the trenches for these pipes, installed them, and buried them neatly. Nothing remained to be done now but to make a cover for the tank itself.

This cover had to be made in sections, Longin decided, and the only place level enough, yet out of the way, was the floor of the garage. So here he made forms and poured concrete, and by the time the slabs were cured and ready to be installed, the Meteses had come for the summer, and Grandpa Musat too, and his son Jon, who was Rozeta Metes' brother, and Jon's wife, Eleanor, and their two little boys Jon and Victor Musat, and the Meteses' boys, Jon, George and Nicky, and some school friends of Jon and George. Everybody came down to help install those slabs, and it made quite a procession coming around from the garage: Longin on the tractor with the first slab of concrete suspended from the tractor loader, a squad of young men striding behind, small children darting about like dragonflies, Mikey bringing up in the rear with an assortment of tools he had hopefully scrounged, and in the lead, directly before the swaying slab of concrete, Grandpa Musat, alert, ready to grab that slab and steady it, should it tip too far. All the men were stripped to the waist, because it was a hot day and they were engaged in heavy work, but Grandpa Musat prudently wore a Maurice Chevalier straw hat, because of the strength of the sun.

When all the slabs were in place, we consumed a couple of gallons of lemonade and I felt somebody ought to make a speech.

"Well, *that's* done," said Longin, and spat on the nearest slab.

Grandpa Musat rubbed his hands and flexed his arms. "What next?"

"Silo."

"You ready to work?"

"Have to make foundation first."

"Okay, you let me know when you need help." He squinted at his grandsons. "Let them know, too." Gathering up his clan, he headed up the hill. He was a busy man and had no time to waste. His vegetables needed to be watered, weeded, and spoken to encouragingly. Grandpa Musat had shrugged off our congratulations over his unfrosted garden. Naturally it hadn't been damaged, he had planted it during the proper phase of the moon. He had planted gardens during that phase of the moon in Roumania—same moon shines on Vermont—what did we expect?

Longin had already planted corn for Jenny's silage, and for this we would need a silo. Obviously. His plans for the summer consequently included building a silo as well as a barn, while mine stressed raising and freezing enough vegetables to carry us over until the next year's harvest, not to mention the usual daily grind of meals, dishes, laundry.

In view of our program, therefore, I felt it excusable if the housecleaning continued as before, a once-over-lightly whenever I had time. My own personal appearance was something else again. Every time I glanced into a mirror, I recoiled. Even my own sister, up for a week end, told me I was too old to let myself go like this, I had to take time at least to use a lipstick, she said, and couldn't I do more with my hair than hack at it with a razor?

Eleanor Musat came to my rescue. "You need a home permanent," she said. "I'll roll it up for you."

"You're an angel," I said gratefully. "You know what my sister said? She said, 'At your age, Melissa, you have to *try*.'"

And so, one lovely summer morning, Eleanor came down, and we retired to my bedroom and she tackled my hair with chemicals and incantations. The Dutch door stood open, and in the orchard scarcely a breeze stirred. It was so quiet we could hear the bees humming in the wildflowers under the motionless apple trees.

All of a sudden we heard a rumbling. It began as a low muttering, rapidly grew louder and louder until it was climaxed by a frightful crash. The instant of silence following was so complete not even a bird clacked in alarm.

[118]

"An avalanche!" I cried, having once heard one, in the movies. We rushed outside, and there was the barn, down at last.

"Time—time to neutralize!" said Eleanor, and rushed me back in.

"Damn it," I mumbled, my head over the basin. "Sometimes we go for weeks here with nothing falling down."

Kitty came dancing in. "Look, Mama," she called. "I found a foolish clover. It means good luck, did you know? The barn fell down, *that's* good luck. Look, Mikey—" non-stop, she danced outside again—"I found a foolish clover. Come see the barn, Mikey, it fell down!"

Pat and Chris burst in.

CHRIS: Hey, the barn fell down and we didn't do a darn thing to it! Hey, what's that awful smell in here?

PAT: Yeah, what stinks in here? What are you doing? Why don't you go out and see the barn?

ME (with dignity, my head wrapped in a towel): Can't you see I'm busy? I'm only doing this so I'll be beautiful.

CHRIS: I gotta get outa here. I'm gonna be sick if I stay in here.

PAT: I tell you what. Women are nuts, that's what.

Exeunt snorting]

Eleanor sighed. "Men," she said indulgently.

When I was at the penultimate stage, my hair in little whirls pinned tightly to my head, Eleanor and I could at last go out and inspect the ruins at our leisure. It made a most interesting debris. A couple of hundred berry boxes had shot out of nowhere, and some slatted shutters that turned to powder when you touched them. They must have been in the upper part of the old barn, where no one had dared explore lest he plunge through the rotted floorboards into the depths below. Over all hung a fine cloud of dust composed of exceedingly ancient and well-dried cow dung.

"There's a perfectly good wagon wheel," Eleanor said.

"And an oxen yoke," I said.

"I want those boxes, Mama," Kitty said, and sneezed. "God bless me," she added.

[119]

"You stay out of there," I warned. "There must be a million nails sticking up."

"It's going to be an awful job to clean it up," Eleanor said.

"That's the trouble with the country," I said. "There isn't anywhere to clean anything up *to*, know what I mean?"

"In Cleveland," Eleanor said, admiring our view, "a trashman comes every day. You need a pig, if you ask me."

"I have made up a song," Kitty announced. "Would you care to hear my song, Mama? It's about a star. It goes like this:

> If I were a star
> I'd wonder who you are—"

"Please, Kitty," I said. "A pig would be a very good idea, Eleanor, though of course you can always bury that sort of thing. Makes good fertilizer. Naturally it wouldn't help for tin cans and stuff like that."

"What do you do with the things you can't bury and can't burn?" Eleanor asked. "Rozeta is collecting boxes of broken glass and old rusted metal from the stone walls—"

"I've made up another song," Kitty said. "Listen, Mama. Listen, Aunt Eleanor.

> I'm just a friendly wildcat
> As lonesome as can be.
> I promise I'll not eat you up
> If you'll only play with me!"

Eleanor swept her up into her arms. "I could eat *you* up!" she cried. "I love little girls like you!"

"And I love you!" Kitty hugged her ardently. "I love everybody!" She hopped down and danced away, singing as she went, "I love every bit of God's beautiful world, God's beautiful world, God's beautiful world . . ."

"I hope she always feels like that," I said huskily.

"She will." Eleanor was confident. "That's Kitty."

"About those tin cans and trash—" We smiled at each other. It came to me with a touch of surprise that I had known Eleanor for exactly one week. "We stash them in boxes and load up the

Chevy and lug them to the town dump. We also," I added honestly, "borrow the Bests' dump. With permission, of course. It's way down in their woods where it can't be seen from anywhere. We'd start one of our own, but Mikey would be sure to find it." We strolled back towards the house. "I've been getting bushels of broken glass from our stone walls, too. I swear I think the people who used to live here just went to the door and heaved their trash in every direction. Didn't they see what they were doing, I wonder? Turning their own dooryards into a dump—"

"Messing up God's beautiful world," said Eleanor with a smile.

"I'm getting old, I guess," I said with a sigh. "Crotchety. I get mad every time I see a beer can chucked in the ditch beside the road."

Eleanor laughed. "You must be mad all the time."

"Oh, I am," I assured her. "Simply livid, every time I take the wheel."

By now Longin and I were avid readers of *Farm Journal, Rural New Yorker,* and *The New England Homestead.* I had barely begun to grasp the fact that there was much more to farming than I had realized. Perhaps our decision to farm was justified, perhaps it was the only way we could keep Mike with us. Nevertheless, we could not count on admirable reasons or good intentions to carry us through. We would have to acquire a vast store of specialized knowledge, and acquire it in a hurry, before our cushion of cash, dwindling so rapidly, became too small to keep us afloat.

After perusing the ads anxiously, we decided on a Unadilla silo, which came all ready to set up, said the ad, everything provided but the foundation, everything cut to fit and treated against whatever a silo should be treated against.

"That's what we want," I said, "a nice, conservative, wooden silo, none of these jet-stream concrete or tile or glass-brick jobs. Just a sweet little do-it-yourself silo."

"Also it's cheaper," said Longin, and disappeared into clouds of higher mathematics. After a while he returned to my mental level and announced that our farm could eventually feed fifteen cows, when the land was brought back to fertility, and that the silo should, therefore, be of a size to hold silage for fifteen cows, but that we couldn't afford such a size, yet, but not to let this distress me, because so far we had only one cow. We would get the ten-by-twenty silo, and when that was no longer big enough, we should be making enough money to afford another, and we would put grass silage in the second, a recommended procedure in this climate where the June hay crop is so vulnerable to the June rains.

We sent off a letter to Unadilla and by return mail received instructions how to make the foundation, plus bolts to sink therein, and this Longin proceeded to do at once. He finished off the foundation with professional smoothness, using a cement smoother he had fashioned out of one of my good aluminum cookie sheets. We scratched our initials in the wet cement, MBC—LBA—1952, and were draping it with wet feed bags, to cure it properly, when a truck came hurtling into the yard, and there was our silo, looking for all the world like a set of gigantic jackstraws.

Now we had further instructions. "This should be easy," Longin said. "You just keep inserting one board into another, dowel them together as you go along—" mumble, mumble—"add hoops—" mumble, mumble—"make sure it's perpendicular, two men on a rope to haul it straight, that'll be you—"

"What'll be me?"

"The two men on a rope." He skimmed on down the rest of the page. "Add roof, doors, et cetera. Tighten hoops, et cetera. Well, let's get started."

It really did go up as easily as claimed. Of course, it would have gone up faster if we had had money for lumber and built a proper staging, instead of trying to do the whole job from stepladders. But we got it up, and it is perpendicular, and I performed satisfactorily like two men on a rope while Longin did all the work that required the nerves of a steeplejack. I think it is a beautiful silo. It has grace and simplicity and such a good, useful look that whenever it catches my eye, I enjoy a nourishing sensation of achievement.

If Longin doesn't feel this same sensation of reward and accomplishment when he looks at his barn, he certainly ought to. He designed it, he drew up the plans, he staked out the foundation, he saw the entire project through to completion, in spite of the weather, always fickle, but now downright cantankerous, in spite of time, or the lack of it. The days flipped past with frightening speed. The more we had to do, the less time we had to do it in, and there was so much that had to be done *right now*. Scarcely had one week begun when it was ending and another beginning.

We got the silo up just before the corn ripened in September. Meanwhile, young Turner had come with his crawler and shoved aside the remains of the old barn, and Longin made the foundation for the new one. The dimensions of the barn were determined not so much by the size of the excavation for the old barn as by the needs of the farm which, no matter how fertile the land should become, in all probability would never support more than fifteen milking cows. There isn't much a man can do about land too steep for anything but a woodlot.

Against the ramp of earth on the west there was to be a solid wall of concrete, and all other walls were to be supported by foundations sunk four feet down, with footings well below the frost line. Longin borrowed a portable cement mixer and did these foundations himself, but for the west wall a vast amount of concrete must be poured swiftly, in order to avoid cracks and joints; Longin made the frames and braced them heavily, and then we were treated to the spectacle of a cement mixer rolling in and dumping its load, once, twice, thrice.

And meanwhile (I love these blithe "meanwhiles"—meanwhile *when?*), meanwhile, as I say, Longin had cut and dried his hay and stacked it in the field. And meanwhile, he was milking Jenny in the pasture. He had built a rude shelter of poles supporting a roof, using materials salvaged from the old barn, and here he put her manger for grain, and in bad weather he would milk her here. In good weather he strolled about the pasture, milk pail in hand, and milked her wherever he found her. She was a good cow, cooperative and intelligent, standing quietly when required, and coming to meet him when he called her name.

Jenny would need a female companion during the winter, Longin told me. A barn can be a chilly place with just one cow to warm it. I must go to an auction, and buy something suitable to be fattened up for beef.

There was a sale in New Hampshire. A farmer was selling out his milking herd, and Pat, Chris and I drove over. It was a new experience for us. We watched in amazement and disgust as the animals staggered out, thin, listless, heads wobbling weakly, patchy-skinned, some with open sores on their legs. The boys were fascinated by the selling prices, and kept urging me to buy. "Listen to that, Mother! They're *giving* them away!" "Hush," I would mutter. "Of course they are, and no wonder. Who would want to eat such creatures? And they're too wretched to give any milk." We stayed only because the catalog listed three or four cows from another herd, a large dairy in southern Vermont that was apparently doing some culling before it was time to put cows in the barn for the winter. Culls from a good herd are often better than the best cows in a small herd, I explained. Maybe we could pick up a bargain.

The first cow on consignment came out, and she looked nice, she really did. The catalog gave her lineage, and it was similar to Jenny's, and really, she didn't look bad, and Jenny would soon be dry . . . "Sold to the lady in the red jacket, for one hundred and forty dollars!"

"How could I leave her there, when they were practically giving her away?" I asked Longin when I got home. "Look, she has some Remus blood, and the same grandfather as Jenny—"

The truck came, and Ronna limped wearily down the ramp. For a moment I wasn't even sure it was the same cow. Her back sagged, her hip bones jutted alarmingly, her right rear hoof seemed to be giving her trouble. "Next to Jenny, no cow would look good," said Pat, but it was hollow comfort.

Clifford and Vivian came up to see her as soon as they finished their evening milking.

[124]

"Do you suppose I was deceived," I said worriedly, "and thought she looked like a good cow because of all those miserable, practically decayed critters I'd been staring at?"

"She has a splendid long tail," Vivian said consolingly.

"That's good?"

"Oh, yes. A milking cow does better if she has a good long tail to keep the flies off with."

"She looks hungry to me," Clifford said. "Give her a little grain and her back'll straighten." He chewed on the end of his pipe. "If you're worried about her, I'll buy her from you for what you paid," he offered.

Naturally this made me feel much better, and Ronna joined Jenny in the pasture. Ronna, whether by nature or from experience I wouldn't know, was a bovine doormat, much too submissive to dream of challenging Jenny's autocratic ways, and the two got along famously. They would both come up to the pasture gate to check on the progress of the barn, Jenny slightly in the lead, as befitted her rank. Jenny was due to calve early in December, and she was concerned about her winter quarters.

As September sped by and October raced after, work on the barn was stepped up to a kind of frenzy. We had all sorts of help. Chris's godfather drove up from Connecticut and spent the week end nailing studs to the joists of the pen stable. Lassie and Charlie Smith drove up from Washington once, when Charlie had a few days off from testing the Navy's jets, and it poured the two days they were here, a cold, 33° downpour that drenched Charlie and Longin through to the skin as they stubbornly persisted at nailing the floorboards for the hay mow. My father came up from New Jersey whenever he could, and helped look after Mike, and helped raise the rafters, and helped Pat and Chris with the siding. And Bruce, too, was there, driving every week end from Schenectady, and helped raise the rafters, and worked steadily at siding, roof sheathing and shingles.

Even so, we didn't make it. As October slid into November, the nights were too cold for the cows to stay in the pasture. Longin borrowed four heifers from Bests to help warm the stable, and he put Ronna in with them. The roof was not completely shingled, and the rain came through, and Jenny, in her delicate condition, needed better accommodations than this. So Longin constructed a pen in one half of the garage, all carefully fenced and bedded with hay, and a little manger for her grain, and her own private salt lick, and a bucket as large as a bushel basket for her water. All through November, I could hear her on the other side of the door connecting my bedroom with the garage. She made companionable sounds, gentle stompings and sighings, occasionally murmuring softly, in the way that old women will mumble patiently to themselves. I noticed the smell, of course, but I didn't mind it. It was a good, clean, animal smell, nothing more.

The barn was nearly ready, there was nothing more to be done but finish up the big door and install it on its track, and then move the hay in from the stacks in the field, when we stopped long enough to celebrate Thanksgiving. Late in the afternoon, Jenny dropped her calf, a little heifer calf. She had not yet got the calf licked dry when she dropped another, a bull.

Poor Jenny! I know just how she felt. She stared from one to the other, and roared with outrage. *Who's playing tricks on me?* she roared. *One is enough! Do you think I don't know one is enough?* Turning her back on the little heifer, she licked the bull dry, and let him suck.

"Poor little shivering thing," I crooned, as Longin mopped the heifer off with a grain sack. Jenny was making such a fuss over the bull, it did seem unfair. She poked him to his feet, and began lowing to him, using a soft, deep tone I had never heard before, sweet and tender and throbbing with maternal pride.

I went to phone the Bests. Such magnificent news as this, *twins*, was too good to keep.

"Oh," said Vivian. And after a moment, "That's too bad."

I asked her to enlarge on this theme, and she did so. All my delight drained out of me, I went back to report to Longin.

"Vivian says what a shame," I said, watching him wrap the heifer in the detachable plaid lining of my ancient winter coat. "She says twins are very hard on the mother, and often spoil the whole lactation. She says nobody would want to buy the bull for a herd sire, they'd be afraid he'd breed their cows to twins. She says a heifer twin to a bull is sterile, nine times out of ten."

Longin looked up. "Nine times out of ten, eh?" He cupped his hand and let the calf nuzzle it. "So we gamble. We raise her and see."

"Sure," I said. "We can always eat her," I said, trying to be consoling. I was shocked at the sound of my own words.

Longin stood up and glared at me. "*You* eat her," he snarled. "I will not come to the table!"

I said feebly, "Let's not quarrel now—"

"You might as well understand," Longin said, pounding with his clenched fist on the railing, "what kind of farmer I will be. I will farm *Polish*-style. I shall not hack off cows' horns and make them look ugly, no. I will get golden balls and put them on the ends of the horns. When I get rich, I shall not cut hay in the field and haul it into the barn green and there have a big oven to cook it dry, no! I will dry it in the field and heap it on the wagon all sweet-smelling and when the rain clouds threaten I'll race like hell for the barn. None of this modern, scientific, kill-the-calf-maybe-she's-sterile stuff for me!"

He thumped Jenny approvingly on the hip.

"*Women!*" he sneered, for no particular reason that I could see.

CHAPTER V

As it turned out, we didn't eat the calf, we ate Ronna. There came a time when it was obvious that Ronna was not, as advertised, "safe with calf," so we called the breeder, or bull-cheater, to use the more pungent term, and he came and bred her. And then, some weeks later, it was further obvious why Ronna had been culled from the fancy big herd and sold at an obscure little auction miles from home: she had some mystifying structural defect which made it impossible for her to carry a calf to term, and thus function like a milking cow. The vet pronounced her healthy, but good only for beef.

All of which calls to mind the saying, don't name it if you're going to eat it. A juicy beefsteak you can enjoy; it takes a certain stoicism to chew and swallow when the children, forks poised in anticipation, ask brightly, "Is this Ronna?"

For country living, stoicism is nice to have, but not, fortunately for me, vital. It's not easy to list what are the necessities of life in the country. It depends on what you mean by necessity. If you mean only those things without which you actually cannot exist, of course country necessities and city necessities are the same: food, water, air and warmth. If, however, you mean those things without which life may become damned unpleasant, the list becomes longer and somewhat specialized.

In spite of the astonishing experience of Mrs. Ferncliffe, living for two years on our hill with no car, I think I would put *adequate transportation* at the very top of my list. If you have some way to get out and in, you are in touch with civilization, and all its attendant riches: light bulbs and fuses, a piece of hose for the washing machine, plumbers' cement, more washers for that faucet the lime in the water continually wrecks, a can of caustic soda which may (or may not) clear the pipes to the septic tank, matches, the newspaper, a bottle of shampoo—all the thousand items which smooth the wheels of family life, without which it is perfectly possible to exist, but not so easy to live.

And in our large family, there may, at any moment, be yet another emergency: the pitchfork through Pat's foot; the unidentifiable head-to-toe rash of Mary Lee; the nail in the board in the schoolyard, knelt on at noon by Chris but not reported (there being still no phone handy) until he returned home, late in the afternoon; Pat's chopped finger ("Mother!" Pat called politely, outside my window where I was typing away, "I hate to bother you but this is an emergency, I chopped off my finger!") which turned out to be not chopped off completely, but the speed with which Pat plus fingertip reached the surgeon in Hanover had a lot to do with the fact that Pat and fingertip are now firmly grown together. And with Mikey home, emergencies might multiply uncontrollably, becoming, at any moment, a disaster. It would give me a very queasy feeling to live out where we do, and not know we can get out whenever we have to.

By the fall of '52 our Chevy gave every sign of premature aging. It sought to prolong its life span by conserving its energies, and became very reluctant to do any work. Super-special oils, high-powered cocktails in the gas tank (something called Drigas), a new battery, new fan belt, new spark plugs, new ring job, even new snow tires—all these were as nothing. It whined and complained it had lived out its time and only wanted to die in peace. Did we need a pail of calf feed? It couldn't care less. Running low on shingle nails? Baby needs a booster shot? Aching tooth needs dentist? Too bad. Chevy is all tuckered out.

As I was chief errand-runner, I would be the one to start—pardon, *try* to start—the Chevy, and it was female pride that kept me at it until the battery was run down. I couldn't see how the Chevy knew if it was a male or female toe pressing the starter, but it did. Many a time the car would start for Longin when it wouldn't start for me, and he didn't touch my adjustment of the choke, either. I found this humiliating.

When the Chevy took to not starting unless shoved or pulled, Longin would get out the tractor, hitch the tow chain, and get the Chevy moving, while I played with clutch pedal and choke like a musician coaxing music from a pump organ.

When the driveway was icy, our difficulties were compounded, because then Longin couldn't drag the Chevy towards the road. In that direction the drive slants up, though very slightly, and the tractor wheels would spin and the Chevy stay put. We would have to go the other way, and drag the Chevy towards the field. It was all one to me which direction we went—as long as the car *did* start.

Once I could not get the motor to catch. We reached the brink of the hill and still the motor played dead. Longin unhitched the tractor and moved it out of the way, ordered me over into the passenger seat, started the car rolling with a mighty shove, and leaped in. We jounced down the hill, the car bucking and bobbing over the bare, frozen ground, the motor turning over . . . turning over . . . refusing to catch . . . refusing . . . "Hurray! She's started!" I cried in relief, when there was nothing ahead but swamp and a stone wall.

A good thing it did, too. Otherwise it might be there yet. It hadn't occurred to me before, but perhaps that's how all those other cars got scattered about the countryside. Take a short drive in any direction and you'll see them, rusting patiently, sometimes three or four together but more often one alone, perched on a pasture slope in full view of a house. They puzzled me. Why were they left there? Did they possibly have some religious significance? Were they a fetish of some sort? A tribal symbol, like a totem pole, mute testimony to ancestral affluence? How prosaic if these relics should be nothing more than evidence that someone couldn't get the durned thing rolling one final time! And if close inspection indicates that same frenzied soul hacked at the radiator with a hatchet, let no one cry shame. There was once I might have done the same, had I been alone.

It was in December of '52, and I had an appointment with the dentist. The roads were packed with snow, the kind we often get that early in winter, snow which halfway melts, and then freezes again, polished to a high sheen. Chevy of course balked, and Longin tried to conjure it into starting, by oath and legerdemain, but without success. So it was out with the tractor and haul the Chevy towards the road once again. And could I coax that motor to run? No, I could not.

It was bitter cold and my gloved fingers grew stiff. It was even colder up on the tractor, I knew, where Longin's ears were turning crimson in the wind. After every jerk of the tow chain, I had to be very careful not to let the car roll into the tractor, and Longin's face, as he watched my clumsy efforts with clutch and brake, was growing ferocious, and I was growing correspondingly nervous. The wind and the noise of the tractor motor confused me. I couldn't hear what the Chevy's motor was doing. Once I thought it had caught, but I did the wrong thing, and it died. I smiled at Longin in desperate apology.

"Damn it, I'm glad you're enjoying yourself!" he roared savagely. "What the hell is so funny, I'd like to know?"

I burst into tears of fury. "I certainly am *not* enjoying myself!" I sobbed. "I *loathe* this car, why the *hell* does it have to act so, and why the *hell* do you have to be so hateful?"

We had reached the top of Bests' hill, and Longin was so incensed he decided to start the Chevy by rolling it down that ski jump. I refused to get out. I said he could damn well put up with me in the car, I wasn't going to hike after him like a squaw. Down we plunged, and halfway down, the Chevy began its reassuring racket.

At the bottom of the hill Longin got out and I drove off, neither of us bothering with the amenities. All the way into Woodstock

[131]

I counted over my grievances as a miser counts gold. How *could* I stand him? So arrogant, so moody, so hateful! I *loathed* him!

Any addict of fiction on film could have told me what ailed me. I was suffering from Plot One, Grade B, of course. It's a wonder I hadn't seen it for myself.

Howsoever . . . we worked it out. We turned in the Chevy for a jeep station wagon, and we decided to get married.

But not right away, of course. We took an appallingly intellectual approach to our planning, and decided we would say nothing to anybody, not until right before our plans were to be put into effect. In this way, much yak-yak-yak over a long period of time could be avoided. Because of course we couldn't get married until the farm was paying for itself. Gracious, no. It Isn't Done.

Well may you ask, why isn't it? I don't know. Longin and I didn't really know, then. We just had this vague feeling that it would be so much *nicer* if the farm were a going concern, showing an actual cash profit, not just the intangible kind, full freezers and bushels of potatoes and pork from our own pig and the daily two to three gallons of milk for the kitchen. I pointed out that if we had to go out and buy all this stuff, we'd go broke in a minute, and furthermore look how much healthier we were all getting, full of prance and dance. But even if we put a cash value on feeling full of the old zzzazz, Longin said, we were still a long way from recouping our investment in land, barn, animals, and machinery. I agreed.

Now in 1953 many dairy farmers were making less than thirty-five cents an hour, not counting the labor of their wives and children, and I don't suppose a decision made at that time to postpone marriage until Farm Is Profitable could really be defined as rational. It was purely an emotional one, based on nothing but the fact that we had a certain pride. And pride, in the country, comes at the very bottom of the list of necessities. Come to think of it, it doesn't belong there at all. It ought to head the list of handicaps!

There is, however, a quality distantly related to pride which you cannot possibly get along without, and that is *self-confidence*. You must, if you are going to live in the country, have an unshakable faith in yourself, faith that somehow, come what may, you can take it, you can bounce back, too dumb, if you like, to know when you're licked. Longin and I both have this amateur's ignorance which prevents recognition of defeat, and we both have the kind of self-confidence which blithely assumes we can do anything if we just try hard enough. We knew, though, that no one else thought so, that my relatives and friends were sadly waiting for us to trip and smack our faces in the mud; hence our desire to prove we could succeed at one thing before we took on another, greater challenge.

Another thing. If you are going to be happy living in the country, you have to keep clearly in mind that that is where you are—*in the country*. I think it's nothing short of simple-minded to move from the city to the suburbs, and then start complaining that the suburbs aren't like the city. Or to move further into the country, and then fret because the country is different from suburbs or city. Of course it is. Different, mind you—not worse. *Different*.

So I am simple-minded, because at first I did a lot of fretting. I kept my nails lacquered, for example. I had worn them that way for years, they were part of "me," I thought. And I tried to keep them that way, and would put on gloves when gardening, if you please. It finally seeped into my mind that the state of my nails was of little cosmic importance; if I had to grow vegetables, and harvest them, and put them up for winter, then I had to, so enjoy it, and the hell with Pink Passion polish. You can't grow anything, I found out, if you're afraid to get your hands in the dirt, and that goes for children as well as swiss chard. When I went down to New York to get myself a dress to get married in (this isn't a suspense story—we do get married by the end of this chapter) I decided to live it up and I had my hair done and my nails, too. The chic little maiden picked up my paw and gasped, "What has madame been *doing* with her hands?"

"Using them," I told her happily.

[133]

Human beings, I suppose, could use some of that amazing stuff the seed stores sell, which is added to the water you pour around the roots of a plant newly moved from one location to another. It cushions the plant against the shock of being transplanted. Keeps the plant from wilting, from losing its joie de vivre. . . . A little would help us poor human transplants, yanked forcibly out of one environment and told to grow and like it, adapt, adapt yourself, and no neuroses, please.

This period of transition, when the shock of having been transplanted is wearing off, is a painful period, not because of any large-scale adjustments you are called upon to make, but because of the little ones. The big things—the silence, the time to think, the sweep of the seasons and the imperative demands of the weather, the feeling of being far away from crowds—these are the reasons you moved to the country in the first place. These things come naturally. It's the little things . . .

For me it was not bathing every day. Longin not shaving every day, either. Home haircuts. Seldom if ever attending a party limited to adults. Ordering my shoes by mail. The virtual elimination of the following topics of conversation: books, good movies, politics, military experiences and strategy, politics, the absolutely vital and urgently imperative pay raise for the Army, politics. The addition of the following topics of conversation: the economic importance of the weather, the machinations of the Department of Agriculture, the state of the roads, the price of grain, the price of milk, that is, what the farmer gets, what the consumer pays, and the wicked and unbelievable gap between.

As time passed, these new topics of conversation grew more and more fascinating. When, at last, I spent an entire evening discussing the virtues of different kinds of fertilizer, analyzing the wisdom or stupidity of the last decrees of the Soil Conservation people, and verbally tarring and feathering the villain in the Criminal Case of the Price of Milk, I knew I had weathered the worst of my uprooting, and was beginning to feel at home.

I am very much afraid, though, that in order to enjoy, or even to become used to, the number-one topic in country conversation,

[134]

I should have been born here. I mean, of course, Health. *Ill* health, that is. In Vermont, where it has been said it's bad manners to die before ninety-five, almost no one will admit to feeling well when asked, and the innocent greeting, How are you? brings forth such a detailed description of the begreeted's bowels, digestive process, advancement of pregnancy, heart, lungs, shoulder joint, knees, teeth, throat, head, eyes and nerves (which are sluggish, touchy, still not certain, givin' out, weak, lame, swollen up, ripe for pullin', raspy, heavy, spots before and all wore out) that it's no wonder Vermonters are chary of opening a conversation with a stranger. (Let *him* ask how *you* are.)

I don't know why Vermonters are so proud to be sick. Perhaps it's a we've-had-it-tougher-than-anybody-and-look-it's-nearly-killed-us snobbism.

Not all Vermonters, to be sure. I heard one spare old man reply, drily, "Oh, I ain't complainin'. Wouldn't do me no good if I did—nobuddy'd listen."

It was as refreshing as a swig of hard cider.

And there was another old man, an independent fellow who took to a cabin in the woods, who, when asked by passing lumbermen how he did, replied, "I hear tell I'm s'posed to have lost my mind." He waved away their offers of sympathy. "I don't keer if I have," he drawled. "I cain't say as I've missed it!"

Of course, it's the differences in people that are the hardest to get used to. In Vermont, where six months of the year it's too cold to smile, it's only natural, I suppose, for folks to consider thick insulation a virtue. Nevertheless, what I missed most of all when first I moved here was not the heat of the South but the warmth of its people. Sometimes I would have given almost anything to have Dodie come strolling in, southern sunshine in her voice as she sings out, "Hiyuh, Melisse. Looky heah, I brought m' coffeepot—" I know, deep down inside Vermonters, the warmth is there. But it's no warmer for having to be chipped down to, or blasted out by private grief or common disaster, whatever Vermonters may think. Warm-heartedness thrives not on being hoarded but on being spent.

Another thing that was hard to get used to is the way Vermonters talk about other Vermonters. Men are seldom praised, even by other men. Once in a while you may hear that (cautiously) so-and-so is a hard worker, but that is as far as anyone cares to go. If a man escapes being described as drinking too much, being free with his money, chasing other men's wives, or even being an outright thief, you can assume he is sober, prudent, faithful and honest. These qualities are never mentioned, mind you; it is by the absence of remarks to the contrary that you can judge a man to be a good husband and worth-while citizen. Because, if there is anything to be said against a man, it will surely be said. Man's sins are many, his virtues none, don't tell me his good points, what's wrong that he's done? *

When a woman is well spoken of, she is invariably "a good worker"—for the PTA, the Grange, the church. Should she stick close to home, "she minds her own business." If she doesn't criticize anything (publicly), she "fits in nice." A woman's figure is never mentioned in an approving way; if she's slender, she "looks all wore out," and if she is stout, she "sure has let herself go." I have never once heard a Vermonter describe *any* woman, native or newcomer, as gay, or lighthearted, or a fascinating conversationalist, or charming, or beautiful, well dressed, clever, well read, entertaining to know. . . . Never, not once. If there is a woman here who has any of these qualities, her friends are very loyal and never mention the disgraceful fact.

Oh, well, I really don't want Vermonters to be like everybody else. Humanity wouldn't be as much fun, all homogenized. Just the same, why don't Vermonters, with all their splendid qualities of courage and endurance and independence and sheer grit—why don't they ponder the fact that the granite and marble of their hills vastly increase in value when the surface is polished?

There was a young man visiting at Turners' once, a very young man from down country, full of the joy of living, and he used to stroll the roads and sing. The local rumor was that he was crazy.

* Vermont proverb, Mather coinage, Circa 1954.

Once in a while, in sheer exuberance, he would shoot off a gun at the sky. Crazier than a skunk at moonrise.

I shudder to think what must be Longin's reputation. Longin sings, too. When he goes after his cows, he sings. "Come, cows cows cows," and the hills echo back *ows ows ows*. "Come, Jenny, good Jenny, nice Jenny." *Enny enny enny*. And over the brow of the pasture Jenny comes, eagerly, her companions following her.

When Longin rides the tractor, hour after hour, plowing, harrowing, mowing, raking, he sings. You can't make out the words above the sound of the motor, but it's obvious he's glad to be alive, and not ashamed to show it. When he was shingling the barn roof, you could hear him half a mile away, chanting in Polish in time with the pounding of his hammer. "What were you singing?" I asked once. "That's a song about a dog roaming the fields, happy because he isn't married," he said, grinning wickedly.

We had discarded old ways and standards, we had managed more or less to accept new ones, but our visiting friends and relatives had not, and I felt for them. Everything was such a shock. "We don't open the front door in the winter, darlings, come in this way"—"this way" being through the workroom, past the heaps of laundry being sorted for the wash. "Can you climb over that board? We hook it across the stairs because of the baby." "We can sleep two of you in the living room, and set up the cot in the workroom, and if we spread the sleeping bag out of the way in the dining room, no one will walk on you in the night." "Heavens, you won't need a hat and gloves, we're just going to the village." "I'm awfully sorry, but we haven't any water for a bath. No, I don't mean hot water, I mean we haven't *any* water. Just as soon as I get the roast in the oven, I'll drive you down to the brook and you can sponge off."

I suppose whatever it is you don't have always seems to be what it is hardest to do without. In the winter of '51 and the spring of '52, I would have said nothing could be more important than to have water going out. By the summer of '53, water coming *in* would have been at the very top of my list, and written in italics with little stars between the letters.

Some time early in the spring—it was well before we sprayed the new apple trees, I remember, because I remember *that* very clearly, having been feeling very gay at the time and laughing and talking the while, unaware of inhaling spray, until the next day, when my lungs were on fire, and Longin, reading the label on the can of spray, turned white and said, "My God, this is more poisonous than the Army's poison gas!"—some time before this near-suicide of mine, as I say, it rained, and then it seemed to be giving it up, like a bad habit, because it didn't rain again until long after corn-planting time.

The field where we had had our grass fire was to be a permanent mowing, Longin decided, because it sloped away towards the north a bit too steeply to be plowed very often. It was a poor field that had been neglected for years, and in order to bring it back, Longin planned to plant it first to corn and then to grass. Further down the slope the soil seemed in better shape, and the corn rotation could be skipped there. So Longin plowed, and spread lime and fertilizer, and harrowed, and harrowed again, and planted the upper slope to corn, and harrowed the lower slope once more, and rolled the soil there; but he could not plant the mowing, he said, the seed would not sprout until we had had a rain, the soil was like powder.

I had planted my vegetable garden, and the children and I lugged water by the bucketful every other night, soaking the thirsty soil along the rows of spindly seedlings. If we could only keep them going, we thought, until their tap roots had sunk down to the moisture a foot or more deep, perhaps we could save some of the garden, anyway. The children developed primitive superstitions, and performed every trick they had ever heard of which might bring rain: they killed a frog, tossed salt out of doors, beat on my rain tom-tom (a relic of my handicraft days at girl scout camp) and did what they claimed was a rain-making dance of Aztec origin. I, too, tried to appease the angry rain god, and left my washing on the line overnight, and the jeep windows rolled down.

The corn seed wisely remained dormant. Longin, digging gen-

[138]

tly through the powdery soil, could find no sign of swelling life in the dry, hard seed. Just as well, he said. It would only die. Once in a great while we would be promised "possible thundershowers," and the sky might gradually cloud over. But no rain fell, at least not on us. Sometimes we could see thunderclouds beyond the hills to the north, and gray streaks slanting below, and we would say bitterly, "It's raining in the Ottaqueechee valley again." Once a single huge black cloud came and crouched directly over the farm. Then, as we watched hopefully, blue sky appeared along the eastern horizon and began to shove the cloud back. Here and there a single drop of rain splattered into the dust—I felt one on my face—and then the cloud moved sullenly off, and released a downpour on West Windsor that lasted for three quarters of an hour. Longin was nearly beyond speech.

Then the wind swung to the north, and for several days blew hot, dry and strong, against the cornfield and the mowing. And day after day the dark clouds rose over the fields, clouds of soil, tons and tons of priceless soil, centuries of soil, blown away on the wind, blown away forever. Wherever I worked in the house, I could hear the wind, never stopping, robbing us of our wealth, our treasure of soil, irreplaceable in our lifetime or in several lifetimes.

At last the wind died, and it was possible to go outdoors without the taste of soil in one's mouth, the grit of soil under one's eyelids. Longin and I went to look at our fields, and we were heartsick. The corn seed, which had been planted inches under the surface, was exposed, row after row. We walked along, poking the seed under, literally stunned by the knowledge that more than three inches of topsoil had been blown right off the field.

One Friday evening I decided to start painting the barn. Perhaps that would bring rain. I recruited Pat and Chris and we began work on the north side, moving over to the west in the morning, in order to keep out of the sun, which was then rising in the general direction of Greenland. It was a very hot and sultry day, 96° in the shade, and the entire kitchen garden began to look dehydrated. Towards evening, storm clouds gathered. They don't mean a thing, I thought bitterly, taking down the washing and going indoors to do the supper dishes. I'm sick of being disappointed, I refuse to get my hopes up.

Then I heard the children screaming joyfully. "It's going to rain, it really is, *it really is!*" I rushed outdoors. Towards the northwest I could see a gauzy curtain between earth and sky— rain! Across the valley it was, it really was raining!

And then we could hear the rain coming, rustling and rushing through the woods, drumming up across the pasture, and at last it swept across the parched lawn and reached us where we stood. The children stretched their arms out to catch the falling water. Oh blessed, blessed rain! Longin had his eyes closed and his mouth wide open, and his upturned face, in spite of such distortion, wore an expression of sheerest bliss. My hair flattened and dripped delicious wetness down my neck, and I slipped off my shoes and pranced about in the soaked grass like a happy savage. Mikey was smiling in delight as his shirt and jeans became sopping wet. The rest of the children had leaped into swimsuits and were now splashing noisily in the puddles that appeared like magic in the driveway.

It was only a thundershower. Before dark the rain stopped, and in the morning, when we probed anxiously into the ground, we found that the moisture had penetrated only a few inches.

Every now and then I read about water shortages in the suburbs. Folks aren't supposed to wash their cars, it seems, or water their lawns, or change the water in their swimming pools. Newspaper editorials advocate that civic-minded men skip shaving every day. When things get really tough, some political appointee (surely not an elected official) may suggest that perhaps air-conditioners should be shut off.

That is not a water shortage. A water shortage exists when you turn on the faucet, and *nothing comes out.*

A trip to the cellar shows the fuse for the pump still works. A trip to the pump house shows the pump itself in fine fettle, though mysteriously idle. A further exploration, to the spring, shows the source of trouble, all right, if (calamity!) no longer any source of water.

When our spring went dry, as it did early in July, we had a goodly choice of things we could do. We—that is, Longin—could dig deeper, hoping to find another vein of water. The only other time this spring ever went dry (a statement which bewildered me, because I could distinctly remember being told this spring *never* went dry)—the only other time, Burke or Bowers or whoever it was living here at the time, Clifford said, started digging and the water came in so fast he nearly drowned before he could climb out. So Longin dug down, and down, and down, with pick-axe and crowbar and spade, and rented the town's air-hammer, and drilled through rock, but all he accomplished was to get the mud at the bottom of the hole to be a little bit wetter.

During this time Longin was hauling water from the Meteses, who had very kindly offered us as much water as we needed from their overflow, but in due time the Meteses' spring began to get low, and there was no overflow; and the Bests' spring (which also had never gone dry) was threatening to do so, too. Longin, who "meanwhile" had made a trailer for his tractor, borrowed some of Clifford's extra milk cans and hauled water for the cows from the brook in Jenneville, nearly a mile away, and, for the house, from the spring there, just below the cemetery. We didn't bother to have this water tested for purity; all we asked was for water that was wet. The children said they had lots of times taken drinks from this spring, when they were waiting for the school bus; I accepted this as evidence that the water was not lethal. I did forbid them to make any remarks about the location of the spring, as I frequently find their sense of humor too earthy for my appetite. This spring also has never been known to go dry, and it deserves its reputation, because all through that summer it gave us to drink, and the Alfonses, and the Meteses, and no doubt the Jennes, too, of Jenneville.

Another thing we could do was to inquire about ponds, and the digging thereof, and the paying therefore. (One way to weather a catastrophe in the country is to take action so it can't happen again—you hope.) A pond might trap some of that water seeping so wastefully below the spring, water which had turned nearly two acres into a swampy place too wet to plow and too wet for tender grasses and therefore useless for pasture even if the cows wore galoshes. A pond, we learned, costs hundreds and *hundreds* of dollars; not only must we pay the cost of excavating and the cost of transporting enormous machinery miles and miles to get here, but we must pay for the lumber to prop up the bridges on the lower road so that the enormous and expensive machinery will not collapse them. Should that occur . . . well, the results could be bankruptcy and prison, at any rate that's what we were given to understand.

It was at this point that we heard a most enchanting rumor. The Government—whoever that is—is all in favor of farm ponds. Every Farm Should Have a Pond. The Government is so very much in favor of farm ponds that it, or they, will go shares with a farmer wanting a pond, providing, of course, the farmer wants his pond for practical reasons such as conservation of water, irrigation, watering livestock, etc. If the farmer (or, more likely, his children) wants the pond for fishing, canoeing, swimming, ice skating, or as artistic background for a barbecue, he would be advised not to mention this until after he has his pond. And then he would be advised not to mention this to me.

We put in our application for a pond. Then we waited for the proper surveyors to come and survey. The Government likes to be sure the pond will be dug where water will flow into it, and where water will stay in once it gets there. While we waited, Longin watched with understandable impatience as the bridges on the lower road were propped up with sturdy lumber for the passage of road-building machinery. This lumber was the property of a private construction concern, now busy making a driveway for a well-to-do retired couple who were restoring an old stone house on a hillside above Jenneville; once the job was done, the lumber might be removed.

"We ought to dig now," Longin said. "It wouldn't cost us anything to get the machinery over the bridges."

His impatience increased as the dragline arrived at Bests' to dig a drainage ditch along the mowing. "Dragline is right next door!" he exploded. "I have surveyed, I know where pond should be, soil there is good clay. Why don't the surveyors come?"

We didn't know what to do. We needed water desperately, and we needed it at once. Would it cost us less to go shares with Clifford on transportation, and pay the whole cost of excavation, or wait until later, pay all transportation costs, and have government help on the excavating costs? And after all, we were not conservation experts, hydraulic engineers, or dam builders. Maybe we had not chosen the pond's site wisely. What if we should spend all that money and water wouldn't stay and there we'd be with a huge expensive hole. . . . We decided to wait.

Late in August the surveyors got around to surveying and they said Longin's choice of site was excellent, his verdict on soil was quite correct, it was clay and the proper depth. Pond site was approved; pond construction was approved. Now we had merely to wait for our turn at the machinery, which, by now, was miles and miles away.

So we waited. We waited through the fall of '53 and the winter and the following spring, which was a wet spring and therefore pond-digging would have been difficult, and into the summer, when at last we received a communication re our pond. Approval for assistance for our pond had been withdrawn, said this communiqué, because our farm *carried insufficient cows to justify the expense.*

Longin's temper flared like a skyrocket. Why couldn't they have said so when the dragline was right next door? How the *hell* did they think the farm could carry more cows until there was water for more cows? Who got aid from the Government, anyhow—just the farmers with big ideas, big operations, big incomes? The *hell* with aid from the Government!

Longin called Lyman in North Hartland, who enjoys a splendid reputation locally of having great skill with a bulldozer, and Lyman came, bringing his bulldozer, and in exactly one day, or, to be more precise, four and a half hours, he bulldozed out not one but *two* ponds (true, not large, but the cows can drink from them) and a ramp for loading cattle on the truck, and a lane over the hill to the far-west field, and a smooth place in the barnyard where machinery can maneuver to go into the pole barn. The bill: $29.

"The *hell* with help from the Government," I echoed.

I used to think, when I was young and slightly more foolish than I am now, that it is absurd to live in a house with an attic. I no longer think so. Now I long for an attic, large and rambling, where the sounds of life in the rest of the house reach only faintly, where it is quiet, and cluttered with memories happy and sad, and crowded everywhere with all the things I have learned at last not to be so silly as to throw away, because I shall need them again some time.

The children's cribs, highchairs (we have two of each), rocking horses (three, in assorted sizes); pup tents, bedding rolls, duffel bags and canteens; sleds, skis, ice skates, wagons (assorted sizes); easels, mine, and two smaller; various battered suitcases, trunks, and musette bags; ski boots; lamps with broken necks; Bob's letters from overseas in '44-'45; Bob's letters from Louisiana maneuvers, '41; my letters from England, '39; the puppet theater I made at the age of ten, and the box of Rumpelstiltskin puppets; the box of Nazi decorations and such which Bob picked up on his trip through Belgium and the Siegfried Line, except for his Luger pistol, which was swiped by the moving men when we left Monroe; the box of clothes my dressmaker-grandmother made during the first decade of the twentieth century; our choice collection of Halloween costumes; my wedding dresses (two); the box of beautiful baby clothes my mother made for my brother Ted, with the yards-long baptismal dress worn by all her children and all mine, except Chris, who was enormous, and which, pray God, my many many grandchildren-to-be will wear . . .

Oh, an attic is something I long for. Because all these treasures of this family are now stashed here and there throughout the house, wherever the roof doesn't leak, in boxes under the beds, crammed underfoot in the clothes closets, stretched out on the joists of the garage, and just generally cluttering up the place everywhere. But they are *there*, which is the important thing.

In addition to an attic, I would like to have a handy cupboard for Useful Articles Needed on Short Notice, such as, for example, flashlight batteries. There are occasions in the country when the electricity does go off, and I am not referring to those times on Sunday afternoon when I am about to cook dinner and the stove will not heat and a phone call to the local power and light corp informs me that mysterious things are being done to the wires, as per a notice which I received in Monday's mail. No, I mean the times after supper when two or three of the smaller children are playing porpoise in the bathub, and *blink!* no lights. At such a time, flashlights are imperative, and in our house somebody has always "just turned it on to see if it still works"—and left it on. Hence the supply of batteries to fix the flashlights so I can find the matches and the kerosene and the lamps (which had to be kept hidden from Mikey), and if there isn't any kerosene then for goodness' sake find the box of candle ends, isn't it in the carton of Christmas wrappings?

No, it isn't.

Once in a great while the power fails in the winter, because of snow on the lines, and this is a delight. There is brilliant dazzling white glittery beauty from every window, and inside the house such peace and quiet as to be almost tangible. No rattling heater in the bedroom, no pulsing oil burner, churning washing machine, rumbling freezers, patient complaining refrigerator. There is no sound from outdoors; no cars pass, no one is cutting wood in this wet snow, and if there are soft cluckings in the henhouse or gentle sighs in the barn, the sounds are too faint to travel through the storm windows. It is good to be reminded, once in a while, of how silent real silence is.

Naturally such power failures must be of short duration to be enjoyed to the fullest. There is no pleasure in a house, no matter how quiet, which is getting chilly because the oil-burner's recess is turning into a vacation. Nor does Longin care to milk his cows by hand, cows being very strongly devoted to the serenity of ac-

[145]

customed routine, and likely, should he try to milk them by hand, to cast a sour look at him, as if to ask has he taken leave of his senses, and then they will not only refuse to let down their milk, one or two may try to boot him out of the barn altogether.

I'm afraid my idea of a storage place for Useful Articles Likely to Be Needed isn't such a very good idea because the things one may need the most can't be stored anywhere. Such as the ability to read the future, for instance. A small dollop of this would enable me to buy *this* trip the replacement for the spool of yellow silk which is going to roll into the crack in Chris's room's floor *next* week, without which he cannot finish that dry fly for trout and/or small-mouthed bass, a task of highest priority because it's only five weeks to fishing season and gosh, he has only seven dozen flies on wires strung across his wall now. . . . In a large family, it would be so much easier to keep the peace if one never never had to hear the wail, "But *when* are you going to town again? I have a great big rip in my rubber boots!" Or, "But I *told* you every single pair of my socks is too small! I suppose you want me to go to school *barefoot?*"

Off I go again, grimly wishing I could read people's minds, read the future, or read the riot act, effectively, I mean. Off to town again, and I swore I wouldn't go in again this week. Oh for a well-padded sitzer, isn't the town truck ever going to smooth out those ruts? I swear the roads have never been so—tha n k-you, *ma'am!* —wretched—*scrunch!*—what was that? Look back, did anything fall off?

I can understand how it came about, before the advent of paved roads, that a man's house was his cherished refuge, inviolate to unauthorized intruder. No wonder it was cherished, no wonder it was considered almost sacred. It was so difficult to get there!

I feel the same way about our home, every time I return from town. When at last the car and I pant exhausted but triumphant to the top of Bests' hill, or we ease cautiously down over the ledges from Meteses', and I can see the house once again, windows wandering casually and skinny chimney and the bushes I planted for

[146]

foundation planting all crushed from last winter's snow, it may be just a plain, rather bleak, and certainly crumbling house, but it is *ours* and I am *home* and I say, "Well, look at that nice house! I wonder who lives here?" And the children say (I almost always have some of the children with me) "Probably somebody pretty *nice!*" And they giggle.

Once, when I was alone, I thought to come home from Woodstock through South Woodstock and up the road for Felchville. This way is ten miles, versus seventeen through Four Corners. The only drawback about the short way is that once I have negotiated the mountain road past the meadow where the beavers have their pond and past the old cemetery slumbering forgotten under the butternut grove, and have turned due east by the apple orchard, I very shortly am out of Woodstock and into Hartland, and there the fun begins. In the spring the water runs down the center of the road and I feel like an adventurous trout. Let there be a rainy spell, and the road makes like Mud Season and is exceedingly difficult to get through at all, even in four-wheel drive, low gear. Well, this time that I speak of, there had been rain and the road was muddy. I was churning along at four miles an hour and feeling rather anxious lest my speed slacken to nothing, for it is a lonesome spot in which to get stuck, when I spied a spotless new sign perched on the bank. HARTLAND (it read), SPEED LIMIT 35 MILES PER HOUR.

You may think that the roads are consuming more than their share of our attention. Not so. Drive over them once . . . or drive beside them, as we did the first spring we were here, taking to the grassy bank below Belisles' hill, the road there being too soft to support a car; or use the old road through Bests' pasture, as we did only last year during Mud Season, the new road, the one with the accursed hump at the top, being such an unbelievable morass that I got stuck going *down*, and the jeep sank in until it was resting helplessly on its underpinnings, and David Best had to haul me down the hill by tractor. . . . Well, sample our roads any way you please, and you will see why they absorb some fifty per cent of our local tax money, and why they dominate our conversation.

Speaking of Bests' hill and getting stuck, let me tell you about our wedding.

Longin and I did, of course, come to our senses and realize that to wait until the farm made a profit was a highly impractical plan. So when at Easter time in '53 Dad came to spend a few days, he and Longin had a very formal talk, both being sticklers for tradition. After that we decided that Saturday the second of May would be a convenient date, relatives and friends thus not having to lose time from work, and the children could attend the ceremony without missing any school. (This sort of reasoning, my dear children, is the ghastly kind of practicality that afflicts people past thirty.)

I was rather anxious to see what Bruce, Ted and Mary would think of all this. Bruce, the laconic type, never expressed himself one way or another, as I can remember. Mary said to me, "Lucky lucky lucky *you*," which was precisely how I felt, too. And Ted wrote:

> DEAR MELISSA,
> Best wishes and felicitations and stuff.
> We're both awfully happy that you and Longin have decided to join forces. It is seldom that a bunch of children get so adequate an opportunity to break in a new papa. . . .

Ah, so. Very true.

I don't suppose many weddings have been planned with such blithe disregard of what is done. We did send off announcements to the newspapers of our coming marriage, giving pedigrees and blood lines of the principals, and we phoned a number of people in town to urge them to drop in after the ceremony. Before I managed to send word to friends elsewhere, I received an indignant note from Natalie Krebs, who had been my best friend fourth grade through high school, that she had read in the Caldwell, New Jersey, *Progress* that I was getting married, and what the heck, weren't she and Karl going to be invited? She'd missed

Bob and me because I hadn't let her know in time—was that the sort of thing of which to make a habit?

I wrote back quite truthfully to say certainly she and Karl would be invited, just as soon as I got my spring housecleaning done and had the time to write invitations. And then I went off on what Longin has always referred to as my honeymoon, a week in and around New York during which I spent two days helping Mary clean the attic in our old home in Essex Fells, saw old school friends at breakfast, lunch and dinner, took in three shows, and even managed to accomplish what I had gone for in the first place —I bought my wedding dress, hat, and shoes.

Dad drove me back to Vermont, where I promptly came down with Virus XYZ, and for two days, if asked, couldn't have said if I wished to live or die. On Thursday the last day of April, I sprang from my bed and began slicking up the house. On Friday I drove to Windsor for groceries and flowers for the table, and returned home to find Dad hacking away with a sledge hammer at the ledge on Meteses' hill. Longin was in the cellar propping up the beams.

"Can't you make Dad stop?" I said. "He's out there with a sledge hammer."

"You make him stop," Longin said. "You've known him longer than I have." He was hammering away at a prop under the kitchen. "It will give very common tone to our wedding if everybody falls through collapsed floor."

I went back upstairs, thinking it would certainly spoil the whole ceremony if my father collapsed, too, and wishing there were some way you could do something with men.

After a while my father came in, tossed his cap jauntily onto a peg, and announced that *that* ledge, at least, would give no trouble to city-bred cars. He seemed very pleased with himself.

Saturday morning the second of May dawned cold and snowy. It was what I always like to think of as a Typical Vermont Wedding Day: four inches of snow on the ground, caps of white on the daffodil blossoms, clusters of snow like cotton-wool on the lilac buds. The ceremony was scheduled for ten o'clock in St.

Francis' Church in Windsor, and long before I was ready to leave for the church, I had occasion to think some deep thoughts about marriage, which I here record for the guidance of the reader: It is best to wait until after marriage to have children, for reasons not so much moral as practical. Preparations for the ceremony, difficult enough under the most ideal circumstances, become almost impossible when complicated by concern for the whereabouts, behavior, and appearance of the children of bride and/or groom.

Evidence of this follows:

KITTY: You mean you and Longin are going away *alone*? Without us? Well, I never heard of such a thing!

CHRIS: Why do us kids have to have separate punch? What's going into the grown-ups' that we can't have?

PAT: Gee, Mother, you sure are all dressed up. Hey, Longin, you ought to see how dressed up Mother is. She sure is taking this seriously!

KITTY: Mother, shall I just go and see if Longin has the ring?

ME: *No!* Leave him alone! Leave me alone! Go away and get yourself ready! Brush your hair, wash your hands, but *go away....*

CHRIS: Why can't I wear my blue jeans? They're clean.

ME: Because *I'm getting married*, that's why.

By nine-thirty Longin had finished his chores and was ready to leave in the jeep, taking with him Pat, Kitty and Chris. I was to follow with Dad and Mike. I was ready by quarter to ten, which was cutting things a bit fine. And then Dad, overcome by caution, decided to go up the hill past Meteses' and the long way round. The road was ice frosted lightly with snow, and in spite of Dad's herculean labors, we got stuck on the ledge. Back down and try again ... stuck. Back down and try once more ... *made* it. At last (my nerves in state indescribable) we reached the lower road, where my father, his engineering blood outraged by what he

[150]

was driving over, lectured on the improper banking of the curves. Did I realize they were banked the wrong way? Did I realize this forced cars to slide off the outside of the curve? Did I realize the result could be a drop into the brook? Where were the guard rails? And on ice such as this, one must hug the inside of the curve. . . . I could do no more than bleat feebly I hoped we wouldn't meet any cars, and then I chewed my lip to keep from shrieking. We reached the village safely, and the clock in the crossroads store said ten after ten. Route 5 was icy, too, but here we traveled at a reckless clip of thirty miles an hour, and thus I was only twenty-five minutes late to the church.

Longin had not given up and left, as had wildly crossed my mind he might. He and Ellison and Mary greeted me with subdued hilarity. After they had waited for about fifteen minutes, Mary explained later, they had all begun to get anxious, and then the outer door had creaked open and Mary had said joyfully, "Here she comes!" when the inner door had creaked open, and in tottered a very ancient old crone, bringing flowers for the next ceremony after ours.

I shed my boots and put on my slippers and we all walked up the aisle, the Alfonses our witnesses and Dad and Mary and Longin and I, quite informally and just as it struck us as right and proper. The church was icy cold, I was told afterwards, but I never noticed. The ceremony was brief and very beautiful, Father Ready having chosen the form of service with all the lovely old phrases, including "With this ring I plight thee my troth," and Longin and I exchanged rings, and were now man and wife in the sight of God and man. I could only think how wise and good is God to give us such overflowing fountains of happiness to enrich and bless our days on earth, with no nonsense about whether or not we deserve it or have earned it. A gift, like a Christmas present, given because He loves us. . . .

It was raining when we reached the door of the church. Everyone clustered about, laughing and talking, and we managed at last to divide up the children into various cars, Pat to guide the Krebs', the rest to parcel themselves out amongst Dad, Bruce, Myra and

Ted. Longin and I went on home ahead of everyone, and we reached home without adventure, and so did everyone else, except the Krebs', Pat having guided them home the short way. They got stuck on Bests' hill, and Lloyd came rushing out with the tractor and hauled them to the top. This was a new experience for Natalie and Karl, and they vowed they'd never forget it, and I daresay they won't.

In spite of the sleety roads, the house was jammed with friends new and old. Ted was in his element, being, I have always thought, a frustrated news photographer. He took pictures of the Ogdens presenting us with homemade apple champagne which must be aged for three months before drinking; of the children hunched on the stairs with plates of ice cream and cake propped on their knees; of folks sampling the punch, which I was told was sufficiently heady, though I wouldn't know, being intoxicated with joy and nervous exhaustion; of the cake itself, baked by Mrs. Levy of Three Corners, and a triumph of about six dozen eggs, delicious, and expertly decorated with a rich mosaic of flowers; of the daffodils with their ridiculous caps of snow; of Longin coming in from chores in the barn; of Longin and me leaving for our twenty-four-hour honeymoon, courtesy of Dad, who volunteered to milk Jenny that night and the next morning.

The Meteses had driven up from New York too late for the ceremony but in ample time for festivities at the house, and they it was who remembered rice, and some of our more jovial new friends attended to the string of tin cans. Off we went, windshield wiper snapping at the snow, jeep in four-wheel drive.

On Sunday the third of May the sun came out, and we drove into the White Mountains, and there were ten inches of snow where we crossed the ridge, and we passed a snow plow. And shortly after noon we turned back, and headed south, towards home.

"I wonder if children are all right," said Longin.

"I miss them," I said in deep contentment.

CHAPTER VI

Now I must confess that for some time our life had not been as idyllic as I have been painting it, because it had developed a kind of schizophrenic split. On the one hand we were dealing with the relatively light problems which had to do with things. One can always do something about mere things: we could patch the leaking roof, we could brace the sagging foundation. But how could we solve that weighty problem, that hassel of historic proportions, that brouhaha known for miles around as the Hartland School Fight? For, like all school fights, it had to do not with things but with people.

Not just people. Vermonters.

Not just Vermonters, either, but Hartlanders.

The Hartland School Fight did not, you see, follow the usual pattern. Ordinarily such a fight is a battle between those whose children still must be educated and those whose children (if any) already have been, and the issue is most likely to be what to do about outworn, outgrown school buildings—should they be repaired, expanded, or replaced? Once the school board has reached a decision, the problem comes down to getting the voters to okay the plan and to ante up the money. All this may take some time, and a great deal of heat may be generated, and a number of friendships severed, noisily, with vitriolic letters showered on the newspapers. In New England, there will be bitter outbursts in Town Meeting, the mine-are-already-educated lamenting the rise in the tax rate and predicting mass bankruptcy, the ours-are-still-in-school orating on our sacred obligation not to lower further the standards of education in this the greatest country of the world.

All this is normal, and the righteous anger which shakes the impassioned voices is normal, too, and healthy. Because, sooner or later, something good is going to come of all this. The proper plan will be voted, the money will be raised, and there, on that old hill pasture on the outskirts of town, well back from the highway and surrounded by a comfortable number of acres in which to run about and holler, there will be yet another excellent new school modest in concept, flexible in plan, nothing fancy (for this is New England), just a plain, useful school. A good school, with the emphasis where it belongs, on good books and good teachers.

The Hartland School Fight did not follow the usual pattern, in that no good came of it. Although it began long before we moved here, and it went on and on year after year, in the end nothing was really settled. Something has been done about the schools, true—but nothing wise, or economical, or far-sighted. It can even be said that in a certain sense Hartland has no school. That this should be so can be blamed on one single factor in the Hartland School Fight. As it became more and more impossible to ignore the appalling condition of Hartland's schools, Hartlanders, the majority of Hartlanders, did not become righteously angry at the state of the schools; instead, they became angry *at the people who were angry about the schools.*

Well, who can blame them? The things we said! Perhaps we should have remembered that the schools are the outward sign of the inward grace of a town, they are the windows of its soul. What a town is, or wants to be, its schools are. Hartlanders are just as aware of this as you or I. And when we protested that the schools were unsafe and unsanitary, naturally it was taken to mean we were saying Hartland was neglecting its children. When we pointed out that the local schools were not supported as generously as elsewhere in Vermont, we were implying that Hartlanders were skinflints begrudging the children an education—weren't we? So what difference does it make if there aren't enough books to go around? What's the matter with those out-of-date maps? Who says $1,800 isn't enough for a beginning teacher? That there shouldn't be fifty children in one room combining the first and second grades? That there ought to be dictionaries handy and good reference books and globes and all that stuff?

Well, I said it, for one, and Longin said it, and Ellison, and Jules, and quite a number of other parents, and one or two teachers, and—rarely, but still often enough not to destroy my shaky faith in the human race—even a mine-are-already-educated would say it. We made quite a lot of noise saying it, so much noise that we got ourselves confused, and thought there were more of us than there were, and so we would be more astounded than anything else when we got voted down, as we did, again and again and again.

The trouble was, we couldn't really prove anything we were saying. How can one prove a child's mind could have been better trained? It's as impossible as proving that a malnourished child could have had a strong, sturdy body, given better food. So when we declared passionately that better school facilities, smaller classes, fewer grades per room, would mean better education for the children, "Prove it!" we were challenged; and when we could not, not to anyone's satisfaction but our own, "Huh, the schools aren't good enough for them!" we heard, and then, "Why'd they come here, then, huh?"

Ah, touché.

Ignorance, pure ignorance is my plea. I don't know what Ellison's plea is, or Lefty's, or those noble teachers (native-born!) with the courage to speak up on our side. All I can say is, I was bemused by the legend of Vermont. When I came looking for the farm, I was under a spell cast by the state legislature, which, you will recall, in order to legalize its payment of ten dollars a month to each Vermont soldier in Federal service, declared on the sixteenth of September 1941 that a state of "armed conflict" existed between Germany and the United States. How could I have dreamed that in the very same state capable of such a magnificent display of noble self-sufficiency there could exist a village with such a lackadaisical attitude towards formal education?

"I told my kid I never went to high school myself, but if he wants to go, I won't hinder him none. I won't help him, neither— he c'n walk if he has to, I told him. It's only ten miles."

"The neighbor's girl wants to go to college. What d'ye s'ppose got into 'er? I told 'er she'd do more good to stay to home and breed us some sojers."

It wasn't until after I had purchased the farm that I got my first inkling of the local standing of the schools. Mr. Potwin and I were driving back from the farm, having just made final arrangements with Mrs. Ferncliffe. As we neared the village of Four Corners, we passed an isolated schoolhouse, a bleak wooden structure staring at the road with large blank windows.

"That's where your kids'll go to school," Mr. Potwin said.

I screwed my head around to take another look. It didn't appear to be very large, and I said so.

"Two rooms, four grades to a room."

"All Hartland's children, to this little school?"

" 'Nother one just like it in the next village. Three Corners. And in North Hartland, too. Nothin' wrong with 'em," he went on comfortably. "Went to a one-room school myself. So did most of my kids. Never hurt 'em none, as I could see."

Oh, well, I thought, we'll only be here for a year or two. Just till Bob gets back. That shouldn't seriously cripple the children, and I can make up at home whatever the school lacks.

"I should think you'd want to send Mike, too," Mr. Potwin said. "Seems to me he'd be better off spending his days in school with the other kids."

How could I explain what it was like with a child like Mike— the endless search for a school willing to let him sit in the classroom, the rebuffs and humiliations and disappointments?

"Of course he would be better off," I said at last. "But it wouldn't work out. He's not easy to manage, and his not talking gets on the teachers' nerves."

"They was a kid once went to school here never *did* talk," said Mr. Potwin. "Never said a word, all through the eight grades."

I digested this. "You mean he was passed along from one grade to the next—"

"Graduated," said Mr. Potwin, nodding.

"But didn't the teacher mind?"

"His not talkin'? Oh, I expect it bothered her at first. The way I heard it, after a couple of months, and she couldn't get a word out of him, she went to the kid's house and asked his mother how about him? Is he scared or something? His mother says she dunno what the teacher is talkin' about. Says he talks at home. 'Well, what does he say?' says the teacher. 'When he gets real excited,' says the kid's mother, 'he shouts *hoy!*'"

At that time I thought this reflected great credit on the school. Humane. Tolerant. The fit and the unfit in democratic desegregation.

During the fall and winter of '51-'52 I was so concerned with the bare essentials of survival it was enough for me to know there were schools off to which Pat and Chris went each morning, Pat to the Four Corners school, Chris to Three Corners. Mr. Potwin's information had not been up-to-date. The schools no longer housed eight grades each, but, ever since a savage battle between parents and school board a few years previously, school board *pro* change, parents *anti*, there were only four grades in each building, two per room.

I had heard of this battle. The echoes of it were still rumbling about the hills when I moved to the farm. During the spring of '49, Ellison, then a rank newcomer from Ohio, had attended a special school meeting which had been called to discuss what to do about the overcrowded schools, and there she had heard an idea proposed by Mrs. Mabel Lobdell, a former teacher with experience in both one-room and graded schools. Would not better instruction be facilitated, Mrs. Lobdell suggested, if the load on each teacher were lightened? Why not use the two school buildings, which were not much over a mile apart, as essentially one school? Put four grades in one building, four in another, and in this way each teacher would be responsible for instructing two grades instead of four.

This seemed an excellent idea to Ellison, and, when nothing seemed to come of it at the meeting—or of much else, the problem of how to expand the schools being referred to a newly formed advisory committee—Ellison asked Mrs. Lobdell if she might try to carry it further. And so it was that Ellison wrote to the school directors, urging consideration of this sensible plan. She received no reply, although she heard, via the grapevine that passes news about in country places, that the school board was having a meeting. Then, a few days later, two women knocked on Ellison's door, thrust a paper at her, and asked if she would mind signing a petition.

"Sign it!" Ellison said, recognizing her own letter, word for word. "Good heavens, I wrote it!"

She signed it once again, and so did a sufficient number of others, and a meeting was called to vote on the idea.

Now the board had the authority to shift the children about as they wished, but they felt the plan would work out very much better if the board's decision had the backing and approval (in Hartland these do not necessarily go together) of the parents. For a long time it didn't seem likely the board would get either. The Three Corners folk did not want their children being trucked to Four Corners . . . out of their own village . . . to that awful school, in that awful neighborhood, filled with those rowdy children from Four Corners. They said so in loud, hoarse-with-anger voices. They shook their fists under the noses of the parents of children from Four Corners. The Four Corners parents shook their fists right back. "So our kids ain't good enough to associate with yours, huh?" they shouted furiously. "Well, your kids ain't so damn perfect, neither!" Both factions shook their fists under the noses of the school directors, who were upset, white-faced, and, at least in the case of the woman chairman, close to tears; but the board stuck to its guns, refused to give way, and stressed again and again that the children would learn better, the children would get along together, the children must be thought of, first of all.

This went on for nearly two hours.

Ellison, so far silent in deference to the unwritten law that Newcomers Must Not Speak, at last could contain herself no longer. Being new to Vermont, she didn't realize that what she was about to say was sheer, downright heresy. She stood up, drew herself to her full five feet, and in a voice trembling with righteous anger said, "I think we ought all to be *ashamed* of ourselves."

Vermonters are never ashamed of themselves. When they are being tight-fisted or mule-headed, they seem to think they are being quaint and colorful; they cherish these characteristics as tourist attractions.

When everyone's verbal ammunition was spent, a truce was reached, and it was decided to try the idea for one year, and then only if the school buses would come to Martinsville so these children no longer would have to cross Route 5. And for a long time nothing was said about reverting to the old eight-grades-in-each-school system, and one might have thought this battle over.

But it wasn't. The things that were said at that meeting, the insults shouted and the prejudices aired and the petty personal digs indulged in, these were not forgotten. They festered beneath the surface, and the time was to come when their virulence would infect the entire town.

I did my best to ignore any other rumblings of trouble I happened to hear. A charming young woman from Four Corners stopped by one day to collect some stuff for a white elephant sale the PTA was having, and Kitty danced up to ask, "Mother, if you're going to town, may I go with you? Please, I want some gobble gum."

"Won't you be delighted when she starts school," the young woman remarked drily. "Then it'll be, 'Hey, Maw, kin I go, huh, Maw?'"

I smiled politely. I wasn't sure I quite got the point.

Nevertheless I was distressed one afternoon when I stopped by the school to observe Chris and his classmates file past the teacher as if she were a post by the door, not looking at her, not speaking to her. "You must not forget your manners," I chided him on the way home. "You must remember to say good night to your teacher."

"She told us not to, Mother," Chris said earnestly. "She said she didn't want to be bothered with all that stuff."

Why in heaven's name does she teach? I wondered. The voices of her children bidding her good night . . . Doesn't she realize she's rejecting as counterfeit ninety per cent of her pay?

When Chris reported, at first with surprise and later with relish, who had received a "shaking up" that day, and, in due time, how many he himself had received, I thought vaguely these "shakings up" could hardly be anything objectionable or Chris would not be so proud to have achieved one. Perhaps, I thought, a child has to be "shaken up" in order to be accepted by his peers.

Then one day Chris came home and reported that the teacher had slapped him in the face. He reported this calmly, as if it were nothing at all.

"Slapped your face?" I repeated, stunned. Anger began to boil in me. Struck him . . . struck my son . . . Christopher, the Little General, the image of Bob . . . *in the face.*

"We weren't supposed to talk, see, and David didn't know what page the arithmetic was on, and so I told him, and she hit me."

He must be hardened to such scenes, I thought. That's the most appalling thing about this, how calmly Chris takes it, like an everyday affair.

"Has she ever hit you before?"

"Nope. Not really. Sometimes she socks kids on the head with her ruler, but she hasn't me. Sometimes she whacks 'em on the hands. Most of the time she just shakes 'em up."

"What is this 'shaking up' you keep talking about?"

"Oh, that's when the teacher yanks a kid out of his chair and—well—shakes him." He grinned. "It doesn't hurt, Mother, you just feel sort of *silly*, all right."

And in the Army, I thought furiously, an officer is subject to court martial if he lays a finger on an enlisted man. But in Vermont a child is at the mercy of a teacher's self-control—or lack of it.

I went to the superintendent of schools.

"I think this whole incident quite shocking," I said. "Chris says the little boy who did not know the arithmetic page is too frightened to ask questions. How can you justify permitting a teacher to indulge herself in such destructive displays of temper?"

"I'm not trying to justify anything," he said patiently. "I'm just pointing out that the law says a teacher may act *in loco parentis*. She may, therefore, chastise a child as a parent would—"

"How medieval," I said coldly. "Why doesn't the teacher try to show how adults ought to behave? Striking a child in the face! What a violation of human dignity! I'd like to sock *her* in the face!"

His eyes twinkled sympathetically. "I'll speak to her," he said. "I'll see if we can't work something out."

"Yes, you do that," I said, still boiling. "And if any of the teachers are too incompetent to control my children without resorting to force, let them complain to me. I'm an old-fashioned parent and I expect obedience and I get it. I reserve to myself the right of chastising my children. I don't want any neurotic teacher putting calluses on their self-respect, I don't care what the law says."

He did not commit himself to transmit this verbatim, but I did not expect him to. He thanked me for coming, I thanked him for listening, and we shook hands. I like this man, I thought. An Irishman.

As I say, stray bullets such as these whizzed over my head from time to time, but I was busy having Mary Lee and all that sort of thing, and it wasn't until the PTA meeting of January, 1953, that I realized these bullets were not just stray, there was serious ferment behind them.

I don't know how you feel about the PTA. Personally, I am not an addict. I can take it or leave it alone. If a PTA looks upon itself as the legitimate lobbyist for the rights of children, as an electric-shock supplier to galvanize the community into action,

I'm with it. If it's just a kind of filler for a social void, no, thanks.

You can spot this second type of PTA if it's glad to have any-body join, grandmas, maiden aunts, lordy you don't have to be a parent *or* a teacher, to belong—all you have to do is claim you like children, or something. You don't have to vote for anything that benefits children, or against anything that doesn't, or even think about such things, one way or another. All you have to do is pay your fifty cents' dues, and throw yourself with wildest enthusiasm into such projects as suppers and bazaars and lawn parties, which raise money for boxes of Kleenex and first-aid kits and hot lunch platters for the school. This is all very worthy, and who am I to say such things should come out of the school budget, and the members of the PTA should devote themselves to matters which take not only time and energy and money, but also courage?

Like what? Like, for example, the overcrowding of the schools.

Ellison was program chairman that year and she had flown in the face of local tradition and had invited the Special School Committee, formed, you may remember, back in 1949, to give a report on the results of its studies. The meeting was to be held in the Ladies' Aid Hall. That's the large wooden structure on your right as you come into Four Corners from the north. It looks as if it might have been the first building put up after the town was settled in 1761, and it is just about the only building of any size in town that no one has suggested be used as a temporary school building, not because it lacks heat and formal plumbing (it has plumbing of a sort, which you can smell as you come upstairs), but because it is of such noble age that its timbers are tottering and its floors bend gracefully beneath the slightest burden. The meeting was on the second floor, and Longin and I walked cau-tiously up the stairs (but quickly, so as not to have to breathe en route), and we found ourselves in a large room half filled with curving rows of ancient deacon's benches. At each seat there was a booklet with the challenging title, "Our Schools Are What We Make Them."

In order to know what all the shouting is to be about, we had better take the time for a quick eagle's-eye view of Hartland. Imagine yourself, if you please, sufficiently high in the air to have a good view of the entire town. You are looking at a mountainous area roughly six miles square, bordered on the east by the silver ribbon of the Connecticut River. Those glints of silver near the river are the tracks of the Boston and Maine. The depot is being torn down now; there haven't been any passenger stops there for a long while, and not much freight any more, just an occasional carload of fertilizer for the farmers. Hartland hasn't grown much in the last hundred years, but it hasn't shrunk much, either; the population is just about the same, a little over fifteen hundred people. In those days, though, the people were scattered all over the hills, on farms, and in little settlements, each with its one-room school, its cemetery, and perhaps even its own chapel. As you can see, there aren't many people living up in the hills now; most of them are in the three villages, North Hartland up there to the northeast, Three Corners here in the southeast, and Four Corners a mile to the west of Three Corners. As Mr. Potwin said, each of these villages has its own two-room school. If you look sharp, you can see all that's left of the more than two dozen one-room schools the town once had. Up there in Grout, that cluster of houses in the hills west of North Hartland, there's a school which has been in use ever since 1846; and there in Center is the first school the town built, sometime before Grout's, but how long before, no one knows now, the town's records don't go back that far. Now follow the Lull Brook road west out of Four Corners. A little more than two miles out there are four or five houses that mark Fieldsville; the schoolhouse there has been converted into a house. Another two miles up the valley, marked by a cemetery, a crossroads, and an outhouse made over into a shelter for children waiting for the school bus, is Jenneville; its school has been closed for several years, and now the building has been sold and is waiting to be removed.

It's a pretty town, seen from way up here. Pretty, and peaceful, and pleasant. Too bad we have to get down to earth for a close-up of the schools. Somehow, after counting the children packed into

[163]

the classrooms in Three and Four Corners, the town may never seem quite so pleasant again.

Thirty-four children in the seventh- and eighth-grade room, thirty-seven in the fifth and sixth. Forty-eight six- and seven-year-olds crammed into the classroom for the first and second grades. There would have been fifty-seven in the third- and fourth-grade room, but the school board had divided this group and put the third grade into a converted storage room in the cellar of Three Corners school. And still the school population was climbing, and no end in sight.

The speaker for the Special School Committee rose, and I was momentarily disarmed by the fact that he reminded me of my grandfather Mather. Grandpa had had just such a long, lean face, the "long English face," my mother had called it, though nowadays, I mused, it was thought of as a Yankee face. Grandpa's suit was always rumpled, and his hair grew longer than was fashionable, until it encircled his head like a silvery halo. This man's suit was in excellent press, and his hair was close-cropped and gray, and his voice, too, was gray, and close-cropped, and well ironed. His voice, and the things he was saying, didn't remind me of Grandpa Mather at all.

The first thing to decide, he said, was how many rooms do we need altogether. Seven, or two more than we have now. But we'll have to build three new, because we aren't supposed to keep on using the temporary one in the cellar.

The second thing to decide, he went on, pulling out a rough sketch of the roads of Hartland, all of them leading like the ribs of a fan to Three Corners, is where to put these new rooms. As you can see by this map, he said, Three Corners is centrally located, with Four Corners and North Hartland balancing each other, you might say. Besides, Three Corners is the center of school population, so that's the place we should start expanding.

I glanced at Longin. I could tell by the frozen look on his face that he was distinctly unimpressed. I supposed that he, too, had never thought of Three Corners as the center of anything. And how could you tell where the most children were unless you counted them? As far as I knew, nobody had counted mine. . . .

The cheapest way to expand, the speaker was saying, was to add a two-story structure on the back of the school, because in this way we'd get four new classrooms, two upstairs, two down, twice as much space for our money. Just bulldoze away the ground—

I heard Longin muttering. "What did you say?" I whispered.

"Not true," he hissed. "Foundation has to be heavier to carry two stories. Steel beams under upper story cost money, so does space for stairways—"

A good local builder could do the job, the speaker was winding up. No need to get any fancy drawings by arch-itects, just get some local carpenters, working by the day. . . .

No one seemed to feel strongly about the plan. There was no enthusiasm, no marked objection. Coffee was being poured, plates of cookies were set out, and it looked as if this plan were being accepted, though with an indifferent shrug.

Now the one thing that stuck in my mind at this point was the classroom for the first and second grades as I had seen it about a week before. A teacher's desk, a piano, some shelves, and desks and chairs for fifty children so cluttered the room that I had had a hard time to make my way through it except by edging sideways. There was only one way in, a door opening onto the school's center hall. What would happen to those children if a fire were to make the hall impassable? Perhaps the Special School Committee was planning some extra measures for fire safety?

Balancing my coffee cup carefully, I went over and asked the speaker about this.

No, he said, the committee hadn't thought anything about it. The children could always go out the windows.

"But they're so high!" I said. "Nearly fifteen feet off the ground—"

He gave a little whinny of amusement. That wasn't high, he told me. Why, a child that couldn't jump that far was hardly worth saving.

I have a very low boiling point, I admit. I went speechless with anger. Righteous anger, I like to think.

The next morning I called Rowena James. I had worked with her on KP for the hot lunch program, and she had let drop remarks which had led me to believe she wasn't too enchanted with the schools as they were. Furthermore, she was a "native."

"I don't have any sense of humor when it comes to schools," I told her. "I simply cannot laugh a merry ha-ha at the idea of first-graders forced to leap out of windows. What do you think?"

What she thought was precisely what I thought. We both thought it was time the parents did something about the schools. And that's how the Citizens' Committee for Better Schooling came to be formed. We chose the name blithely, none of us having any idea what resentment and suspicion that name would arouse, how sinister it would be made to sound. *Citizens' Committee, eh? Now what do you suppose they mean by that?*

We started out with eighteen members, including the town constable, the town lawyer, a couple of schoolteachers, a member of the school board, two farmers, not counting Longin, some men who worked in Windsor, and an assortment of wives and mothers. At our first meeting we decided to start out by doing a survey of the town's five schools, and report the conditions which we found to the school board. We sent off a long, chatty report of this meeting to the local papers, and wound up by hopefully inviting "all interested citizens" to volunteer their help.

Where, looking back, did we go astray? Well, for one thing, Longin and I cast a taint over the whole thing. We were *newcomers*. I had heard, of course, that it is considered a virtue by natives for newcomers to keep their mouths shut for five years, ten, twenty—the length of time varies, but not the essential point of saying nothing, doing nothing. I hadn't given this rumor too much credit, because it struck me as out of character. Surely Vermonters would not want only the meek to move here. Vermonters like spunky folk—they are that way themselves. *Vermonters* won't put a time lock on democracy.

Won't they, though!

Our survey turned up some facts which certainly surprised us newcomers. Not one classroom in town met the state minimum

[166]

standard of space per child. Out of the nine classrooms in the five buildings, six still had wood stoves, crowding the rooms still more. On the day we checked, it was below zero outside and over ninety at desks ten feet distant from one of the stoves at Four Corners (1930). At Center, two buckets for drinking water were brought each day from a near-by barnyard. At Center, too, there was only one toilet room, and the toilet was the hole-in-a-plank type, and the toilet room was filthy, and the air unfit to breathe. All the other schools including North Hartland (1895) had separate toilet rooms for boys and girls, but in the Three Corners School (1915) and at Four Corners there was neither a window that opened nor a ventilating fan. Not a single school had a telephone, nor any place where a sick child might be separated from the other children, for there were no teachers' rooms, either. The teachers used the same latrine as the children, and no provision whatsoever was made for them to have five minutes' rest during their long day. Not even their lunch hour was time off, because they must then supervise the children at table or on the playground. Naturally, the care of the wood fires was theirs, too, and in three of the five schools, the janitor work also.

I felt I might have been just a bit hasty in condemning the teachers' dispositions. It looked as if there might be some justification for worn nerves and exhaustion.

On February tenth we met with the Special School Committee at Alfonses', and I gave a digest of our findings so far. I also laid considerable stress on what I thought were the nuclei of danger from fire: the stove at Grout that stood by the one entrance to the room, and the line of coats hanging just behind; the lack of panic bars at Three and Four Corners schools, and the door that opened in, with faulty latch; the fuel stored in the cellar at Three Corners, and the wooden door between the furnace room and the stairway; the fact that no classroom in these two schools had a second way out except via the windows. . . .

I became aware that I was not en rapport with every one of my listeners. The chairman of the SSC and some of his committee gave me to understand (politely) that they considered me somewhat hipped on the subject. "There hasn't ever been a school fire in Vermont, as we c'n remember," they told me.

Vermonters are very good at building stone walls. I had just run into one—head on.

Renfrew Quackenbush was not present at this meeting, although he was editor of the *Village Crier*, a little mimeographed publication of a few pages that came out every two weeks, devoted to news of a very local character and to the expression of Quackenbush's personal philosophy of life, politics, and civic responsibility. Perhaps he ought to have been invited. However, he was not. If Mr. Quackenbush were there, some members feared, all anyone would get to talk about would be the virtues of the one-room school.

With ominous forebodings that it is unwise to antagonize the press, the rest of us agreed that Mr. Quackenbush would not be there. Nevertheless, his spirit was. He had allowed it to be known that he himself thought one very likely solution to the shortage of classroom space would be portable one-room schools which could be moved from section to section in town, as the school population shifted about, so that all children could walk to school. Walking to school struck him as having an extraordinary great value in any educational program. Such a solution could be reached, he had told Longin and me, by the construction of quonset-hut schools, as was already being done in New York State. He furnished us with pictures of these structures, and I had to admit they looked a lot better than the schools we had, at least on the inside, where there seemed to be lots of light and space. Naturally we didn't fall in with the idea that these be one-room schools, but there was nothing to prevent erecting them behind one of the present schools, the school board said, particularly if they should be economical to construct. I said I'd be glad to show them at the meeting, and let him know what everybody thought. I did so, and the idea received a cautiously favorable reaction, and Ellison said she'd write and find out how much they cost, and if the folks in New York State liked them, and let him know at Little Town Meeting, and this message I relayed to Quackenbush.

Now Little Town Meeting was, at that time, a yearly feature originated and sponsored and conducted by the Quackenbushes. It was held two weeks or so ahead of the regular Town Meeting, in one of the large rooms in their pre-Revolutionary house. The house, as well as his newspaper, was an extension of Quackenbush's philosophy of life, which was, as near as I could make out, a kind of revolt against the twentieth century. The house had the peace and quiet which comes from the non-running of furnace, freezer, or refrigerator, which weren't running because they weren't there, and they weren't there because there was no electricity. The house was heated by quiet, well-disciplined fires in several fireplaces, and it was lit by large kerosene lamps.

But as we arrived at Little Town Meeting, Ellison and Rowena and I, we did not yet know how formidable was to be the opposition of the Quackenbushes, and we were in great warmth of enthusiasm if not of body. There were perhaps twenty-five of us sitting on straight-backed chairs in the second-story room, where the winter sun was streaming in almost horizontally from the south. Ellison had the letter on quonset-hut schools in her purse, and we were afraid its contents might prove disappointing. "On the suitability of this type of building in your climate," the letter went, "not suitable, unless you have a cellar under the quonsets or a much better heating arrangement than we have. Price of the six, approximately $75,000 . . . We are at present building permanent quarters which will not require repairs and improvements . . . in such a short time . . ."

Quackenbush opened the meeting with the statement that this was to be "off the record," we could speak freely and not worry that our soundings-off might appear in print to embarrass us. He then took up, one by one, the items on the town Warning.

The Warning is a listing of the things to be voted on at Town Meeting. It is supposed to be published at least five days in advance, in order to give the voters time to think things over. As our Town Meetings went then, there might not be much time to think at the Meeting. Election of town officers always came first, and this was done by separately nominating and voting for each officer, a most time-consuming process. The voters wrote their choice on a slip of paper, and then "forwarded their ballots" by filing past the ballot box; the ballots were then counted, and if no candidate receive a majority the balloting was repeated until somebody finally got more than fifty per cent of the votes. Once the election of officers took nearly four hours, and since the meeting didn't start until ten, and there was an hour out at noon for dinner, it was three o'clock before we could turn to the rest of the items on the Warning—and at five, the farmers had to leave to do the milking, and the womenfolk to cook supper.

This year, once we got the officers elected, we would have to make decisions on the following assemblage of articles: the amount of money to be spent, per mile, on the roads; whether or not to pay tuition for children to go to high school in Windsor, White River, or Woodstock, and if so, how much; whether the town would cooperate with the state and pay $200 towards control of white-pine blister rust; whether the town would buy a truck; how much to give the fire department; how much to spend on an appropriate observance of Memorial Day; whether $2,000 should be spent on a furnace for the North Hartland school; should the town control billboards along the highways; when taxes should be paid and if they should be paid to the town treasurer (this pure routine, I presume—so far as I know, the town never voted no, let's pay no taxes, or let's pay them to the eighth-grade beauty queen); whether to give the selectmen authority to borrow money in anticipation of taxes; how much, if anything, to give the libraries (there are three tiny ones in town); whether to vote more money to complete the bridge in North Hartland; what should be the tax rate; whether the town should employ a town manager; should the town elect its officers by Australian ballot in 1954; should the town spend $200 for preliminary plans for the additions to the schools; will the town allow the school directors to accept gifts from whatever source may feel so inclined, the Federal Government, the State of Vermont, or private individuals (and don't

[170]

think this pure routine—once in a neighboring village a public-spirited old man wanted to give fifty thousand dollars with which to build a school, and the town voted to accept the gift by a margin of one vote); whether or not the town should add a two-story, four-room addition to the Three Corners school; would the town spend $30,000 for this addition; will the town spend any money towards replacing the bridge across Lull Brook below Lobdell's; will the town start a town forest.

Ellison thought this quite a chunk to hack through, after three P.M. and before evening milking, and she had been responsible for the petition which had been the legal lever to get the item about the Australian ballot on the Warning. Such a ballot, routine in neighboring communities, not only would save time but would also make it possible for Hartland men who worked in the shops (factories) in Windsor to vote, at least for town officers. A few of the shops gave their men the hours from eleven to one to vote. If any wished to attend the entire Town Meeting, they were given the day off, but without pay. Clifford, who was at that time working in the shop as well as farming (with the price of milk what it was, his pay check helped greatly to keep him farming), told me that for a man to take the day off and spend it at Town Meeting might cost him, including loss of overtime, as much as twenty dollars—quite a poll tax for a man to pay.

Ellison expressed herself freely on all this, and Quackenbush replied it cost the farmers money, too, to spend the day at Town Meeting. I did not feel in any position to speak for the farmers, Jenny and Ronna and Jenny's doubtful-heifer daughter scarcely giving me sufficient backing; but it seemed to me, as I sat there mulling this over, that Vivian went to Town Meeting, and Vivian was practically a full-time farmer all by herself, and she and Clifford had done chores and milking before they left, and would do them again in the evening after his work in the shop; and meanwhile their cows were behaving themselves and making milk just as efficiently as if Vivian were home. In early March, what else ought Vivian, the farmer, to be doing?

While I was arguing thus to myself, the discussion proceeded

[171]

from the North Hartland bridge to the Lobdell bridge on the lower road. This bridge was swaying and sagging as if weak in the knees. The state was insisting that the new bridge be a concrete structure costing close to $30,000, of which the town would have to pay less than $5,000. Quackenbush felt that such an ambitious structure was unnecessary. For about $6,000, he said, a wooden bridge could be built, not very wide, to be sure, probably at that price it would be one-way—but look at the saving of money! Of course such a bridge would not meet approval of the state, and therefore the *town* wouldn't save any money, having to pay the entire $6,000 ourselves. The important thing would be the principle involved—no dictation from the state in town affairs!

"But Mr. Quackenbush!" I protested, "the bridge that's falling down is nothing but a wooden bridge. It can't stand the load of milk trucks and lime trucks and all that. In a farming area like this we have to have bridges that can carry—"

"This," said Mr. Quackenbush firmly, "is *not* a farming area. It's a commuting area. For the few farms still being worked, use smaller trucks."

I tried to rally my stunned wits. "But the lime truck—it's enormous—"

"Unload it on one side of the bridge," he said, flicking this objection to one side. "Transfer the sacks to a smaller truck on the far side. Now, about billboards—"

Rowena at this point made an excuse and left. Ellison and I stuck it out, but we saw no point in trying to contribute further to the discussion. When the next issue of the *Village Crier* came out, we were glad we had said no more than we did. Ellison found herself misquoted on the Australian ballot, how the present system of electing officers was "unfair to the working man," who was not given time off to attend Town Meeting.

"I didn't say exactly that!" she protested. "I said they don't get paid—oh, what will Jules' bosses think! He said he wouldn't quote!"

"I thought 'off the record' is practically a sacred phrase to a newspaperman," I remarked.

"I'm glad I didn't read the letter about quonset huts," Ellison said. "I'll read it at the special school meeting."

"Where the intellectual climate may be more favorable," I said hopefully.

This special school meeting was to take place a week before Town Meeting. The school board had expressed itself to the Citizens' Committee as quite disappointed in the recommendation of the SSC, and had not wanted to put the item about the two-story addition at Three Corners on the Warning at all; they had only done so, they said, because the town had voted to have the SSC, and ought, therefore, to have a chance to accept or reject its plan. The board, however, had a plan of its own which it would like to discuss with the voters. It was most unlikely there would be time at Town Meeting for a proper discussion, hence the special school meeting. Could the Citizens' Committee have its report ready by then? It looked to the board as if our findings would back up their plan.

We would, we said, do our damndest.

We had already gone out and counted the children, house by house and trailer by trailer and shack by shack. Longin, who had had considerable experience preparing visual aids for Army training lectures, made a map of Hartland about five feet square, and on it he put every road and every house, and marked the routes the school buses were taking, and by each house he put a dot for every child, green for a child already in school, red for a preschooler, every child born up to January 1, 1953. And we made a graph showing the relative number of children in the two villages. There were 110 children in the Three Corners area, including Martins- ville; there were 190 in the Four Corners area, or 224 if you in- cluded Center.

Our graph showing the school population for the next five years indicated that there would shortly be only about ten children attending Center school. It would be wise to close this school, we thought, and bring the children down to the graded school in the village. By making this mild suggestion we waved a red flag of intense luminosity under the outraged noses of the Supporters of the Preservation of the One-Room School. "Close that school?" they cried indignantly. "What for? What's the matter with a one-room school? *I* went to a one-room school, and look at *me!*"

We had to admit the one-room schools certainly sent forth their scholars armored in self-satisfaction.

Nevertheless, the special school meeting was distinguished by its peaceful proceedings, each side presenting its case to its courteously attentive opponents. The Special School Committee briefly outlined its plan for adding on at the back of the old Three Corners school. We showed our map and graphs. The board said they had in mind four rooms separate from the old building, though adjacent to it, and in Four Corners, which, they said, seemed closest to the center of school population, had twice the playground space of Three Corners, and less traffic, being located outside the village and not on a state highway, as was the school in Three Corners. They would like very much, said the board, to have the Town vote the $200 for which they were asking, and with this money they would obtain plans for such a building from an architect. They had heard a report, the board said, that there was a surplus in the state treasury, a surplus to be used for school construction. Towns willing to meet certain minimum requirements as to classroom space, playground area, and so forth, would receive State aid up to twenty-five per cent of the total building cost.

Mr. Quackenbush then made a plea for the one-room movable school, and advanced the quonset-hut idea as an economical solution. Ellison, with a timing most tactless but certainly effective, then rose and read (dead-pan) the reply to her inquiry about quonset-hut schools. And I wasn't a bit sorry for Mr. Quackenbush. A newspaperman shouldn't have climbed out on such a limb.

At Town Meeting the following week, the voters gave the board the $200, and the board went out and got plans, and an estimate, and it turned out the town could get an addition at Four Corners for just under $44,000, of which the state would pay roughly $11,000, leaving the cost to us a bit over $32,000. Looking back, this seems as fantastic as bread a dime a loaf or butter a quarter

[174]

a pound. For this sum we would have had four new classrooms, window-walled, radiant-heated, each with a door opening directly outdoors, with the necessary lavatories, storage rooms, and a teacher's room, plus a heating system adequate for the old building as well as the new, and in this way the stoves could be removed from the older two classrooms. The six lower grades could be put in these two buildings, out where there was the least traffic, and the Three Corners school could be for the seventh and eighth grades, a sensible division of facilities, as Damon Hall (the town hall) was just down the street from Three Corners school, and was used for graduation exercises. Some day, when the old buildings were no longer usable, they could be sold, and, at least at Four Corners, removed, and another four-room building constructed there, and behold, there would be a fine graded school for the south end of town. Who knows? cried the enraptured board, perhaps someday a graduate of this fine school might even donate a room for a library. . . .

Now to bond the town for $32,000 and pay off the principal and interest would cost the individual taxpayer only twenty-six cents on the tax rate, or (the average taxpayer in Hartland being appraised at about $2,000) roughly $5.20 a year. A couple of cartons of cigarettes, a tankful of gas at Vermont prices . . . figure it any way you like, it would have been a mighty small investment for such tremendous returns.

Could we get it? We could not.

Late in June, quite unexpectedly, in the middle of haying season and on a Thursday when the men in the shops couldn't get there, a school vote meeting took place, and the voters, the few who came, duly voted, 41-30, to build two rooms at Three Corners, for $27,000 less state aid if they could get it.

The Citizens' Committee was astounded that this totally irrational plan should be voted. True, a number of people who favored the school board's plan didn't hear of the meeting until it was over. True, the board's plan called for the use of an architect and a bonded contractor, and architects are well known for their addiction to costly frills; as for bonding a contractor, why, those are city ways, we were told, "Up here we trust each other."

The *Village Crier*, too, had been blowing on the embers of the old bitterness over sending children from one village to another. It called for the preservation of the "neighborhood school," extolling its virtues and decrying the soul-destroying factory-type school, from which no good citizen could ever emerge. The school board's plan for six grades in one place was nothing but the beginning of a consolidated school—and in the *Crier, consolidated* is a dirty word.

All in all, the Citizens' Committee was outraged by the vote, the timing of it, the lack of sufficient notice, and the failure of the board to explain in detail what its plan was. There was nothing to do, we felt, but have a revote, by golly.

Now to get a revote we needed a petition signed by five per cent of the voters. We needed, in other words, forty-three signatures.

That doesn't sound like many. It is quite a number in our hill country, because once you get out of the villages the houses are often half a mile to two miles apart.

I took my copy of the petition and went out Route 12 towards the north, and up the tributaries leading onto it. Route 12 goes up what is called on the map Alder Meadow Valley, but it is known locally as the Skunk Hollow road, though why this one road should be so singled out I do not know, as skunks have not preferred it exclusively to all others. The valley is narrow and very picturesque, the road winding and climbing and sometimes giving a view of Mount Ascutney to the south. All its length there are groves of birch and second-growth hemlock, and blighted, overgrown orchards separated by run-out hill pastures, and in the narrow ribbon of meadow next to the road a little grass snake of a brook undulates its intricate way. Perhaps only to a tourist (or an artist) is it beautiful. To a farmer there is something heartbreaking in the sparse woods, the thin grass in the pastures, the rickety, senile barns clinging to the heights.

I went into all kinds of houses. Some were new, and very small (they didn't look much larger than a nine-by-twelve rug), and were neatly clothed in mail-order sheathing, with a row of geraniums thriving in tin cans on the porch railing. Others were ancient, crumbling farmhouses, with rusted tin roofs and sagging steps. There were one-room schoolhouses now being used as one-room houses, semi-detached plumbing. There were dilapidated house trailers whose nomadic years were so far behind them moss grew on their foundations. And every now and then, way up in the hills where the lanes start their downward plunge into the valley, there would be an old house, cherished, freshly painted, set in a green lawn, and bordered by peonies, poppies, hollyhocks, and daylilies.

Some of these houses were clean in the casual way my own house is clean, with a cluttered look that indicates busy people with no time for more than the bare essentials of housekeeping. Others were desperately, frantically clean, as is a house where isolated women are left too long alone, too poor for any pastimes that cost money. And others, not many, but enough, were quite the opposite.

The houses varied. The standards of living varied. But in every home, the greeting was the same.

"Please to come in, ma'am."

"I surely will sign, ma'am."

"Anybody with any sense a-tall knows the place fer the school is Four Corners, we got the land fer it there."

And then, always the same refrain: "We *got* to have a good school. I never had a chance, nor my man, neither. It's too late for us, ma'am, but our children, they got to have a chance. They got to have the best schoolin', somehow. That's the only way they'll ever get out of the rut we're in."

I'm not making this up. I have what is called an auditory memory. I can hear their voices as if it were yesterday. The anxious, eager voices. Hurried, as if afraid I might not give them time to finish.

One woman told me of the son who ought to be in the eighth grade now, but who, last year, was sent home by the teacher with the flat order (delivered publicly before the grinning class), "Don't come back because you're too stupid to learn anything."

[177]

Another woman, whose floor looked clean enough to feed a baby on it, told me of her young son whom she had caught slapping and pummeling his playmate. When she had reprimanded him, he had answered, "But Mother, we're playing school and I'm the teacher!"

And another, caring for a state child (as Vermont children are called who are, for one reason or another, assigned to foster parents), told how the child had returned from school one day with all the buttons ripped off his sweater, so hearty had been the shaking up he had received. "I sent him in the same sweater the next day," she said, "hitched together with big safety pins. I hope that shamed her!"

Perhaps it did. I wouldn't have bet on it.

They said more. They said what I never had thought I'd hear in these democratic United States, not north of the Mason-Dixon line, anyhow. They said, "You talk for us, ma'am. We can't talk in Town Meeting. I dunno's I kin even vote, I ain't got my poll taxes paid yet. But you talk—you don't owe nobody in town money!"

Vermont's poll tax does not apply to voting for President. But in order to vote in Town Meeting, or have one's signature count on local petitions, or even to be eligible for a state driver's license, your poll taxes must be paid up.

I was getting a close-up of financial segregation, and I didn't much like what it was doing to people. I didn't like the hopelessness in their eyes, in their voices. It's very easy to say some of them should spend less on beer and more on soap. But a can of beer can take the edge off a man's despair. And what drives a woman to scrub and scour her house clean? Why, the fact that her mother kept hers clean, and her mother before her. And if neither Mama nor Gran'mama knew how, and the one-room school in the hollow never taught them to, why, then, let's bring the children down out of the hills, I thought.

Not that what we had to offer was necessarily the best of the twentieth century.

About a month after Kitty started first grade, she remarked over her lunch one Saturday, "You know, Mother, we've got some niggers in our school."

I said, "Where did you hear that word?"

"What word?"

"Niggers. Where did you hear it?"

"That's what the kids call them," she said. "Isn't that what they are?"

"You have *never*," I said, with such emphasis that she looked a little frightened, "you have never heard me use that word, have you? I know the children you mean. They are sweet, clean, well-mannered children, and they have some Negro blood. The word is *Negro*."

Chris said, "What's wrong with 'nigger'? That's what the kids in my class say, too."

"It's just that it's a word I never expected to hear in Vermont," I said. "It's a fighting word that one Negro sometimes calls another; a white person, if he is courteous, never uses it. Of course there are always people with shriveled-up souls who try to make themselves feel bigger by mixing other people with mud, but don't *you* do it."

"Yeah," Chris said, "like the kids call those other kids, not the nig—Negro children, they wash, but those others, you know who I mean, the kids holler at them and say corn's growing from your ears, and stuff like that."

"That certainly isn't very nice," said Kitty severely.

"What can you expect?" Chris said. "Jeepers, there's the teacher asking 'em right out in class do they sleep with their clothes on. Jeepers, I thought *grown-ups* were supposed to have some manners!"

We needed forty-three signatures, and we got 133. Sixteen of these were no good to us, being of folk unable to ante up their poll tax, $9.50 for '52. But, armed with the 117 legal signatures on the petition, the school board was able to convince the selectmen that the next step was another special Town Meeting, and this was scheduled for Saturday, the first of August.

The Citizens' Committee was determined that everybody should have heard of this meeting. We had been getting all kinds of bulletins and facts and figures and advice from the National Citizens Commission for the Public Schools, and now we sent off for free posters, and we inked in the date and time and place of the meeting, and nailed the posters to barns and fences and trees all over town. "Big-city high-pressure tactics!" sneered the *Village Crier*.

I came home one day and repeated what I was stupid enough to think was an amusing bit of gossip: someone, not a member, had objected to the name of the Citizens' Committee on the grounds that not everybody in it was a citizen. To my astonishment and dismay, this so cut Longin to the quick that he said he was out of it, he was through, he would have nothing more to do with it. I said *nonsense*, and *don't be silly!*—but there are few more proud and touchy souls, I found out, than those still knocking on the door asking to be let in; and I could not move him.

So it was that Longin did not go along when Lefty and Rowena James and I went to Montpelier and had a long and most interesting talk with the State Department of Education. We were told we must determine our goal: Is it merely to get a minimum program to qualify for state aid, or is it to meet the needs of the children? And when we start to build in one place, we were told, we must continue to build at that place whenever further construction is needed in the future. There will be no state aid if we attempt to add two rooms at both locations, the exact wording of this warning being, "The Department will not look with favor on . . ."

We wrote these statements down very carefully. Then we reported to the school board what we had been told. And on Saturday, the first of August, we reported to the voters what we had been told. Unfortunately it had not occurred to us to have our conference tape-recorded, as had Mr. Quackenbush when he had gone to Montpelier a few days before us. It was, therefore, only our word that the town would receive no state aid if we built in two places. It was only our word, too, that the present site in Three Corners would need considerable additional land

[180]

purchased in order to qualify as having sufficient playground space. Such money, we said, would far better be spent on the school itself.

I'm not sure if it was at this meeting—we had so many of them —that we hashed out whether or not there would be a business depression should the war in Korea come to an end. Naturally in that case Hartland mustn't find itself trying to finance a new school. And what if Hartland, unique in the United States, were about to die out due to an inexplicable snuffing out of the birth rate? What would we do with a new school building then?

But I am quite sure, having newspaper clippings to jog my memory, that it was at this August first meeting that a former town representative to the state legislature, faced with our report that we must choose one site or the other, or forfeit state aid, rose, leaned back against the edge of the platform, and gave us the benefit of his experience in Montpelier.

"Now I'm not questioning the motives of those who want to build in Four Corners," he said. "I don't know this lady—" he indicated me with a casual gesture of his hand—"but she seems to have an honest face." He stopped, and peered at me doubtfully. "But we ought to remember that these things can always be worked out." He went on to explain there was nothing rigid or hidebound about the State Board of Education, which consisted of men and women appointed by the governor, and which ranked the State Department of Education, who were career men. The Board could okay or veto whatever the Department decided.

The arguments went on for nearly two and a half hours, mostly about what the Department meant when it said it *would not look with favor*—did that mean it would just frown and look cross, or would it say No? But no one offered any conclusive proof we had not been told what we said we'd been told, and so, when at last the first vote was taken, whether or not to rescind the vote for two rooms at Three Corners, it was in favor of rescinding, 110-104. This was a pretty narrow squeak, but after that we had no difficulty in getting the four rooms at Four Corners to be voted.

But not the money.

In order to bond the town, the warnings in the newspapers had to be published three consecutive weeks plus five days before the meeting, and this had not been done, explained Mrs. Lobdell of the board, because the board hadn't been aware of this requirement until just a couple of days ago, and therefore there was no sense in voting for the money because we would have to have another meeting, to satisfy the bonding companies.

I was ashamed of myself for wishing Mrs. Lobdell weren't so honest, so unshakable in her scruples. But I felt cold with apprehension. We ought to vote now, I thought. We've come so far, let's finish. Vote the money now, and then, later, vote for it again. . . .

The voting for the bond was to take place on the last Saturday in August, by ballot, with no discussion. I posted our map and graphs, and a listing of all the children in school, and all the preschoolers, and I hoped these would speak, though silently. We were filled with foreboding, because the political climate, barely temperate on August first, had cooled rapidly and was now bitter cold.

For one thing, there had been those rumors. Who started them we could only guess, but word went with the speed of a grass fire from one frightened person to another, that the twenty-six cents on the tax rate meant that the average taxpayer would be paying for the new school not $5.20 but *fifty-two dollars a year*— and if the town couldn't pay, and defaulted on the bond, somebody would come and seize the taxpayers' very homes!

Even more disastrous had been the affair of the teachers' certificates. Just a day or two before the voting, four of Hartland's teachers found that their temporary certificates (which had been renewed again and again without any question, in one case for nearly twenty years) were not renewed, and no one knew if the teachers would have their jobs, or the schools any teachers; and feeling ran high, not only against the Department of Education (the withholders) but against the superintendent of schools also, and *they* were on the side of the Citizens' Committee, weren't they? So blame lapped over onto us, too.

[182]

Where all the voters came from, we never knew, but come they did, folks who hadn't bothered to vote in years and years. And the vote went 221-122 against the bond.

When I stopped in the village to get the Sunday paper the next morning, I went into the hall to collect my charts and map, and I found them torn from the wall and hurled in twisted, angry pieces on the floor, and (apparently) stamped on. Which really wasn't necessary, I thought, picking up the pieces with a sick sensation. We lost. Why should anyone hate us when we lost?

While the school board now attended to the urgent business of finding temporary quarters for the fifth grade, the *Village Crier* blistered first the board for having listened to the recommendations of the Department of Education, and then Lefty for having deferred to the judgment of the board. Now Lefty was an outspoken and energetic member of the Citizens' Committee whom Longin and I had regarded with special affection ever since we had found out he had been a captain in an infantry outfit which had fought right along with Bob's Third Armored Division across northern France and through Belgium and the Siegfried Line. I was not particularly pleased, therefore, to read the *Village Crier's* open letter to Lefty, which advised him to remember he "is no longer a captain taking orders from above." It was quite a long letter, and I read it with mounting bewilderment.

". . . There are some in Town who believe that you are an innocent tool in the hands of a group or even one person assigned the job of preparing Hartland for the coming of the socialized state. That you are innocent of any such motive, I am sure. Neither can I believe that Mrs. Amrbos [*sic*] or Mrs. James or any other of the women leaders of your committee are deliberately playing along with the welfare state people. But the effect is the same, whether you are doing it deliberately or not . . ."

Longin came in for a drink of water—he was mixing cement by hand, a hot job—and I said numbly, "Well what do you make of this? Is Mr. Quackenbush calling us Commies?"

Longin looked at me as if I had taken leave of my senses. I handed him the paper. He read it. He turned on his heel and went out. About ten minutes later he came back in. "Where's that lousy smear sheet?" he said. I fished it out of the wastebasket. He read it again, then stuffed it in his pocket, and saying no more than, "I'll be right back," he got in the jeep and drove off as if all the devils in Hell were after him. And he didn't come back for two hours.

Naturally during that time I imagined all sorts of picturesque goings-on. Longin walloping Quackenbush and being carted off to the clink. Quackenbush walloping Longin—less likely, but after all, he did stand a head taller. What actually happened was not particularly conclusive, one way or another.

Longin kept reminding himself as he drove that Melissa Is Pregnant and therefore Cannot Do the Barn Chores and therefore he, Longin, Must Not Get Arrested. Therefore he must goad Quackenbush into taking the first blow. (Longin's knowledge of law is as shaky as mine.) He had tried to goad Quackenbush into swinging at him, and had called the *Village Crier* a (censored) smear sheet, and Quackenbush himself a liar.

Mr. Quackenbush would not get mad. He said he was terribly sorry Longin took all this so hard. He pointed out he hadn't said anything against Longin, he'd been talking about Longin's wife.

"Well, *Gawdammit!*" Longin roared . . . and for the life of him could not stay raging, and had to laugh.

Longin had then, rather unreasonably, tried reason. Neither his wife nor his friends could possibly be working for the Communists, and he not know it. If anybody in Hartland knows what Communism is, he does. "If it were near me, I could smell it," he said. Not for nothing had his uncles disappeared into Siberia. Not for nothing had he gone to school under Russian occupation.

"You know how they teach the little children to hate God and love Stalin? They have the children cover their eyes, and pray, 'Dear God in Heaven, give me candy.' And open their eyes, and there is no candy. Then they say, 'Now pray to the good Father Stalin,' and the children cover their eyes once again, and the teacher runs along putting candy on the desks."

I suppose Longin thought that if he could get Quackenbush to grasp enough of the real nature of Communism, he would stop printing slurs against the members of the Citizens' Committee. "I come from one of the poorest parts of Poland," Longin told him. "Anybody with two cows was thought to be a rich man. But when the Russians came, they kept marveling at how well we lived."

But it was all in vain. Quackenbush continued to imply that we were "unwittingly working for the welfare state" not only in his own *Village Crier* but also by letters to other local newspapers, repeating his charge as much as a year later. But always carefully in the negative . . . "Neither can I believe . . ."

Longin came home very much annoyed with himself for having stooped to discuss the matter at such length. "I was a fool to waste two hours talking," he growled. "I have more important things to be doing. I don't stop to argue with Butch every time he barks his fool head off." But before he went back to work on the milk house, he went down cellar and brought up a jug of hard cider given us by the Quackenbushes some time before, and this we ceremoniously poured out on the lawn.

Our usually taciturn neighbors, who, like everyone else in Hartland, took the words "Communism," "Socialism" and "Welfare State" to be synonymous, troubled to walk up over the hill and assure Longin they "knew it was all nonsense." And other new friends, Vermonters, stopped me on the street and said, "My God, to print such stuff about you, of all people!"

I said lightly, "Oh, you really don't know how subversive my background is. Why, my own mother resigned from the DAR—two days before Eleanor Roosevelt did, and for the very same reason!"

Just to keep the record clear, I should stress that Mr. Quackenbush is not a native Vermonter. No native attacked us personally, though they had a superb target, had such been their nature. I mean, of course, Mikey.

Everyone in town must have heard about Mikey by now. Word of such a child always travels swiftly, but especially in a small town where one can hardly sneeze without everyone shouting *Gesundheit!* Possibly the full details of our interview at the Rutland Rehabilitation Center were not known. Shortly after Mikey had come home to stay, my father and I had taken him over in the hope that he could be enrolled in the Center's day school for handicapped children. We were told, gently but finally, that the Center had all it could do to care for and train physically handicapped children, there simply was no room and no time for "the other child," as Mike was called.

No doubt our search for a private tutor for Mike was well known—I had had total strangers stop me in the village store and ask me, in anxious concern, whether I had succeeded in finding help for my child—and no doubt the disastrous consequences were known, too: the talented young woman from Woodstock, whose efforts to teach Mikey even such a simple concept as *like* and *unlike* (a circle is *like* another circle but *unlike* a square) had caused such tension to build up in him he had struck her, with force; the elderly woman, for many years a kindergarten teacher, who had tried to help him express himself, even though without words, but using crayon and chalk and paint, and Mikey had struck her, too, with force. After that we had given up looking for teachers for him, and had tried only to keep him safe and happy—and those around him safe. We could only hope that the times we had not been completely successful in keeping the other children safe were not the subject of widespread gossip . . . the number of times when Mike had threatened to strike Mary Lee; the rock hurled in anger; the paper napkin thrust suddenly into the candles of a birthday cake.

Mikey himself had a certain flair for self-dramatization. One evening, when a group was meeting at our house to discuss the coming vote on the bond, Mikey wandered over into his favorite haunt, the swamp meadow across the road where the cattails grew, "Metes' field," the children call it. Mikey had got to playing in the mud, and after a bit, feeling cold and uncomfortable, he came home, black mud from head to foot like an animated tar baby. The swift look of shock that crossed their faces told me my friends had read, quite accurately, the implications of his appearance.

But no one ever said, or implied, or even seemed to think, "Who does she think she is—arguing about better schools—her with a half-witted child?"

So now school had opened, the fifth grade was installed in the basement of the town hall, the second grade in the cellar of Three Corners, the third grade in the cellar of Four Corners, and everybody else above ground. I kept canning and freezing and prayed for an early frost. And the frost came, and October seemed wintry, but it was not yet, fortunately, deer season on the night of the PTA meeting when Mikey was lost.

The topic for the meeting was "Help Your Children to Health" and there was to be a guest speaker, a Mrs. Mildred Hatch from St. Johnsbury, who lent books on nutrition by mail, no charge except for postage. I had got reading these books and was, you might say, a convert to good nutrition. I took it very seriously and applied it in every way I could, and was feeling peppier and peppier in spite of being more and more pregnant. The children were having fewer and fewer colds and practically no cavities in their teeth, and even Longin, who disapproves of "nutrition" and so has to have it sneaked into his food—even Longin was losing some of his traditional Slavic pessimism. So I was looking forward very much to meeting Mrs. Hatch, which as program chairman I was supposed to do; she would arrive by bus in White River in the afternoon. I was to drive her to Three Corners where she was to give a talk to the seventh and eighth grades on eating right so their teeth would not rot; then she was to come out to the farm for supper and then back to Four Corners for the PTA meeting.

Mrs. Hatch arrived, and gave her talk, and then we drove home and I fixed fried chicken while she read to the children. And then the chicken was ready, and Longin came in, and everybody washed up. Except Mike. No one had seen Mike, not for hours.

We went outside in the dusk and called. Patrick scampered up through the orchard, Chris went across the road to Meteses' field. We looked wherever we could think he might be. No one could find him.

It grew darker. We searched farther. Then we searched where we had already searched. Had anyone seen any rabbit hunters? I asked, and tried not to think what might be huddled in a ditch.

I called Alfonses. Had they seen Mike? Oh, no, but then he very seldom ever came that far. But they would look. And they went out into the dark, with lanterns, and looked, and Jules drove slowly over the back roads, down to Jenneville corner and along the lower road a ways, and then came back, and came to check had we found him? And we had not.

And I called the Bests, because sometimes he did go down over the hill, as far as their mailbox, but usually the sight of their hunting dogs hitched by their doghouses had sent him home again. No, they had not seen him, but they would look. And they did look, and after a while, Clifford came up over the hill, on foot, bringing one of his hounds on leash. I was to get a piece of Mikey's clothing, he said. . . .

When Longin thought of the tractor. Perhaps, in the dark, Mikey thinks it's a game to hide from us, Longin said. But he always runs to see what the tractor motor means. That was so, we all agreed. Mikey likes to follow behind the tractor, mile after dusty mile, as Longin plows, or rakes the hay.

So Longin got out the tractor, and, its motor roaring reassuringly in the darkness, he started up the road. Very shortly he came back, followed by an impish, grinning, muck-covered Mike, who, just as Longin suspected, had been hiding from us all.

I thanked Jules and Clifford, who went home, and we cleaned Mike and then sat down to chicken as overcooked as any I ever tried to eat. Mrs. Hatch, who all this while had been quietly confident Mike would be found, and found safe, now assured me the chicken was delicious, but I could not eat. The whole process seemed pointless.

We set out for the meeting. I knew we would be late, but I thought it couldn't matter less if we were, and I was driving along

[188]

slowly and not really thinking much of anything, when Mrs. Hatch said, "Tell me about Mike."

So I told her, briefly. I was too cushioned by exhaustion for any of it to hurt, and besides, *she's very aware*, I thought, and found her easy to talk to.

"And after you gave up looking for a teacher, you took him to Hanover?"

"Yes. And the doctor there really laid it on the line. Mike is hopeless, he said. He'll never be any better than he is now. As a matter of fact, he'll be worse, because the older he gets the harder he is to control. He said he could go in and operate, but there wouldn't be any point to it, he knows what he'd find. A brain that doesn't work, that never grew. And he doesn't, he said, have any spare brains in good working order with which to replace it."

I hoped Mrs. Hatch could make sense out of this muddle. Apparently she did, because she said quietly, "And what did he say you should do?"

"Oh, he said we must put Mike in an institution as soon as possible. Partly for his own sake. I never thought about that part of it before, but the doctor said Mike would be happier where the world was geared to him, instead of all the time having to obey a lot of rules that simply don't make sense to him. And then he said—" I groped for some way to say it easily, but there are no smooth words for some thoughts, so I went on harshly—"he said that unless I wanted to see Mike put in an asylum for the criminally insane some day, where, he said, there are a lot of people who ought never to have wound up there, but their families didn't take the proper steps to protect them early enough—unless I wanted something like that to happen, I'd go ahead and do something now to see that that *couldn't* happen."

We were pulling up in front of the school. Mrs. Hatch made no move to get out. "Have you started to look?"

"Oh, yes," I said wearily. "I've written every place I ever heard of. Some places won't take a boy as old as Mike, some won't keep them after they're fifteen. Others expect a child to have an IQ of fifty, and to fit in with what they call their 'academic program'—imagine! And all of them are horribly expensive, anything from a hundred and fifty a month up to four or five hundred." I slid out of the car. "We'd better hurry. You're the program, you know."

We found we had arrived just as the business meeting was ending, which was good timing. I introduced Mrs. Hatch, and then I retreated to the kitchen where I sat huddled on the woodbox and drank cup after cup of coffee. From where I sat I could look out at the cellar classroom for the third grade. I could see the faces of the members of the PTA, and suddenly I hated them. I despised them. I'll spend every cent I've got looking for help for my child, I thought, and I'll tear my guts out trying to give him a chance at a decent existence, and I can't even teach him to come to supper. And all over the country the mothers and fathers of all the other Michaels are doing the same thing, and there you sit, so damn smug and satisfied with the little you do for your children with their good minds, you won't even fight like hell for a decent school for them, you won't even spend five dollars and twenty cents a year to put a decent roof over their heads. . . .

And then I didn't despise them, I pitied them. Because they didn't know what they had. They looked at their children and they didn't realize how lucky they were, how blessedly lucky. They've got gold in their pockets and they don't know it, I thought. All the wealth in the world sits at their supper tables; and they? They're afraid. . . .

Mrs. Hatch wrote the most unusual bread-and-butter letter I have ever received. "You must consider what is best for Mike," she said. "Sooner or later he is going to have to leave you. You know this. It will be easier on him if you can find the courage to do it sooner. Have you considered the state institution at Brandon? It has an excellent reputation—far better than most, I understand."

What a grand human being she is, I thought, rereading this letter so carefully worded to avoid unnecessary hurt, yet to reach in and help. I don't care what anybody says, all Vermonters don't build stone walls around their hearts. . . .

It now appeared that our chance for four rooms for $32,000 was irrevocably lost, because the State Department of Education put forth a ruling that with new construction of four rooms, there must also be a multi-purpose room, or the project would not qualify for state aid. Were we to succeed in getting our four rooms voted once more, our share of the now higher cost would be $45,000. How to raise the extra $13,000? Could we do it ourselves? said the Citizens' Committee. How about a series of bingo games? said Peg Stillson. How about a big barbecue, said Longin, with him doing a parachute jump as a crowd-getter?

But the school board was utterly discouraged, refused to try further, and let it be known that the member whose term was to expire would not be running for re-election, and the other two members were going to resign.

So for a while the winter proceeded quietly, though not uneventfully. Longin became a citizen. Victor Robert Ambros was born. And then Ellison called for an inspection of the schools by the State Department of Health. The results made quite a splash in local newspapers.

REPORT SHOWS POOR LIGHTING, TOILETS, AT HARTLAND SCHOOL, said the *Vermont Journal*. STATE HEALTH DEPARTMENT CRITICISES HARTLAND SCHOOLS, clacked the *Daily Eagle*, across the river in Claremont, New Hampshire. The *Rutland Herald* gave details: "In the Four Corners basement classroom the ceiling was two and a half feet under the State minimum . . . inadequate window area . . . dirty toilets, foul air, no soap or towels in the lavatories, in fact no lavatory in Damon Hall, where the children were washing their hands in the kitchen sink . . . no proper fresh-air ventilation in a single classroom. Worst of all was the lighting. State requirements called for twenty foot-candles on desk surfaces, yet in Damon Hall cellar classroom the light available was five foot-candles, in Four Corners cellar classroom, four foot-candles . . ."

Parents and townspeople responded with cries of outrage. "Who does Mrs. Alfonse think she *is*, anyway?" "What business is it of hers, anyway?" "What an awful thing, all this publicity about our schools—all over the papers for everybody to read!" As far as I know, no one thanked Ellison. Not that she was looking for thanks. She was looking for action, but she didn't get much of that, either. Not to amount to anything, although a certain amount of shamefaced scrubbing took place, and I believe soap and towels no longer were kept in the teachers' desks instead of in the washrooms in Three Corners.

Ellison next called for an inspection of the schools by the State Department of Safety. Even the *Village Crier* gave details on the results of that inspection: Exit doors must swing out at Grout, Center, and North Hartland; panic bars should be installed on doors at Three and Four Corners and North Hartland; Grout, Center and Four Corners should have trash removed; electric wires should be removed from pipes at Grout (we'd missed that completely in our Citizens' Committee report a year before); take the clothing from behind the stove at Grout; fireproof the new furnace room door at North Hartland.

Mr. Quackenbush then added the following: "EDITOR'S NOTE: It seems to me . . . that the Citizens' Committee is out to show that our schools are all falling apart and that all we can do is sell what is left for junk and start off all new . . ."

And here and there, the little seeds sown by such statements took root, and it was said (and not by certifiable fools, either) that the Citizens' Committee was out to bankrupt the town.

We are now, in case you have lost track, approaching the Town Meeting of 1954. The feeling of an ordeal ahead, of a kind of obstacle race to be run, is familiar, isn't it? Probably will go on and on, just like last year, because they didn't vote to elect officers by a single ballot, did they? No. And look at the items about the schools: To see if the town will vote $32,000 for *two* rooms, teacher's room, and supply room with heating plant at Four Corners . . . three rooms for $40,000 . . . one-room schoolhouse for $9,000 in Fieldsville . . . ditto for same price on Route 12 . . . four rooms plus hot lunch room, etc., etc., for $44,000, location not mentioned. Plus items covering bonds for these. Plus—what's this? Another request for money for the Lobdell Bridge? Didn't it get voted last year?

I will rush you through Town Meeting. I don't want you to get cynical, as some of us have, and start thinking of this last evidence of "pure democracy in action" as "just a chance for every ass to bray in public."

Again, no Australian ballot. About the Lobdell Bridge, well, maybe it would be a good idea to replace it before it collapsed and somebody sued the town; $8,000 was voted as the town's share, not the previous year's $5,000, building costs for bridges having gone up right along with building costs for schools. And nothing was voted for the schools, not of any size, at any price. Who can blame the voters? Obviously the board couldn't make up its mind what should be built—what were the people to do, say eeny meeny miny moe?

The new board was voted in: Lefty James, Citizens' Committee member, parent of two school-age children, development technician in one of the shops in Windsor, to replace Mabel Lobdell, whose term had but one year to go; Danny Trivet, replacing the member from North Hartland; and Carson Scott, elderly retired gentleman now dabbling in dairy farming, a newcomer to Vermont. Lefty's election was naturally a source of comfort to the Citizens' Committee. We weren't so sure about Danny Trivet— wasn't he the man who had said that labor by the day, instead of bonded contractors, was traditional in Vermont, because "up here we trust each other"? As for Mr. Scott, we knew nothing about him; we'd have to wait and see.

The new members of the board were to be bonded at the next town officers' meeting, and afterwards, when Lefty caught up with the others on the steps of Damon Hall, they remarked that Mr. Scott might as well assume chairmanship, didn't he agree? Lefty, though knowing it was traditional that the member serving the last year of his term also serve as chairman, deferred to Mr. Scott's years and his prestige as a Ph.D., and let the point ride.

Mr. Scott went off on a trip to the West, and Lobdell Bridge, as if pleased that now it could have everyone's full attention, chose a soft summer evening to collapse. This was shortly after the end of school, and it was an empty lumber truck, not a filled school bus, God be thanked, which did it. Even the driver escaped unhurt, with such considerate gentleness did the beams twist and lower towards the brook.

Now we had to drive six extra miles in order to get to Four Corners. We had to turn sharp left, just this side of French's Bridge, which had been a very narrow and skittery structure when I first moved here, and which had been replaced, over Mr. Quackenbush's anguished opposition, by a large culvert which he henceforth referred to as a quonset hut. Just this side of the culvert, then, we had to head up into the hills, seeing many magnificent views we would not otherwise have seen, and jarring over many bumps and ruts we would not otherwise . . . oh, well. This detouring continued for some five weeks, while the selectmen and the state came to an agreement, and machinery arrived, and then work was halted while Quackenbush slapped an injunction (or had an injunction slapped, I don't know the legal term) on the building of the concrete bridge, and wrote invitations via the newspapers to other towns to come and see where their tax money was going to be wasted. Somebody made him see reason and withdraw his injunction, and work was started, and the very first thing the state did was to build a temporary bridge in Lobdell's pasture and we were at last able to cut out the wild-goose chase in the northern hills.

When I would tell visitors this sort of thing, they would look at me in awe and say, "You don't *need* TV up here!"

Now from this point on it must be understood that the term "school board" refers to the Scott-Trivet majority only. Mr. Scott, as chairman, was in a position to schedule the board meetings, and arrange conferences with architects, lawyers, and officials in Montpelier, send out correspondence and notices in the name of the board, and call special school meetings, particularly as he could count on Mr. Trivet's vote, should a vote for any of these steps be needed. A letter was sent to the voters, calling for a discussion meeting on June 26, the purpose of which was to decide

which of *five different plans* should be selected to be put on the
warning for a vote at a special school meeting to be held later.
At the beginning of this letter there was a ballot which was to
be mailed in, unsigned, indicating the voters' preference (only one
ballot per married couple was furnished). Lefty was willing to go
along with the board on a vote indicating popular preference, but
he felt such a vote should be taken at the end of the discussion
meeting, not by unsigned ballots mailed in ahead of time. Lefty
said so, and in print, and this was taken as a most serious sign
of insubordination by the board.

Chairman Scott conducted the meeting, and it was apparent almost at once that his sympathies lay with the "village school." He
had gone to a one-room school himself, in the Middle West, many
years ago. Must that mean, I thought in despair, that now Hartland, with nearly two hundred children swamping the school
facilities in the southern part of town, would have to maintain
indefinitely two school plants, and buy two of everything, two
furnaces, two hot-lunch rooms, two teachers' rooms, two sewage-
disposal plants?

It was a hot evening, and tempers grew hot, too. Particularly
the tempers of the parents. Our children were involved, not just
our pocketbooks, and we could not achieve a detached, sophisticated attitude. We could not view the school fight as quaint, or
amusing, or even as a bore. And we resented deeply any nuance
of such an attitude.

We didn't want anything wasted, not money, nor time—teachers' or children's—nor the children's minds. We didn't know just
how to explain this so it would be convincing, particularly when
we felt we were being understood very well, and our points were
well taken, and then they were being dismissed as of no importance. Tempers rose, and voices rose, and it began to look as if
the evening would end in verbal violence, anyway, when Clifford,
who had also gone to a one-room school, and who makes no bones
about the fact he wants none of that sort of education for his
children, Clifford rose and said in his slow, easy drawl, "It's like

this. You ask a teacher to teach two grades at once, it's like you ask your hired man to ride two tractors at the same time."

All through the summer of '54, while Longin cut hay and piled it in the barn, and he and I built the chicken house (with some help from the boys) and he finished the milk house and I painted it, and we harvested the corn, and filled the freezer with fruits and vegetables of our own raising, and I stacked quart jars of applesauce and pears and plums and tomatoes and cucumber pickles by the dozens and dozens on the shelves in the cellar, while we tended the cows and fed the children and turned them out reasonably clean for school in September, all this while we waited for a decision to be reached about the schools, and work for a solution to be started.

It turned out that the popularity-contest-by-mail in June had had a very small return, and so, in August, the board sent word to the voters that there would be a runoff vote on the 17th to choose, finally and for good, what would go on the *final* ballot. The runoff vote was to be between the board's pet plan, two rooms in each village, $50,000 less state aid, and Lefty's plan, which he hoped would get around the sentimental tug-of-war over which village should be favored, four rooms plus multi-purpose room at a new site, $80,000 less state aid.

Now Lefty had taken the trouble of getting an accurate figure from an architect, and $75,000 was the figure given him, not the $80,000 as printed on the warning. Where the board got their figure of $50,000 for their plan, no one was able to determine. Rumor had it that the wife of a pro-Three Corners property owner was asked how much she thought such a building might cost, and she plucked that neat round figure from thin air. Maybe so. Certainly the board's architects refused to admit it was their estimate. In fact, they refused to say anything at all about it, when asked. But that figure of $50,000 would get votes, my, yes!

On the day of the voting, it turned out that the land, the ten or more acres of splendid, rolling, ideal-for-a-school-site land, which was owned by two elderly brothers and which was for sale, for purposes of a school halfway between the two villages, so

Lefty had been told (but Lefty had "trusted one another" and had not got this statement in writing), was *not* for sale. Not any longer. Why not? No one knew. The chairman of the board had called on one of the elderly men, a day or so before the voting, in order to make sure of the status of the land. And now, at the meeting, he had to report that unfortunately it seemed it was not for sale.

Of 250 voters who turned out, 135 declared themselves for two rooms at each village. So be it, we said.

Perhaps we should have petitioned for a revote. It would have been easy to get enough signatures. But the voting had brought a strong turnout, and we felt we had to accept the result. In a democracy you have to yield to the will of the majority, we told ourselves glumly, even if the majority is behaving like a jackass.

Now appeared a strange state of affairs. It seemed—oh, no, not again!—but yes, again. *The meeting had not been properly advertised.* Therefore the voting for the bond would not satisfy the bonding companies. What had gone wrong this time? The first notice in the newspaper had had the date wrong. . . .

Does this mean there is going to be another voting? Maybe we can get the whole shebang voted down? Nothing can possibly be built until spring, now—maybe we can somehow get a real school voted by then?

We didn't know. Lefty didn't know. If the board knew, it wasn't telling. The board was holding meetings, cozily, just the two of them, with the architect, and with officials in Montpelier, and it got so that these officials, embarrassed at being party to such a state of affairs, took to notifying Lefty when the board was coming, in case he wanted to come, too; and they sent him carbons of correspondence which he, as a duly elected member of the board, had every right to see.

Mr. Scott, surprised that such a trivial error as one mistake in the date should cause all this rumpus, sought advice. Would there have to be a revote? Lefty heard that Mr. Scott had been told yes, by Vermont lawyers. So off Mr. Scott went to New York, where he asked some New York lawyers, and they said yes, too. And all this little jaunt cost the taxpayers was $250 for the lawyers' bill (almost twice one year's budget for new textbooks).

Now Lefty had learned at the last board meeting to which he had been invited that the board's architect did not think the plan which had been voted could possibly be constructed for $50,000. Lefty felt that no one had a better right to know this than his fellow townsmen, who soon were to be asked to revote the money for this plan. So he told them. And the board was furious, and told him he was "disloyal." The board was so much put out with him, that when they took their architects' plans to Montpelier to see if these plans would meet state approval for state aid, they neglected to tell Lefty they were going, or what was said there.

Lefty felt that enough is enough, b'gosh, and fired off a letter to the *Valley News* revealing this state of affairs. Naturally the board felt an answer was expected, and naturally they denied what Lefty had said. In particular, they denied that the architect told the board $50,000 was not sufficient for the proposed building program. And they expressed shock and repugnance at Lefty's behavior, "losing his temper," his "misrepresentation" and "innuendo" and "crocodile tears" and his pose as "a bit of a martyr."

Lefty let fly another salvo. He lost his temper, he said, because Mr. Scott stated he would not vote for acoustic tile if it cost as little as $1,000 extra, that he would not favor tile on the concrete floors even at $100 a room, that he couldn't understand where Lefty got his crazy ideas. Lefty went on to say that he had not been greatly enthusiastic about Mr. Scott's trip to New York to see about the legality of the vote; he had wanted, he said, to take a day or two to find out if such a trip were necessary. Unh unh. Gotta vote now, said the board, and it did.

All this made pretty fascinating reading in the papers. Circulation rose right along with the Citizens' Committee's blood pressure. What right had the majority members of the board to withhold information from the minority member? How were we ever going to get a good school voted, with all this squabbling? Something ought to be done. The PTA, with all its fine talk of working for the welfare of the community, school, and children—

how about the PTA urging a little cooperation amongst the members of the board?

So I wrote a letter to the president of the PTA. It wasn't a tactful letter, and it had no pussyfooting phrases, and it soothed nobody's ego. It simply said what we thought:

> . . . A three-man school board is small enough to lay the most onerous burden of responsibility on each member; for two of the members to usurp all power of decision, or, worse, for one member to act independently of any check on his judgment by the other two, denies the town the right to have a representative school board.
>
> I believe that no organization claiming to work for the welfare of the community, school, and children can possibly remain silent. For not to protest is to condone . . .

The corresponding secretary read the letter, hurriedly, and to the muffling accompaniment of vulgar belches from the furnace in the corner of the room—we were meeting in the cellar classroom of the town hall. And then the next I knew, a motion was being made not to discuss the contents of the letter, as "the PTA is not to mix in politics or administrative matters." Consultation of the rule book failed to settle whether or not this particular matter fell under such prohibition, so a vote was taken, whether to discuss (i.e., think) about the letter, and it was a standing vote. I was mighty interested to see who would stand up and be counted as willing at least to think. Up rose two teachers, and Ellison, and I, and precisely five more. And twenty-four rose to say nay, let's not even talk about it; and the PTA's record of nothing-that-takes-courage was preserved, unsullied.

Late in November the State Board of Education did an unprecedented thing: it voted to convey to the Hartland school board that they thought it unwise to build in two places. This communication cut no ice whatsoever with the board. On November 23 they sent a letter to the voters reporting that, due to some "trifling" flaws, the vote of September 8 was "marred" and a new vote on December 18 was scheduled. Sweetly and without a blush the letter reported that the architect's estimate for the board's plan of two rooms here and there was *sixty-four* thousand dollars. There was no apology to Lefty. On the contrary, there followed some rather nasty cracks at him and his "cohorts." (I presume this meant the Citizens' Committee, although I'm not quite sure, *Webster's Collegiate* defining "cohort" as "In the Roman army, one of ten divisions of a legion." Well, then, how about "A company or band, esp. of warriors"? Ah, that's better.) The board implied that the "minority member of the board" had "misrepresented" by his "broadcast far and wide" that the plan could not be built within the limits of the bond issue of $50,000. The board then goes on to state quite blandly that indeed it can't, it's going to cost an estimated $64,000. Of course, if the town gets state aid, the cost to the town will be only $48,000. Certainly . . . who said anything else? Lefty's whole point had been that *the board was not bonding the town to cover the entire cost of the building,* as it should, according to accepted procedure. If there was any chance that the total cost would be more than $50,000, Lefty had said, then the board ought not to be asking for *$50,000 less state aid.*

Naturally, the letter did not make plain these points. But it did include a number of other shallowly plausible statements, such as "a central school means a more costly building; it means more spent, year after year, in transporting pupils. . . . Fine buildings and long bus trips are no guarantee of good scholastic training. . . ."

Cohorts, indeed! Lay down your swords, Romans; up, scribes!

"We've got to tell the people the facts!" we told each other, naïveté shining in our eyes. "They must know a school in Four Corners means not one cent more transportation cost, that to build in one place will save at least twenty per cent, that to talk of 'long bus trips' is silly when you remember Four Corners is closest to the most children. If the people have the *facts,* they'll vote down the board's plan—"

We were very much concerned that, should the vote for two rooms at each village be reaffirmed, the board might interpret this as approval of multi-graded classrooms, and start once again sending the children of each village to each little school. We thought that perhaps a sampling of opinion of the parents might help prevent such a step. So we circulated a petition among the parents, and anyone acting as a parent, of the children who would be going to the village schools. The petition stated that those signing wanted the present one-grade-per-room system to be preserved, no matter what choice of building plan was finally accepted. By promising not to release the names to the *Village Crier*, we obtained a surprisingly strong expression of opinion. We took the petition and the signatures to the town clerk, who counted the names, and notarized the result, and posted a statement in his office to the effect that our petition was indeed signed by the number we said it was; then we sent the petition to the State Department of Education, to be on file in case it were needed. Mr. Quackenbush tried to get a list of the signers, but the Department honored our pledge not to release them, and refused him the list.

We sent out ten newsletters, and of course we quoted our petition in one of them, giving the number of those not contacted (14), refusing to sign (8), and signing (96). This was an expression of opinion very close to unanimous among the parents, yet we could see that, no matter how strongly we were agreed on what we wanted for our children, we could not vote it through without help from that large majority of voters whose children were not involved.

In the other newsletters, we quoted the architect on the relative cost of building in one or two places. We went over the revised and up-to-date school population figures. We verified every single fact these letters contained until we would have been willing to stake our immortal soul on the accuracy of each of our statements.

Rowena and I did the actual printing of the letters. We whizzed to Windsor every morning, scrounged paper from the superintendent of schools, carted this to her brother's laundry, and there, amidst the heraldic splendor of its second floor, where great and colorful rugs were hung to dry, we ground out copies of the next day's letter, one, two, or three pages each, depending on how much we had to say, hundreds and hundreds of copies, thanks to the laundry's duplicating machine. These were parceled out to several scribes, women members of the Citizens' Committee, who nightly stapled the sheets together, and addressed them, one to each family where there was a voter. We all chipped in on the postage, and bought two-cent stamps by the thousands, and so we flooded the town with our facts.

And, truth to tell, I don't know if it won us a single vote we might not otherwise have had. I did hear of one man in the village who was sure grateful to us, he said, amidst guffaws in the corner store—he'd run outta toilet paper just before the mail came.

The voters voted three to two for the bond.

How did it all turn out? Well, Lefty resigned. Quackenbush and the *Crier* rejoiced. The State Department of Education "did not look with favor" and said no, no state aid; the State Board of Education said this certainly wasn't very good but it seemed to be the best Hartland could do, and overruled the Department, and said yes, state aid.

But only if more land were acquired for playground space at Three Corners. So the school board spent $1,975 for about three acres of playground, and another $400 for a little piece on which to put the septic tank for the enlarged school, and $250 to one of the town's tax appraisers because they held an option on some of his land which they didn't need after all. And construction was started in the spring, and in the fall of '55, there they were, two rooms tacked on at the back of each of the two old buildings, over enormous, unfinished, dusty basements. All this came to $70,300, plus all those little sums for the land.

But that isn't all. It has seemed only fair to spend something on all the other schools, too, so improvements have been made at Grout (1846) for $3,750; and there's been a room added to the North Hartland school (1895), $17,080 for the construction plus $5,250 for three acres of land—pretty steep, but there's a building on it the board hopes to sell for a couple of thousand.

$99,000, all told, $75,000 of it out of our own pockets, but we did get all the children under some sort of a schoolhouse roof. Not enough books to go around, even yet. No "frills" like a school library, or a teacher's room, or even a telephone. But we certainly preserved the vintage—sorry, village—type of school.

CHAPTER VII

Now let's take a lighthearted skip backwards, to the first day of spring, 1954.

The pussy willows were showing green slits in their gray velvet jackets, the apple buds were swelling, and over all these sweet stirrings of new life, there came a light sifting of snow. There is a strong sense of intimacy with the weather where we live, it presses against the windows so that even indoors we are vividly aware of the vast arc of the sky and what it holds for us each day, storm or sun, wind or calm. Outdoors, where the very texture of the ground beneath our feet is of prime concern—has the frost gone?; can we plant yet?; is it too dry for the pasture grasses?— outdoors, it seems to me that the weather is of such supreme importance it cushions us against the terrors of the twentieth century.

On this first day of spring, there came a sign that, as always and always, the earth had spun along its path on the palm of God, and now, as always and always, the new year had come. For the geese were back.

It was Longin who saw them. It was just at dusk, and he had stepped from the barn for a moment, when he heard a honking down in the valley, over our woods. And then he saw them, a huge flock, many more than a hundred of them, coming up from the valley and heading toward Bests'. This had surprised him, for they were coming north-to-south. And at that moment the setting sun broke through the thick clouds, marking precisely the western point of the compass, and the birds turned, flying very low, he said, passing over his head no higher than the silo, their wings wide-spread, spanning nearly five feet, and white with black tips, and the woosh-woosh of them against the evening air was clearly audible. As the geese passed over the barn, they began that rhythmic changing of position that is like a primordial dance, and having demoted their confused guide and regrouped behind a new leader, they headed north, continually chanting signals as they went.

Longin came into the house, to report joyfully on what he had seen. "So now our new year starts," he said. "We must plan, too, for our year. Make sure we know where we're going, not get all mixed up, like that poor goose, for lack of solar orientation."

"I'm going to sell a story," I said dreamily. I had been trying for years to write a story someone would care to publish, in the vain hope of adding to our Fund for the Care of Mike. So far all I had accomplished was to consume quite a stack of paper, envelopes and stamps.

"We get Victor baptized," Longin said, politely ignoring my remark.

"And I'll paint the milk house."

"I need some place to put machinery," Longin said. "And young stock in winter. I better figure on some kind of shed."

"I'm going to get gloriously skinny," I said, "so I can get into all those clothes hanging in my closet since before Mary Lee."

"I'm going to start shipping milk."

"I'll stop smoking. For good, too."

Longin just grinned.

"I will," I said. "You think just because every other time I stopped, I started again—you'll see."

"Plant corn for silage," Longin said. "Plant kitchen garden. Hay."

"Order seeds from Burpee," I wrote. I was making a list, which I find comforting when I have lots and lots of things to do. Write

[205]

them all down and let the list worry. "Order chickens. How many?"

"Better get a hundred, straight run. Fifty hens to lay eggs and fifty cocks to eat will be just about right."

"One hundred chicks," I wrote. "Where are we going to put them? That shack is too small."

"We build a chicken house," Longin said. "And I have to smoothen out the barnyard and put up fences. I don't think I will have time this year to build the new house," he added thoughtfully.

The next morning the boys, too, were convinced it was really spring. The crows were back. They perched insolently in the hedgerow between Clifford's pasture and ours, and from here they swooped with harsh shouts of joy down onto the ground, where they walked back and forth, digging up the roots of the permanent pasture. One black fellow was stationed in an elm tree as lookout. When Longin went out with a milk pail, it paid him no mind. But let him sneak out of the house with a gun, and the lookout would sound the alarm, and away the rest flew. Let Longin walk out with a milk pail and Pat sneak out with a gun—alarm and retreat! But should either Pat or Longin sneak out with a hoe, trying to conceal it as if it were a gun, and chuckles of derision would float down from the elm tree.

Patrick was overjoyed when Longin promoted him from BB gun to the .22. (Longin: You have to make up your mind what you're trying to raise, a man or a mouse. Me: I just want to *raise* him.) He was not to hunt with another boy, however; Longin felt this would compound the danger. So Pat began rising before the sun, in order to be in ambush when the crows came for breakfast. He did not hit one. Longin scored a "probable," the crow having trouble in take-off and dripping blood and feathers as it fled. Clifford was hunting crows, too, and announced plans to shoot half a dozen or so, and put them in Vivian's freezer until cornplanting time. Oddly enough, Vivian's reply to this was a curt *niet!*

April was as wet this year as the previous year was dry. It was difficult to get the manure out, and on any soft spot the tractor would bog down. Once when Longin got stuck in the barway to Meteses' field, when he came back with planks he found four deer sniffing at the tractor fastidiously. They weren't alarmed at his approach. Perhaps it was the continual rain, but all wild creatures seemed disturbingly self-assured, as if they had a hunch that this year the cards were stacked against us.

April melted into May, and still it was too wet to plow, but the pasture grasses surged vigorously upwards, and the tent caterpillars attacked the orchards and the trees along the roadsides and even got into the maples. I had gone out earlier and cut every small tent I could find, and burned bushel-baskets of twigs with little tents on them; and later I went back and, using a rag soaked in kerosene on the end of a pole, I burned the nests I had earlier missed; but still the onslaught of hungry worms was formidable, and our apple trees and cherry trees looked ragged and frayed. But our two magnificent maples were spared. Other folks were not so fortunate, and lost all the leaves on their maples, which must have been seriously weakened by such devastation. A number of farmers whose maple groves mean vitally needed income hired planes to come over and spray their sugar bushes. And it was the middle of June before the attack was really on the wane, and one could again walk under the trees without having something unpleasant drop in one's hair.

If you don't count rain, that is. By the middle of June we were all cursing the rain. Even Kitty, confined to the house when every fiber of her being was bursting to be outdoors, stared at the sodden lawn and drenched trees and said softly, "God, stop raining. Stop raining, God."

Longin had managed to get his corn planted during a few more or less clear days, but Clifford, with a herd three times the size of ours, naturally needed to plant that much more corn, and had been able only to get the fields ready when the heavens opened up again and down came more unneeded and unwelcome rain.

"I wonder if the cows'd mind," Clifford said to Longin, "if I switched to rice."

"Yeah, how are you going to get your corn in?" Longin said.

"Reckon I'll use a rowboat."

The hundred baby chickens came. We put them in a corral on the kitchen table, where they did very well, except for one unfortunate which ate some paper tissue Mikey put in there, and so died. The others thrived, and by the time they were ten days old, they had little tail feathers coming, and their wing feathers were in. They began hopping up on the edge of the board that corralled them, and then they began fluttering down to the floor, where they would run about cheep-cheeping shrilly, until rescued and returned to their fellows. And then they began going further afield. They ventured into the dining room and started hop-hop-hopping up the stairs. And I began to rage at the weather, and declared it *had* to stop raining, we *had* to build a chicken house *now*.

I called Olga Woodruff to tell her when Victor's christening was to be, and to invite her and her husband, Fred, to the party after the ceremony. I had got to know the Woodruffs very well during the school fight, they being ardently pro good schools, and it is their driveway in Four Corners we use as a parking lot for out-of-town vehicles. Olga said she and Fred would like to come to the baptism too, if that was all right, and I said of course, how good of them to want to.

"Darling," she said, being mixed-European and therefore calling people "darling" when that's the way she feels, "Darling," said Olga, "I do hope you have some sunshine for your picture. You must line up your entire family, Longin seated in the center of the front row holding Victor, you standing demurely—"

I hooted. "What a multitude!" I said. "We'll need one of those panoramic cameras—"

"For your flock—"

"Flock, nothing," I said. "That's for sheep. *Herd.*"

"Tribe!" said Olga zestfully. "Of wild Indians!"

"Horde of barbarians!"

"Galaxy!" she cried. "Galaxy of stars!"

On this we parted, with mutual expressions of esteem. I had

scarcely separated the squabbling children more than twice, and reefed Mary Lee back into the house, wiping up the mud behind her, and told Kitty to help me ram half a dozen towels under the windows where the rain was coming in past the rotted frames, when the phone rang six shorts, and it was Olga again.

"Darling!" she carolled. "Larks—that's what you all are, larks! Now guess what are lots and lots of larks."

"A flock?"

"No no no!"

"Covey? Bevy?"

"No, darling! An exaltation! *An exaltation of larks!*"

I lived on that for days.

Victor was to be christened on Sunday the 27th of June. Ellison and Jules were godparents, and the ceremony was at one o'clock in the old St. Francis' church, the little wooden one where Longin and I had been married. We drove to the church through thunderstorm and hail, and Longin had to remove a fallen tree from the road.

It was a beautiful baptism. Victor in Ellison's arms kept reaching for the priest's hand, and for the gilt-edged Bible, and for the candle. The salt of wisdom made him cry (as who, indeed, does it not?) and then shortly the priest was bidding him, "Go in peace, Victor Robert." Mary Lee tugged at my hand and whispered, "Our blessed baby," which made me blink back tears of joy. Then away we went, the Woodruffs and the Alfonses and the Coughlins and the Ambroses, to what was to be a real Polish christening party, in spirit anyway if not in detail.

Longin and I may not have as many friends as we might have, had we been able to "put up and shut up" for twenty years; but those friends we do have—oh, they are true blue, twenty-four carat, sixty-inch wool, and we invited them all to Victor's baptismal blowout. We had planned to have a buffet on the lawn, but it was obvious Sunday morning that any such plan would result in rain-soaked food and drink. Our house could not stand up under the numbers coming, so Longin and Patrick swept out the hayloft, which was empty as it was still too rainy to have done any haying.

They arranged benches around the room, of planks on cement blocks, and they put the dining-room table at one end. I had baked a ham and two small turkeys, and fixed about a bushel of potato salad, and an aspic, and there were several kinds of home-made pickles (recipes borrowed from neighbors) and two cakes iced in white with pale blue frills, and lots of iced tea and hot coffee. Serving all this was no problem at all. When folks began arriving, about two o'clock, the women proceeded to the kitchen and carted everything up to the barn. And afterwards, I didn't wash a dish. Kitchen clean-up courtesy the company (Vermont cliché).

The Meteses could not get away from New York, as they had hoped, and so with no Meteses there was no music; but except for this rather serious flaw, the party proceeded without a hitch. There were mobs of children whizzing past as briefly and unex-pectedly as shooting stars, and then the men began competing with demonstrations of strength and agility, chinning themselves on the rafters and even hanging therefrom by their toes. This was before the weather cleared and before we opened the jugs of wine after the ball game. Victor refused to nap, and I carried him out to the celebration, and he was passed from lap to lap, and so he was there to hear Rowena make a speech in honor of Longin's new citizenship, and present him with a picture of the flag, the gift of his former associates on the Citizens' Committee. And Fred Woodruff read a fine passage from Anya Seton on new life in a new world, and we all rejoiced with Longin.

The last of our guests had just left, about nine o'clock, when Father Ready came to call.

Father Ready said he had been in touch with the man in charge of all state institutions, and had got him to say Mikey's case should be taken care of at once. He urged us to finish about Mike without delay, and spent some time telling us what awful things had happened when people simply didn't do what their minds told them they must do, because their hearts wouldn't let them.

We explained we were hurrying, although it might not look that way.

"It was February before we could get up to Brandon," Longin said, "to look the place over, and have Mike tested. He passed their requirements with flying colors. They think he's about eighteen months old, mentally. And then we had to wait for their social worker to come—"

"That was really something, Father!" I said. "Talk about fine-tooth comb and pocket magnifying glass! You should have heard her. She had to get all about Mike's background, of course, and for some reason she seemed very surprised that my mother and father both graduated from college, and Grandpa Mather too. And when I told her that my brothers both made Tau Beta Pi, and Bruce and I Phi Beta Kappa, and Bob went to West Point, and his brother also, she kept shaking her head and saying, 'Amazing, amazing!' I got the idea she'd always thought mental retardation purely hereditary. Anyway, the next thing she said was, 'And in Vermont there is the highest rate of mental retardation in the United States!' I got to thinking we probably hadn't helped any by moving here—we probably raised it—one out of eight."

"What do you think of the school up there?" Father Ready asked.

"Not bad," Longin said. "Out in the country, not all fenced in. Personnel seems well trained, and there are new buildings."

"They need more," said Father Ready with a sigh. "They're still very crowded."

"I think that's what's taken so long," I said. "The children are grouped according to their mental age, and naturally children as young in mind as Mikey can't stay at home, so Mikey's group is the most crowded of all. But just this week we got word we're to bring him. I guess we have you to thank for it."

Father Ready rose. "Good," he said. "Let me know if you need me further."

When he had gone, I said, "What an absolutely awful conversation. All those frightful examples . . ."

"In his odd way," Longin said, "Father helped."

"Yes," I said thoughtfully. "I don't feel so bad about Dad and Bruce, do you? They don't say anything, but their disapproval sticks out a mile."

"They couldn't take care of him for twenty-four hours," said Longin shortly. "Not now. He's nearly as tall as I am, and I swear sometimes he seems as strong."

I wanted to talk about something else, anything else. "It was a good party, wasn't it?" I said. "What a marvelous place for a whoopdedo the hayloft is! Let's have a party there every year, before haying, what do you say?"

"A christening party?"

"Idiot," I said, and was able to laugh.

The following day, Monday, we went into Woodstock to discuss the affair first with our lawyer and then with the judge who would be the one to handle the business of our signing Mikey away, which we had to do, sign away all control over him, all our rights to him as parents, everything. He was to become a "ward of the state"—the only way he could be admitted to a state institution, even though we would contribute to his support. So we went to talk to the judge, who proved to be a fragile little dried-up leaf of a man about eighty years old, wearing a hearing aid, an immaculate white suit, and a keen and joyous eye. He was most kind. He didn't bother with any of the routine phrases so many people feel called upon to express. He took it for granted we knew that he knew how it was with us; and he explained there would be no formal hearing with lots of witnesses, all we needed to do was to let him know when we would be passing through on our way to Brandon, and stop in with the necessary papers from doctors and town officials, and we would sign and he would sign, and that would be that.

This discussion took place between the judge and me alone in the judge's chambers. The door—a very tall double door recently painted a charming pale green—was discreetly closed. The judge then tried to open it, but it appeared stuck. To my alarm, he began to hurl his aged bones against it, and I begged him to stop, to allow me, being of a construction and bulk more likely to batter

[212]

down a door. *No,* indeed. Wouldn't be chivalrous. The doors suddenly gave way before his eighty-five pounds, and he plunged into his secretary's office.

"Well well well!" he said briskly. "For a moment I thought we'd be leaving via the window, like an eloping pair!" And he chuckled gleefully.

As we went down the courthouse steps, I said, "Longin, did you ever notice, when something tragic is happening, how farce keeps butting in?"

"I have noticed."

We got into the jeep and started home. "I remember when Bob was going overseas," I said restlessly. "We were living in Elizabethtown, Kentucky, and I was getting eggs from a farmer, a sweet old man who used to bring them around to the house, and so when Bob got his orders I told this old farmer not to bring me any more eggs. And he said, 'So your husband's going overseas? Say, that reminds me of a story. There was this man who was a-dyin', and he says to his wife, "Honey, promise me one thing. Promise me that after my funeral you'll drive to the cemetery with my mother in the same car with you." And his wife wipes her eyes and says, "All right, I promise. But I tell you one thing, it's going to spoil the whole trip!" ' "

Longin reached over and took my hand in his, and we drove that way, hand in hand, as long as we were on the blacktop.

That evening we took Mike to Windsor for two doctors to see, so they could sign the required certificate. Mikey did his very best to please them, nodding his head vigorously to everything they said, and finally offering them his hand to shake. They were both visibly upset. "Such a handsome boy," one of them muttered. "How awful."

And on Tuesday Ellison and Rowena went with me, to act as witnesses when I took a petition of admittance to the "Town Fathers," as Longin calls them, for their signatures. I knew this was strictly routine, that I was not asking them for any favors, that it was their job to sign; but it was a painful experience just the same.

One of these officials led the way into his parlor and lowered his bulk into a chair and hitched at his trousers. "You goin' to take him up there yourself?"

I said I was.

He sighed. "Wal, I hope he don't carry on too much. I had to drive a kid up just a couple of weeks ago—nobuddy in the family would do it—and my God, how that kid screamed and cried. Could hardly drag him to the car. It was pitiful. Lord, all the way —it must be all of seventy miles over there—all the way he hollered and cried and begged me to take him home again. Pitiful," he repeated, unscrewing his pen and slowly inscribing his name.

We took Mike to Brandon on Friday, the first of July. Everything went smoothly, the pause in Woodstock to sign the final papers, the collecting of a sheriff in Brandon (you are required to arrive escorted by a sheriff), and the final parting, handled with infinite finesse by the school's personnel. While I went in to have a talk with the doctor in charge, Mike went with Longin and a matron over to his dormitory. That was the last I saw of him that day. There was no scene, and no chance of a scene. When Longin said good-bye to him, all Mikey did, Longin said, was to wave at him indifferently and wander off to play.

All the way home my most intense emotion was relief, utter, complete, shameless. It was over. It was done.

Mike was not in the car . . . I did not have to ride twisted in the front seat in order to keep an eye on him continually, lest he impulsively strike at one of the other children. He was not left at home . . . we would not return wondering whether there had been any close calls: was anything smashed, was Mikey himself all right, was he, indeed, *there?* And supper would be different, and the night would be different . . . no longer watching for a tantrum, no longer listening for the sound of sobbing, bitter and lonely.

Oh, things would be different, all right, and for a while we would feel guilty because we felt so relieved. But we would get over feeling guilty. It would take time, but the time would come, I knew, when we would be able to accept everything the doctor had said.

"You know he is not happy with you," he had said. "He cannot understand your world. To stay clean, not to grab other children's toys, not to hit them—to you these are very simple rules, to him they are bewildering. He would not only be safer, he would be happier in an environment geared to his level. . . ."

In time, I thought, I will really believe this, and then perhaps I won't feel this sensation of abnormality, as if I have just hacked off a diseased arm.

"You've come to the end of the road," Longin said abruptly. "You've been on it ever since Mike was born, and you've been trying to escape from it ever since. Every side road you came to, you took, but they all led back, and here you are, no way out but this. You have to cut him off."

"That's what I was just thinking," I said. "No miracle drug. No wonder cure."

And I was aware of a strange feeling of gratitude. Bob had not had to live through this day. He had not had to take his first-born son and leave him in a shelter for the feeble-minded.

When we got home we found that the two roosters were out again. William and Fred, the Notorious Ghoul, so named because he found pleasure in watching executions of chickens destined for the freezer, were in the barnyard keeping everyone at beak's distance. Fred was not as ferocious as William, even if he did enjoy the sight of blood. William would go into the barn and drink the milk from the cats' dish, keeping the cats at bay until he was through. Once in a while, if in a mellow mood, he would allow them to drink with him.

We caught the roosters and tossed them into the temporary corral we had made for the rapidly growing younger flock.

"I thought you said you clipped their wings."

"I did clip their wings," Longin said. "Haven't you seen how they climb out? They just walk up the chicken wire."

There was some kind of a disturbance going on in the little hut we were still using for a chicken house. Longin went in to investigate, and I heard him laugh. "You think *you've* got troubles!" he

[215]

said, emerging with a half-grown chicken in his arms. "Look at this poor fellow—what a dilemma!"

The chicken had one end of a piece of string caught around his foot, and the other end was in his mouth, and he was eating away at it, shortening the string, hauling his foot towards his mouth. Longin untangled the string from the skinny toes, and reefed the remainder back out of the gullet. He swung it before the critter's beady eyes. "Observe," he said, "that this is not a worm."

Kitty and Mary Lee came in from the meadow, their arms full of flowers. "We picked these cock-eyed susans for you," said Kitty. "To make you happy again," said Mary Lee with her shy smile.

Now in July we began to have short intervals of bleary weather when the sun shone halfheartedly, and in desperation we began haying. It was often touch-and-go whether or not we'd get the hay in undamaged. When the grass is first cut, it doesn't matter so much if it gets rained on, but when it's just about to be raked, or has been gathered into windrows, and then gets wet, not only are lots of the nutrients lost (which means more expensive grain must be fed during the winter), but the hay is less appetizing to the cows, and they'll pick it over in a choosy fashion, and waste a lot of it. If it gets rained on too often, it'll rot, and be good for nothing but compost. This year, blackened windrows and rotting bales were to be a common sight.

This was the year the bridge was down, you may remember. Ordinarily, with the weather so uncertain, we would have hired some one to bale our hay, as in this way getting it off the field and into the barn could be greatly speeded up. But no one would bring his baler over the six-mile-long detour. Nor did we dare wait to borrow Clifford's hay-loader. Longin sent me to an auction of a dairy farmer going out of business (there were a lot of such auctions in 1954) while he stayed at home to rake up the hay ready for the loader I had orders to buy.

Clifford declared he was going to get a baler if he had to mortgage Teddy, the dog, and he did get a baler, and after that we all were able to hay at top speed. As soon as Clifford would finish baling, Lloyd would bring the baler over the hill and Longin set to work with it, while Pat and Chris went down to help gather in the Bests' bales. By the time their hay would be in, ours would be baled, and if the weather looked threatening, as it always did, the Bests would help the boys help Longin rush ours into the barn. My job was to drive the truck, which we had bought second-hand for $200, complete with the most temperamental clutch that ever came out of Detroit.

I wasn't promoted to ride the tractor until this past summer, and I would like to let all you housebound housewives in on a little secret. Mowing the hay, or raking it, is just two jumps this side of heaven. The weather is warm, the sun is shining, behind you the thick grass falls in rich abundance, or tumbles in a continuous, fragrant roll, and all the while the tractor is roaring so you are cut off from your usual distractions, and you can ride and ride and ride, and think all the aimless, dreaming, drifting thoughts you've needed to be thinking for a long time. . . . Don't be sorry for a woman you may see riding a tractor. She's AWOL from housework and she's *loving* it.

There was one time that rainy summer when we had nearly three hundred bales down and a huge thunderhead was menacing us. The Bests and the Meteses both were there, Vivian driving their truck and I ours, Marilyn stacking bales for her and David for me, the boys and Clifford and Longin loading bales onto both trucks, and, in the barn, the Metes boys unloading. On the outskirts of the field, Kitty was stationed to keep Mary Lee and Victor safely out of the way. We were unloading the last truckful when the rain began, and not more than twenty bales got damp, and they dried quickly the next day when Longin carried them out again into the watery sunshine.

It was my feeling that if every other dairy farmer in the U.S. went out of business, Longin would still be at it, stubborn, determined, cussin' the weather, the government, the cows, but come hell or high taxes, he*would*farm*for*a*living. "Though nobuddy in his right mind goes into the dairy business," Clifford told us gloomily.

When we couldn't hay, Longin and I finished up the new chicken house. We built it in the northeast corner of the barnyard, where it has the most magnificent view of the New Hampshire hills of any of the buildings on the farm. Or would have, if we had put a picture window in it. Which we did not.

Our chicken house was not large, designed only for about seventy-five laying hens. We didn't plan to go into the poultry business; we just wanted to be able to raise our own chickens to eat, because our chickens would grow at their own rate, not speeded up by any high-octane capsule stuck in their neck, and we would not feel like a guinea pig when we ate them. We wanted, also, to have our own eggs; not that anything has yet been devised in the way of tampering with the insides of a store-bought egg, but there is a striking difference between the taste of an egg "strictly fresh" in the store and an egg laid this morning. If you don't believe me, I'm sorry for you, because you must never have eaten an egg laid this morning. I didn't know what *fresh* means, either, until I first ate an egg from our own chickens.

That's the trouble with living on a farm. It has spoiled us. We can't stand store-bought eggs, or store-bought milk—imagine, we say, milk with cream so thin you can't whip it! No wonder half the children in school, poor little town-raised kids whose taste for milk is conditioned by the chalky stuff that passes by that name in waxed containers, sometimes all glopped up with chocolate or otherwise not left alone, just to be milk—no wonder these children say, "No, thanks, I don't want any, I don't like milk."

How do they know? They ought to try it some time.

While the boys acquired the habit of polishing off a couple of quarts of milk apiece every day, we were all getting spoiled in other ways, too. With all those eggs on hand, I got to making my own mayonnaise. And ice cream. And custards. We raise our own beefsteaks by selecting the cows whose daughters we would not wish to keep in the milking herd and breeding these cows to a Hereford bull. We have veal when we keep the little bull calves for a few months. Our pig, having dined on our leftovers, winds up the most succulent pork, and savory bacon and ham, and delicious homemade sausage seasoned with our own home-grown sage, carefully dried, only the leaves saved, never a stem. I render the fat into lard, and this, I discover, being lard as it comes right from the pig, makes the most toothsome biscuits and pie-crust, so light, so flaky, so flavorful, that naturally I have stopped buying prepared mixes. I've stopped buying mincemeat, too. Homemade mincemeat is of such spicy goodness someone ought to write a sonnet to it.

I suppose I've got myself into a worse fix than that poor chicken involved with the string on his foot. There seems to be no end to the work I can cause myself. But you know what? We know what it means—"food like Grandma used to cook." It wasn't just youthful appetites that gave Grandma her reputation. Of course she was a good cook—but what she put on the table was *food*.

So do we. Peas picked while still young and tender. Tomatoes with the sweetness of sunshine in their deep red globes. Fresh leafy lettuce, green beans so slender they're the size of a pencil, swiss chard and beet greens and kale picked *young*—when they get the size of what you see on the supermarket shelf, we feed them to the chickens. Corn—oh, I could grow lyrical about our corn. I get the kettle to boiling and then I take a couple of the children and a bushel backet and we pick, and husk, and into the water for never longer than six minutes. Or we all gather up at Meteses' and sit around talking and maybe singing and wait and wait until the fire has burned down so there are lots of white-hot ashes below the grate, and then we roast the ears right in their husks, and then, while the evening light fades from the sky and the stars begin to appear, one by one, we eat and we eat and we eat. . . .

All the extras of all these things I put in the freezer, or, in the case of tomatoes and some of the fruits, in jars in the cellar. I try to put up enough to carry us over from one harvest to the next, which means at least two quarts of vegetables and one of fruit for each day. By this time our fruit trees were doing very nicely, in spite of the fact that I had become too busy to spray them. I always make time to prune them, however, because I get such a savage pleasure out of pruning anything. The classic time for this type of work is, I believe, in late winter, but I don't care to work in drifts six feet deep or in winds boasting it's ten below zero, so I prune the trees whenever I get around to it during the spring, and they don't seem to mind. The second year we were here Longin plowed up the orchard and planted rye, which he harrowed under and then planted a mixture of grasses rich in clover. Since then about all we have done for the trees is, during the summer, to dump where the feeder roots must be all the "gushy-gushy," as Victor calls the manure from the milking parlor. It's true our apples don't look like the pictures in the nursery catalogs, and they seldom are much larger than a tennis ball, but they certainly pack a wallop when we bite into them. It isn't that they're sour, they're not; but they give my taste buds such a jolt tears spring to my eyes.

So we have apples, and cherries, and pears and plums from our own trees. We have strawberries, too. By standing with my head on a level with my ankles for a total of approximately a hundred million years, I had planted one hundred strawberry plants in 1952, which were five hundred strawberry plants in 1953, which were, or seemed to be, several thousand by 1954, and once planted needed constant weeding, and constant transplanting, and, during the season, constant picking of the berries. By 1954 we had all the berries we could eat, and I froze several dozen quarts, and made jam, and offered plants to people, and even berries. Longin said that if ever he had a spare hour or two, he would haul me some sawdust from the mill, and this would help keep down weeds. Ellison suggested we get a goose, as she had heard geese like weeds but not strawberry plants. I said no. I said we already had cows that think they are deer, and cats that think they are dolls, and a dog that thinks he's a wildcat, and roosters that think they are tigers. I said with our luck with animals we would inevitably get a goose that preferred strawberries to all other forms of flora. I went on weeding.

There are secret spots in the woods where the blackberries grow thick, and the children bring home quarts of these, for which I pay them ten cents a quart. They earn it. Blackberries grow in the most tangled part of the woods, where the lumbermen have been, and where the branches, left behind to rot, make traps for children's feet.

There are raspberries growing wild, higher on the slopes than the blackberries, in the pastures now going back to the forest, and in the hide-and-seek sun and shade of the apple orchards. There are black caps, too, as we call the black raspberries. There is a rumor that there are wild blueberries on the ridge across the valley, on those steep slopes where sheep were pastured nearly a hundred years ago, where still the soil is too thin for pine seedlings to find a foothold. We have not yet gone to see if this rumor be true, because for picking blueberries you have to be young and agile as a skier, and for this I am not yet young enough, though I have hopes.

By now, you see, I really was a Reformed Smoker. Shortly before we took Mikey to Brandon, I realized I had stepped up my consumption of tobacco to close onto two packs a day. All of a sudden it seemed I could go on smoking or I could go on breathing, but it wasn't likely I could do both, not much longer. I chose to breathe in this life and leave the smoking to the next.

I went out to the barn and handed Longin my half-emptied pack. And then, having read a book on how to stop smoking—it says *pamper yourself*—I leaped into the jeep and went into town for that very purpose. I bought a bottle of muscatel and a bottle of good sherry, these mostly for me, and a bottle of rum for Longin, whose nerves, I had a feeling, were going to be in for some punishment. Then I bought a copy of E. B. White's *The Second Tree From the Corner*; though I don't think books are luxuries, having time to read them is. And then I returned home quite tipsy with good intentions.

And I haven't smoked since, except once. That was the evening that Lefty and Mr. Scott had words, after one of the school meetings, and I had gone outside and bummed a cigarette from Rowena, and it had made the whole world rock, and my insides, too, and I loathed the thing. Then it was that I realized that I was indeed a Reformed Smoker.

Let me not deceive you. It wasn't easy. At first I thought I couldn't live through the day without one. Or that Longin couldn't live through the day with me. There came a time when he remarked over his newspaper, "Listen to this, will you. It says here Vermont is the easiest state in the U.S. in which to get away with murder. Usually gets written off, it says, as suicide or natural death." And he looked at me thoughtfully.

I said, "Who says so? I mean, how do they figure which suicides or natural deaths are really murders?"

But just about then, anyway, I found myself feeling better and better, in spite of the schools, in spite of Mikey going away, in spite of a work load that, if I did it for money, would be downright illegal.

There is this about having lots of children. They do get older. The boys had by now been able to grasp the idea that all play and no work makes Jack a damned spoiled brat, and they really pitched in and helped. They weeded the corn and picked the peas and brought in bushels of beans. Kitty and Mary Lee and I sat in the shade of the maples and shelled peas. Mary Lee did quite well for a going-on-three little girl, and Kitty directed our work, urging me on to greater achievements, and talking, talking, always talking. I think in some obscure way she derives her energy from her tongue.

Sometimes the Meteses came down, and while their boys helped Longin with his building projects, Rozeta and I shelled, shelled, shelled. When the Musats came to visit them, Eleanor joined us around the overflowing bushel baskets, and we fixed green beans, and wax beans, and picked over heaps of swiss chard, and debated what to do with all that summer squash.

We bought a second freezer, and soon both freezers were

[222]

nearly full, and I grew worried. "We better start eating this stuff or I don't know *where* I'll put the corn!"

Patrick, passing through the workroom in time to hear this lament, let drop the remark, "Now *that's* the kind of problem I like to have!"

Longin was finishing up his milk house according to specifications from the creamery. The creamery is the link between the farmer producing the milk and the consumer drinking it. It is the creamery which sees to collecting the milk at the farm, either by trucks which it owns, or by negotiating a contract with a separate transportation firm; but it is the farmer who pays the cost of this transportation. "Handling charges" are deducted every month from his milk check. Once the milk reaches the creamery, it is weighed, and the amount recorded in the farmer's account, and it is tested for bacteria count and butterfat. Too many germs, and out it goes, and the farmer is notified something is wrong somewhere, he better find out where, but quick. If the butterfat is too low, the farmer's base pay, figured on milk with 3.7 butterfat, will suffer a deduction. The amount of butterfat over 3.7 is recorded, too, and the farmer gets paid for this. All this is called "shipping milk," as a contrast to what we were doing with ours: drinking as much of it as possible, selling what we could to our neighbors, and pouring the remainder into the pig trough. Because Longin couldn't get his milk shipped. There was a surplus, said the creamery, and in order to "maintain the price" they were not accepting any new shippers, not before fall, at least.

Well, I could understand all that. Law of supply and demand, and all that sort of thing. Too much on the market, too low a price. Only thing I would question was the use of the word "surplus." *We* had a surplus on the farm. We couldn't use all the milk we had. But a surplus throughout the country? Nonsense! Not as long as there was a single child with poor teeth for lack of calcium, not as long as malnutrition continued to disguise itself as "nervous breakdowns" or "inability to nurse the baby" or "heart trouble" or "fragile bones" or any of a number of similar conditions that are a downright disgrace in this supposedly rich coun-

[223]

try. Not ship milk because too much was being *produced*? How stupid can they get? I fumed. It's just that they don't sell enough. People don't drink enough.

"By fall things may be better," said Longin, installing a milk cooler (secondhand) and a milk-can rack (secondhand). "By fall maybe enough dairy farmers will have gone broke, we can get into the creamery."

"There's a definition of 'better,'" I said with a sneer, "for which I would not care to be responsible." But I got busy and helped him paint the milk house a classy barn red with neat white trim, matching the barn. It made a pretty picture when we were done. Nothing missing but the milk truck . . .

And then something truly wonderful happened. I became a Selling Author.

I had gone into Windsor and, arriving at the grain store, I was told my husband had left a message for me to phone home. I did so. Said Longin: "You have a telegram."

My heart went thud thud thud.

"From somebody at *Ladies' Home Journal.*"

I shouted, "What does it say?"

"Just a minute. I knocked over the coffee."

I waited.

"Now where is it, I had it right here," said L., that devil.

"Longin Ambros, you read me that telegram!"

And he did. Deciphered, it meant that, after seven years of yarns going forth and coming back like boomerangs, I had finally made my first sale, and to the *Ladies' Home Journal,* and for eight hundred and fifty cool, sweet dollars!

The grain man saw me solicitously out of the store, cautioning me to drive safely, asking me was I sure I had come with just the two children. I drove home with skyrockets going off inside me. Longin gave me a rib-cracking hug, and then I rushed to phone friends the great news. That evening they came pouring into the house, clutching bottles of bourbon (lest I, in my excitement, had lost all mental grip), and I sat there, grinning like a fool, my insides threatening to take flight into the wild blue, while many

[224]

and marvelous suggestions were made what to do with these sudden riches.

What we decided to do was this: Each member of the family was to purchase something special he had long had a hankering for, and the rest would go into the fund for replacing the house. Naturally we did not consult Victor as to his wishes, his idea of a really good toy being my turkey roasting pan, on loan. Mary Lee and Kitty selected sister dresses, Chris a baseball mitt, Pat three woodchuck traps, and I a timer for timing to the second all the blanchings of the vegetables for the freezer. Longin said he didn't want anything. I said he was an awful wet blanket. Didn't he honestly want *anything*? Not even, say, a portable cement mixer? Well . . .

So Longin took his cement mixer into the barnyard and made ready to start his pole barn. This was to be a large structure along the north side of the barnyard, and there, as we had planned at the beginning of our year, he was to put his machinery and extra hay. Pole construction would be cheaper and swifter than conventional heavy foundations, he said, but cement should be poured around the poles to make them firm in the ground. And all this he proceeded to do.

I had already received my annual phone call from Mrs. Ferncliffe, from her wilderness retreat in the mountains of New Hampshire. "How are you, dear girl?" she would ask, each year some time in June, and I would reply, truthfully, that I was just fine, and then I would dig up whatever portion of her left-behind garden she wanted, and send it off to her. This year she wanted some of those orange-spotted lilies that grew tall and looked in the living-room window. So I was surprised to receive a second annual call, in August, and after her, "How are you, dear girl?" to which I said I was fine, and how was she, she said she was about to leave for California. I thought she was going for a visit, and commended her energy, and hoped she would have a good time, but no, she was *moving*.

"To California?" I said blankly, thinking that, after all, a whim is a whim, but *here* is Paradise.

[225]

"Yes, dear girl," she said. "I don't know what else to do. I am *besieged* by porcupines."

It took a bit of doing, she calling on a country line, and I receiving on another, but I did, at last, get the situation clear: Mrs. Ferncliffe was literally being eaten out of house and home by a large family of porcupines, gnawing industriously through sill and joist and floor board. I felt I could not only understand but forgive the move to California. Not a bit too far from such a peril.

Longin had had a brush with a victim of a porcupine. He had come up to the barn with a load of hay and had seen a strange animal in the calf pen. This animal was acting very oddly, swaying and moving slowly towards the calves, who crowded around it curiously. Longin thought the animal might be rabid, and might bite one of the calves, so he ran for his rifle and, taking careful aim, he shot between the calves' legs and struck the animal in the head. It turned out it was a raccoon, maddened by pain and hunger, its nose full of quills.

And I was feuding with a marauding deer. I had noticed the tops of my carrots were nibbled, and then broccoli leaves were chewed, and then—oh woe, woe!—the beet greens were gone, and the swiss chard decimated, and more of the broccoli, and then some of the lettuce, and the bean plants where I was leaving beans to ripen, for soup and casseroles, these too were being clipped off. All along the rows, there were the thief's footprints, so dainty, so carefree.

I raged at Butch, "Why don't you scare her away, you fool?" I strung metal discs on wire, and hung ripe old socks and shirts on the bushes, and applied for dried blood from the game warden, and spread this along the rows. In spite of all this, the deer came back again and again, just before dawn, we thought, although none of us caught sight of her then. Once, just at sundown, an elegant doe with the arrogant mien of a dowager in a fifty-dollar hat came sashaying out of the woods to survey the garden scene. The children and I were thinning the carrots once more, and were in no mood to be the subject of anyone's condescension.

"There she is!" Chris shouted, and hurled a rock.

"This is the limit!" I stormed. "Can't she even give us time to get into the house before she comes checking how much of her food supply we are swiping for ourselves?"

I complained to Vivian, who said we should phone the game warden for permission to shoot her. This was a jolly bit of news, and I phoned at once. The game warden came, looking very official in his forestry uniform, and he observed the bit-off stubs of plants, and listened to my lament that I "need this food for my children." He told me that he was giving us permission to shoot the deer, but we must, of course, shoot her in the garden, we could not just shoot any deer in the woods, on the chance it might be "our" deer. Then we must notify him immediately.

Now all this was said out in the open, in our garden, and we made no effort to lower our voices. And that was the last we saw of the deer. She did not come again, and we lost no more vegetables. But Vivian began to lose hers, and there were the tracks of the deer. Vivian, too, called the game warden, and he came and gave her permission to shoot the deer. And that, too, was the last that Vivian was bothered by a deer. At that time, you understand.

There is a tribe of Indians who aren't satisfied with the terms of the treaty they signed some time ago, and they are suing the State of Vermont for the return of, or adequate payment for, their hunting grounds. I am convinced that the wildlife around here is on the side of the Red Man. I expect any morning to wake up and find chalked on the barnyard fence: PALEFACE GO HOME!

CHAPTER VIII

Hawthorne Turner was very good with machinery, but not so good with fences. Consequently, his horde of Holsteins roamed.

They roamed into the Meteses' garden, first of all. I was driving home the long way round one day in June, when I saw, beyond where Rozeta had planted her iris, a row of big black behinds. There is nothing much sillier than a cow seen rear end to, particularly when she is grazing, so that all you do see is a couple of thin legs and a switchy tail and two slablike buttocks. There was a whole line-up of these, and then, suddenly, heads came into view, as the cows swiveled around to see who was coming.

I got out of the jeep and charged at them, bawling frightful threats. After a brief skirmish, they took off towards home.

Next they roamed into Alfonses' yard. And garden. And rosebushes. And barn. Ellison defended her homestead as best she could, shooing them with her apron, valiantly beating them off with her broom. For some reason they seldom bothered her when Jules was at home, but seemed to schedule their foraging expeditions whenever he was at work. How they knew when Jules changed shifts, Ellison couldn't imagine; but just let Jules start on the late shift, and sure enough, at two A.M. there would be a thudding and trampling and heavy breathing outside her window . . . Turner's cows again.

Every now and then they would come wandering down the road towards our lane, and we would chase them back. Once they mounted Meteses' porch and peered in their windows. Then they took to investigating Longin's hay, which he had planted on a field he had borrowed from the Meteses. Longin purchased a roll of barbed wire and fenced the field to keep the cows out.

Naturally, we did what we could to put a stop to this nuisance. All of us let young Turner know about it, every time his cows were out. He would say, sadly, that they just would go through his fences. Longin pointed out, not too politely, that other farmers were able to put up fences that did keep in cows. Not always, to be sure. Almost every herd will cause trouble in the fall, when the apples are ripe. But most of the time a good fence will keep cows fenced, provided those cows are fed, and provided the fence-posts are driven deep enough so that if a cow accidentally leans on the fence, the posts won't fall over.

Jules, being of a very kindly nature, offered to go and help Turner put up some decent fences. Turner thanked him, and said that just as soon as he purchased some barbed wire, he would let Jules know. And that was the last Jules heard of that.

The children told us one day when they returned from black-berrying, that where the fences were gone completely, Turner had stationed his wife in their little army-style jeep, and there she was to sit, on guard, and when the cows started to roam it was her duty to honk the horn for her husband to come and round them up. I suppose every now and then household chores kept her from her post, and then it was the cows went over the hill.

It is the duty of officials known as fence-viewers to look at the fences which divide one farm from another, and, in cases of dispute, to decide how much of the fence one farmer is responsible for, and how much the other. In this particular case, none of the fences in question involved Turner and Longin, because our land does not border on his. Furthermore, none of the fences (real or nonexistent) actually were on the property line. They lay well within the borders of Turner's open range, and for this reason the fence-viewers could not demand action on his part.

So we fenced our hay, but we did not fence the corn, which, this year, Longin had planted on another field borrowed from Jack Metes, because the field not only was large, of several acres, but also was surrounded by a stone wall well fortified by thick underbrush and young trees. Longin stretched barbed wire across the barways, and hoped these defenses would be enough.

The corn ripened, and Longin began cutting it, using Clifford's corn-harvester, and he brought it on the truck over the hill and along the lane by the orchard, and so to the silo, where, using his *own* corn-chopper (bought secondhand at another auction where another dairy farmer was going out of business), he blew it into the silo. He had harvested about a third of it when the Hungry Holstein Horde crashed through the hedgerow and, charging uncontrollably into this incredible wealth of food, demolished about two acres of the planting before Longin was able to drive them out.

Back along the road went the cows, Longin prancing behind them like an infuriated collie. The critters were in no mood to cooperate, and sought to escape this driver who was slashing the air with a poplar branch, and yelling and cursing at them. So agile was Longin in his anger, and so thick the brush and formidable the stone walls bordering the road, that the cows were forced to keep moving towards home, and could only cast backward glances of anguished frustration at the bovine paradise from which they were thus being unceremoniously expelled.

By the time Longin reached home again he was coldly furious. He called the town constable and wanted to know if there wasn't some kind of a law that would protect a man from this sort of damn nuisance. The constable came right out, and viewed the damage, and was miserable right along with us. Clifford went and looked at the trampled corn, and said it looked to him like two or three hundred dollars' damage. One thing we could do, the town constable said, was to sue Turner. Longin said he didn't want money, he wanted *silage*. Besides, the young fellow had a wife and children. . . . What to do? Well, we could corral the cows when they roamed, said the constable, and he would then come and impound them, drive them to the village, there to keep them, at a pretty sum per day, and Turner would have to bail them out. Maybe he would find this more bother than building a fence, in the long run. Corral those critters? we said. On our land? Near our cows? No, no, our cows mustn't be exposed! Couldn't we just shoot them when they hove in sight? No. Why not? Illegal.

While we were troubled thus by the twin horns of compassion and self-preservation, Turner announced he was building fences at once; there would never be a recurrence of such a disaster; he would come and help lift the mangled corn from the ground, he would try to salvage as much of it as possible. Oh, well, Longin thought helplessly, so we give the poor kid another chance.

That was in September. With the coming of winter, and of snow, we enjoyed a period of peace. Our enemies suffered some losses, we heard. A couple of cows fell into the trench silo Turner had dug, and there died, whether from broken neck or a simple desire to escape from the troubles of this world I do not know. At intervals the children would report another cow, dead from causes unknown, hauled off into the woods.

Longin had not, as he had hoped, been able to start shipping milk to the creamery in the fall. There was only this one creamery making collections up our way, and it was a cooperative, and could not cut off a member unless certain clearly defined regulations were not adhered to, and Turner continued to adhere to them. Longin must look further afield, and this he did, but without any success until sometime in February when he heard of a creamery in New Hampshire which would accept milk from Jersey cows, as this creamery was fighting for the market on the basis of superior taste. Longin said yes, indeed, he had Jersey cows; and a man from this creamery came out, inspected our setup, declared it exceedingly fine, but we could see how it is, we lived too far out for them to send a truck, just for us. Would Longin be willing to take his milk into Three Corners? Longin said he would. And so at last we were able to sell our surplus, not, of course, that we expected to realize any dazzling profit, hauling the cans in the jeep to Three Corners, five wintry miles away, there to meet the milk truck.

It was pleasant to find out what kind of milk Longin's cows were producing. Butterfat 5.6 . . . 5.7 . . . h'm, pretty good. But that was merely to the cows' credit, Longin said. What pleased him most was his bacteria count. Raw, 4,000. Raw, 2,500. (Pasteurized milk in the stores is permitted to have a count of 20,000.) Longin's milk, pasteurized, averaged about 300. H'm, *very* good.

So it was extra galling, early every morning, to see the milk truck whizz past our lane, on its way from Turner's to Bests'. There wasn't a doggoned thing we could do about it.

During March, when we were suffering our annual siege of the Late Winter Desponds, there was one incident which provided, in its odd way, a note of contrast to the general gloom. Longin and I went to visit Mike, and we found he no longer remembered us. He treated us with a kind of distant politeness, docilely exhibited his shoes so we could test them for size, and was indifferent to our leaving. It was a cause for real thanksgiving. He could not mourn for us, nor miss us, because he could not remember.

The grief of Mike I faced long ago. It will be with me as long as he lives, but its bite is dulled because I do not see him every day. I can think of him, not as he is now, his body so uselessly tall and strong, his mind crippled and stunted; but as he was when a little boy, when his body and his mind were matched, and early childhood bloomed in beauty on his face. Let us remember him this way, and now we shall drop this thread of our story, and it will not appear again.

Chris was still spending his days in the cellar of the town hall, which, though better lit now, had apparently had no change of air since school started in September. About an hour and a half of it was all he could take. Then he would be seized with stomach cramps, nausea and dizziness, and someone would phone from the town clerk's office, and I would drive after him, to find him stretched out on a couple of benches in the classroom. After an hour or two at home, his color would return, and he would again feel like living.

His teacher began suffering from similar complaints. One of her good friends suggested to her that possibly she was pregnant. "Huh, if I *am*," she retorted, "so is Chris—he's got the very same symptoms!"

Ellison called the health inspector and asked him to check for coal gas, but by the time he got there the weather had warmed up and the door had been propped open, and he could find no trace of anything lethal in the air. The teacher's wrist watch, about this time, refused to run, and the jeweler found its delicate works choked with coal dust.

I don't suppose that our air at home was actually a great deal healthier, because the new furnace installed just four years before, had acquired an uncontrollable habit of exploding, not once, not just a few times, but over and over again. Something was very much the matter with some kind of a timing device, which, when it wasn't working properly, caused the furnace to begin to hold its breath, until it couldn't hold it any longer, and then WHOOM! ! ! ! black greasy smoke would shoot across the cellar, the covers over the holes for stovepipes in the chimney would be blown out, black greasy smoke would fill the upstairs, and once again we would attempt, in spite of storm doors and windows, to air the house out so we could continue breathing. One time the furnace tried very, very hard to hold its breath, and it held it much too long; when it had, at last, to exhale, it burst itself, slightly, and needed to have its sides redone, here and there.

This was all very inconvenient. I had to wash the insides of the windows much more frequently than I would have liked, but I felt rewarded for my efforts when I saw how brilliantly the sunshine sparkled through the clean glass. Of course, it was hardly safe to leave the children in the care of a teen-age baby-sitter, in a house which might blow up at any moment. We solved this by advising our sitters to bring heavy warm clothing, and when we left for the movies we would turn the furnace off. I tried not

[233]

to think how our lungs must look like the inside of that stopped watch.

Naturally we sent for the plumber-heater man. Naturally Longin tried tinkering with the timer-device himself. No matter who fixed the timer, it wouldn't last. *Couldn't* last, the plumber-heater said. House shook too much, shook everything out of adjustment.

The house wasn't only shaking the living daylights out of the furnace, it was also visibly collapsing. Larger and larger cracks were appearing under the window to the west, just at the foot of the stairs; plastic putty had to be rammed in the crack by the front door, along the floor boards. Cakes baked thicker on one side than on the other, because the kitchen floor was giving way beneath the stove, and leveling the refrigerator became another of Longin's routine chores. If it weren't for the linoleum, I thought, I'd be cooking in the cellar. Nothing was holding up the bathroom but the pipes to the plumbing fixtures.

"We have got to *do* something," I would lament, "before this house comes down around our ears!"

"Nothing is holding it up but its pride," Longin agreed. "I will build us a new house the very first summer that I am not building a new barn or you are not having a new baby."

I sighed. "Now we have to wait another year. But early next spring we will move out into the barn, and get busy tearing down this house."

Of course we had seriously considered repairing the house we had. Pulling the old one down and building a new one seemed a very drastic solution, even to such problems as a leaking roof, crumbling walls, collapsing foundation, and floorboards rotting through. We asked a team of carpenters to inspect the place and give us an estimate, and they told us it would cost somewhere around a thousand dollars merely to replace the sills (but they couldn't sign a contract for the work, they said, because in these old houses "you didn't know what you'd run into"). Thanks, we said, for coming.

When I was considering buying the farm, one of its undeniable charms was the amount of tax Mrs. Ferncliffe had paid that year: thirty-three dollars. This reflected not only the tax rate, half what it is now, but also the appraisal, five hundred dollars. I didn't know there was such a thing as an appraisal value; it might have shaken me a bit to know that the farm which I thought such a wonderful buy at five thousand dollars was, to the cold and passionless eye of the local appraisers, worth no more than $2,000— which is about what a Vermonter would have paid for it.

I very soon became uneasily aware that something was wrong. It seemed to me that with every slap of my paintbrush the appraisal went up. And up. And up. By 1954, our taxes were $118. This year, unless something were done, we'd be paying over $225. Next year—I couldn't bear even to think about next year.

I know by now that it is disastrous to look prosperous in the country. The Vermont farmer who keeps a weather eye out for tax troubles will not, for instance, actually finish his silo. A few heaps of junk rusting here and there are well worth the eyesore they produce, as they give an air of mortified poverty to the place. No one in his right mind names his place. We at least avoided that booby trap. "The farm" it is, and "the farm" it shall be, not "Northern Lights" or "Rocky Ridge" or any other term of affection, not even "Our Achin' Backs" or "The Bottomless Pit."

The trouble with the training Army life gives a woman, it makes her an expert, if not looking like money, at least at concealing near bankruptcy. A gallon of fresh paint does wonders at lifting the morale—and one's appraisal. Books and magazines all over the place—an absolute necessity of life for Longin and me, who will read the blurbs on the boxes of cereal, if nothing else printed catches our eye—do seem to strike the appraisers as unusual interior decoration, and instead of indicating that we are fresh out of cash, no, they apparently hint, "These guys are *loaded*, brother —sock it to 'em!"

I'm just speculating, of course. I really don't know why we got it "socked to us." We were living on a farm without enough land to carry twenty cows, without a good supply of water, with no stand of timber, and with a house literally collapsing before the appraisers' eyes. It is true we had replaced the barn, chicken house, silo and milk house which had been here when the place was appraised at $500, and it is true we had painted the replacements a handsome barn red, with handsome white trim. It is also true that our place was appraised almost as high as a neighboring farm twice the size of ours, well watered, with good stand of timber, larger barn, two silos, and a house that neither leaked nor threatened to tumble down. Now why?

I really think it was this: we weren't "natives." Can anybody tell me any other reason why the two-acre piece I bought at the steep price of $100 an acre was listed not at the customary quarter its sale value, but at full purchase price? ("Sh . . . widder woman livin' alone . . . She'll not catch on . . .") In Hartland, where the tax rate is rumored to be the highest in Vermont, a little slip like that can add $25 a year to our taxes.

What really hurt was this: I didn't have to pay any tax at all, no poll tax, no property tax, until I remarried. Vermont so salutes the widows of its war dead. Bob, having died during the Korean conflict, and in the service of his country, came under this law. All I had to do was to file a statement by the first of April of each year that I was a war widow; but I could hardly file such a statement when I had not been told of the law. Not been told, that is, until *after* Longin and I married.

I thought this so raw that I asked the VA if there were any way I could get those taxes back. The VA was awfully sorry, but it couldn't be done. Ignorance of the law, etc. They really were *awfully* sorry, they said. It never had occurred to them the town officials would accept my tax money, and say nothing.

You know, I'd rather be like me, sitting duck for plumbers and carpenters, a chucklehead that pays the asking price of a farm without quibbling. Yankee shrewdness isn't always something of which to be proud.

Nineteen fifty-four was the year of the quadrennial appraisal, and the result for us had been a doubling of our appraisal of the year before, or nearly five times what it had been when I bought the farm, four years previously. We decided to protest.

The first step in a tax-appraisal protest is to appear, along with a whole passel of your fellow sufferers, at a grievance meeting. Longin did appear, and he pointed out that there is no land in Hartland worth $400 an acre, as they seemed to think that two-acre field was worth. (Unless, of course, someone is trying to sell it to the school board.) The valuation of this piece did come down a ways, but the appraisal on the house and the rest of the farm remained the same.

The next step was to appear before the Board of Civil Authority, which is just as formidable as it sounds. It's an assemblage of every town official one ever heard of, sitting in a kind of coil around the miserable taxpayer, who tries to make a convincing case out of a house they aren't looking at and some land most of them know nothing about. It isn't surprising when an appeal is turned down.

Grasp at one more straw. There's still the state appeal board, which consists of three or four outsiders, non-Hartlanders, who come and look at the place and see what they think. We decided we'd appeal, but we didn't have much hope. The whole matter would hinge, not on how our appraisal compared with that of similar property in town, but on whether or not the appeal board thought we could sell the place for the appraised value; and, no doubt, given some poor sucker from the city drunk on the scenery and used to land values back in civilization, we probably could. The fact was, alas, we didn't want to sell, we wanted to live here. We were willing to pay our share of the taxes; we simply didn't want to pay double our share.

The lister came to look at Clifford's cattle, and Clifford said, "What're you doing here? I thought Ambros was paying all the taxes for this road."

We thought so, too.

The appeal board was scheduled to come on a morning in early spring when there was a cattle auction in Woodstock that Clifford and Longin wanted to attend, some mighty fine Jerseys were going on the block, and each man figured he needed one, maybe two more good milkers. If I could manage by myself, they said, they'd go ahead in Longin's truck and I could follow in the jeep. I said I certainly could show the board of appeal around, I knew all the grim points about this place by heart. So off the men went, and soon the appeal board was here, and they couldn't have been more charming. My, what wonders we had done with the place. My husband had built that barn himself? Marvelous job! We had put up the silo and chicken house—I had helped—why, we were a couple of pioneers, we were! Splendid, splendid what youth and courage can accomplish!

My heart sank. I showed them the cellar and obligingly pulled off a piece of rotten floor board from under the sink, and I showed them the water stains all over the living-room walls from the leaking roof, but I knew it was no use. I mentioned the fact we didn't have water and hadn't been able to get help with a pond because it was such a poor farm, but I could see I might as well save my breath.

I said good-bye to these gracious gentlemen and I went into the house for my pocketbook and to say good-bye to Mary Lee and Victor, who were staying with Emma, a fine cheerful woman from the village, and I went outside again to get into the jeep— and there were twelve black and white bandits in the strawberry patch!

In the strawberry patch!

"Get out of here, you damn beasts!" I screamed, and raced over to defend my precious plants, my babies, my little loves, over which I had slaved for eons of time, my back bent like a hairpin. They were mashing the plants into the soft ground with their damn huge hoofs, they were chomping on the green leaves with their damn teeth. "Get out of here, get out of here before I *kill* you!" I shrieked, racing after them, driving them in a wild morris dance, but I couldn't get them out, as soon as I slowed down, they slowed down to eat, as was only natural, for they looked starved.

I ran to the house for the shotgun. "Emma!" I gasped, "do you know how to load this?"

"No," she said wisely.

I seized the phone and rang the Turners. Poor Mrs. Turner was the one to answer, and she got a blast in her ear.

"I want to talk to your husband!" I snarled, my fangs snapping.

"I'm afraid he's busy—"

"He better not be! He better not be too busy to get right over here and get his damn cows out of my strawberry patch!"

I raced outside again, and picked up a stick and pounded at one flank, and chucked a rock, which missed, and was just about literally frothing at the mouth when Turner came loping up on his horse.

"You keep these damn cows off our land!" I bellowed like a fishwife. "You hear? *You hear?* You keep them *off!*"

I don't see how he could have helped hearing me, unless he was stone deaf. But he gave no sign he had heard. He said not a word, nor even looked my way, which was too bad, because I must have been quite a sight, face purple and smoke coming from my ears.

The cows took off into Clifford's mowing, where they ran headlong, stopped and snatched some food, raced again, stopped, gulped more grass, all the while Turner on his horse was galloping and galloping after them. I got into the jeep and drove off.

I found Longin and Clifford at the auction, and Longin had bought two cows. He listened sympathetically to my story, but he could not keep a straight face when I told of not knowing how to load the shotgun.

"Okay, laugh," I said. "Very funny. You must enjoy Turner's cows roaming all over your fields or you'd have done something about it long ago. Well, *I've* had enough. I'm going to see a lawyer!"

"Sure, go ahead," he said "You see the lawyer and I'll bring the cows home and then we'll go ahead and lynch Turner."

I glared.

"I agree with you," he said. "Enough is enough and in this case it's too much. It's the last straw."

"Oh, berry funny," I said. But I went to see the lawyer just the same.

[239]

There was a very simple procedure we could follow, as it turned out. We could complain to the state's attorney, in White River, and he in turn would check and see if there were any grounds for our complaint, and if there were, he would warn Turner to keep his cows home, or else.

Or else what? I don't know. Just, *or else.*

I shouldn't feel too upset about complaining, I was told. That was one of the things we were paying taxes for.

That did it. I saw the state's attorney forthwith, and told him about the continual botheration of the cows, and the final catastrophe of the strawberry bed. The next day state troopers stopped at the house to say they'd checked and found hardly any fences at all, and they'd told Turner to build some, and also to feed his cows; and they hoped we'd have no more trouble. We hoped so too, and with fervor.

The seasons of our country year had now moved from Mud Season to Fishing Season, and would proceed, not through the conventional summer, fall, and winter of elsewhere, but on through the country's own: Planting, Haying, Harvest, and Hunting. Chris, emerging from his cellar classroom, began to look more like a boy and less like a stalk of blanched celery. On week ends he was up with the sun and would be gone all day, checking in at unconventional hours for food, returning to spend the darkening hours of evening digging more worms for the next day's fishing. He found a mysterious satisfaction in fishing that was hard to understand, as he very seldom caught anything at all, and his fishing rod had a way of coming to pieces in his hands, and his reel never worked properly. His hooks, too, became disembodied as he assembled his gear, and rematerialized themselves later in the sofa cushions or in the dining-room rug, with results not conducive to a peaceful home life. But Chris was a cheerful boy, and took all these contretemps with philosophical calm, and away he would go again, a couple of Band Aid boxes full of worms in his pocket, his rod over his shoulder.

One Sunday he took his bike, saying he thought he'd try his

luck in Lull Brook down in Three Corners, in the deep pool near Route 5. He didn't come home for dinner, but I didn't worry, as that was just the midday meal; probably hunger would bring him by suppertime. At six o'clock he had not returned, and I began to fret. What if Chris had been thinking of something else, and, riding along, had wobbled out in front of a car? I decided to take the jeep and go look for him. I went all the way into Three Corners. On my way home, I stopped here and there to inquire, and I took the long way back, up the valley and through the woods, but I neither saw nor heard anything of him. I got the supper and Longin went out looking. About seven-thirty, Gladys Farnsworth, on the lower road, rang on the line to say Chris had just passed her house and was headed home. She thought maybe I'd like to know. I thanked her, and shortly Chris and Longin drove in, the bike stuffed in the rear of the jeep.

"Well!" I said nastily, "I hope you brought a bushel of fish, considering how late you are!"

"I caught one," Chris said with a pleased smile. He brought forth from his pocket a poor little fish, very small and miserable looking.

"I thought the legal size is six inches," I said.

"This *was* when I caught it," Chris said stoutly. "Before it shrunk."

It was such incidents as these that bolstered my argument that perhaps I was not, after all, being completely selfish in wanting to stay where we were. I had had many long and soul-searching arguments with myself. What if the children were handicapped for life by the wretched foundation their education was receiving? Had I any right to live where I did, just because I loved our hill and our view and the maples and the orchard sloping up the hill, and the meadows Longin had brought back to good use, and the barn he had built and we had painted such a brave fine red, and our cows, year by year more cows, so splendid and healthy and fruitful? What might I be doing to the children, to their future, by staying here? I would worry myself with thoughts like these, until one day it came to me that the children, too, love the sweep

[241]

of the sky, and the privacy, and the wilderness that lies just beyond the stone walls, the wealth of trillium and ground pine and maidenhair fern, the deer in the thickets and the partridges and the blackbirds calling. . . . It came to me I was giving them something they will have all their lives long, I was giving them a treasure that nobody and nothing will ever be able to take from them: a real childhood.

I had gone down to Vivian's to borrow something, I don't remember what and it doesn't matter, and we were standing in her dooryard in the shade of the maples and were discussing how soon school would be over, wasn't it nice, the children would be home all day; and Vivian remarked that all the children had walked up from the school bus and were now down in the barn looking at their new bull, all except Chris, hadn't he gone to school? And I said, oh, yes, but then he was always the last one home, I didn't know why.

And then we both saw him, and it was apparent at once why he was the last one home every day. He came along the road from Red Gates', coming into view and disappearing again behind the clumps of hemlock, and then out onto the flat where the little brook crosses under the road and goes into the Bests' mowing. As he moved, he looked, looked all about him, first at a something by the side of the road, then at a something else perched on a branch. After a few moments, having reached the brook, he stopped again, and stood watching the water flowing, and then he began dropping something, twigs probably, into the water, and watched them move away. . . .

If I were a child, I thought, I'd remember such a walk home all my life.

Only a fool would have wondered why such a boy loved to fish, though he never caught much of anything.

You don't have to explain things like this to children. They know these things, though it is not easy for them to put into words. Patrick will go off with his gun and be gone all day and come back to report how many crows he shot at (hitting none), or where it was he went looking for deer (and saw none), and when

I'd say, "Was it a good day's hunt?" he'd say, "Well, *sure!*" Once he tried to say why it was. "Everything was so quiet. I sat down on this big log and everything was so quiet. . . ." He looked at me helplessly. "Boy, did I have a wonderful day," he said with a contented sigh, and went to put his gun away.

Kitty, who had been too young when we moved to Vermont to remember any other way of life, took all such things for granted. It struck her as perfectly natural and the only way, really, of growing up at all, to learn to ski at the age of four—"Come on, Mother, come on! You won't get hurt!"—and paddle in the brook at the age of five, and beg for a pair of ice skates, and learn to use them on the frozen pond at the age of six. Hills were for climbing, and by the time she was seven, a skinny second grader with flying red pigtails and muscles like steel springs, she thought nothing of hiking two miles into the valley, three miles up the hill on the north ridge, and five miles home again. "There are fox holes up there, Mother—Walter and Cathy and I found a fox hole and Walter says there are fox cubs in there and there *are*—I could smell them!" Being female, she loved words, and words poured from her as water from an inexhaustible spring, as she tried to trap, in the concreteness and everlastingness of human speech, the evanescent excitement of her days.

"We were jumping in Alfonses' barn! From the rafters, down into the hay! Oh, it was such fun—*way* up high, Mother, as high as this room! I jumped down ten or twelve times and I would spread my arms like this—" demonstrating—"and *sail* down!"

"Like a bird!" I said appreciatively.

"Yes! And do you know, it was *such* a jump, from *so* high up, that on the way down I had lots of time for *thinking!*"

When she came home she always came with armloads of flowers, in the summertime, lilacs from beside an old cellar hole high on the ridge, daisies and goldenrod and black-eyed susans from the orchard, wild apple blossoms and bunches of violets and columbine from the hedgerows . . . so much beauty everywhere, so much to see, so much to do, Kitty's days were never long enough to suit her.

She knew all the cows by name and peculiarities. "That Sapphire!" she would say. "So stubborn!" Or, racing into the house, "Mother! Iris is in heat again and Longin is awful mad! He says he's got to call the breeder again and if she doesn't start a calf this time we're going to have lots of beef this winter!" Like all farm children, Kitty found the business of the bull (or the breeder) and the cow and the calf not only perfectly natural but really the only way such things could be arranged, don't you think so, Mother?

Certainly, I say.

Late in the summer Kitty came to tell me that the cow Longin had bought in Woodstock in the spring had dropped her calf unexpectedly. "Down in the woods!" Kitty said. "Were *we* surprised! She didn't have any sign she was going to have that calf, bag wasn't awful big, or anything. My, such a *sweet* little calf!"

"Bull or heifer?"

"Heifer. *Real* nice, Longin says. What shall we name her?"

"How about Fern?" I suggested. "Since she was born down in the woods, you know. And her mother could be called Violet, being shy—what do you say?"

"All the other cows are jealous," Kitty said. "I guess cows must naturally like calves, don't you think so?"

"Naturally."

"The way *we* like babies, don't we? Girls and grown-up women, I mean."

"Of course," I told her, and felt all warm and womanly.

"I certainly am glad you're going to have another baby," Kitty said with a contented sigh. "I was big enough to give Victor a bottle, but this time I'll be big enough to give the baby a bath, don't you think so?"

"Well—" I said doubtfully. "Maybe we'd better wait and see. They wriggle a lot."

I was pleased that Kitty and the rest of the children were pleased there was going to be another baby in the family. Some of my friends were being just a bit tiresome about it. (Dear Prolific Melissa, they would write me.) I told Longin I thought it was

[244]

a shame that women who had had one, maybe two children themselves thought seven such an uncouth number.

"Tell 'em we're going to build a barracks once we get the new house built," Longin said. "Tell 'em if that isn't big enough, I'll add on a loafing pen."

I was hoping Kitty didn't get cows and people too much confused. That had been our trouble when first we came. I could remember feeling so sorry for cows in stanchions. "How would *we* like it?" I had said. And I had been pleased to see the literature giving expert advice had been all for the pen stable, injuries would be less, cows would be healthier, chore time would be cut down.

Well, what kind of cows those experts were acquainted with, I couldn't imagine now. Certainly not the kind of cows we had. Our cows, loose in their approved-by-experts pen stable, trampled not only on their own udders but on each other's, too. The more timid cows got the least to eat, the more aggressive cows ate too much and had a tendency to get sick. Some of the cows lived in mortal terror of Jenny, who, to defend her rank as chief, took to sharpening her horns to a stiletto point by scraping them on the cement wall of the stable. One cow, poor shy Violet, was afraid of every other cow *but* Jenny, and wished to spend all her time by Jenny's side, for protection, and in order to maintain this location, she caused a great deal of turmoil among the others. Chore time dragged on and on and on, because immense amounts of bedding were needed, and keeping the manure cleaned out meant trip after trip with the loaded wheelbarrow.

"Before I can possibly start the new house," Longin said, borrowing some of my hand lotion for Lilac's sunburned tits, "I have to change whole arrangement here. Put in stanchions, cement the floor. Otherwise I will go on spending all day doing chores, taking milk to the village, doing chores—there will be no time to work on the house."

The summer passed peacefully. I proceeded with my canning and freezing at a somewhat slower pace than usual, as the baby was expected shortly before deer season. Longin worked on his pole barn in between chores and taking milk to the village, and he also did the routine haying, harvesting the oats, and making ready to put the corn in the silo.

Just before the Meteses were to return to New York, we had a Chicken-Killing Bee. Longin set up an old door on a couple of saw horses, for a work surface, and he had a big kettle boiling over a fire. Grandpa Musat presided at the table, his sleeves rolled up and a very large apron tied around his lean middle, and an array of exceedingly sharp knives by his hand. Longin slaughtered the fifty chickens destined for the freezer, and as fast as he and the children could defeather them, Grandpa Musat removed heads and feet and insides. The little children then rushed the chickens into the kitchen, where I chilled them and wrapped them and put them in the freezer. Everything proceeded with splendid dispatch. The children enjoyed themselves immensely. They enjoyed watching the whole process, from the dramatic catch of the cocks, to the flapping of the corpses which have got the axe, right on down through the loss of feathers, extremities, and insides.

"Mommy!" Victor shouted, coming into the kitchen where I was involved with freezer tape. "Those chickens out there by the big hot kettle—they haven't any pants on!"

They do look awfully naked without their feathers.

Work on the new school additions was proceeding, too, though more slowly than hoped. They wouldn't be ready when school should start, so there would be a week or two extra vacation. The additions, jutting out behind the old schools, looked from the road for all the world like enormous woodsheds. Kitty, riding with Longin one morning along Route 5, looked back towards the Three Corners school, and began to scream with joy. "Oh, *look*, Longin!" she shrieked. "They have *windows*—did you see? I was afraid they wouldn't have any windows!"

So they did, along the southern exposure, a lovely row of windows with very little overhang of roof over them. When school started, Kitty, who was in one of the new rooms, said the teacher was being very fair. "We take turns sitting where the sun cooks us and gives us headaches," she said.

"Very democratic," I said. But the room *was* sunny. It is only fair to admit it.

Longin was harvesting his corn now, and everything favored him, weather, machinery working without breakdown, and his own cows not breaking out of the pasture to get drunk in the orchard. The work of filling his silo was proceeding smoothly, until one afternoon as he drove the truck back into the field and drew near the corn binder, he saw the tips of the uncut corn start to sway, and then through the stalks poked a number of black and white faces, followed by hollow-ribbed black and white bodies.

Cursing furiously, Longin drove the cows before him back through the corn, and onto the road, where, by a combination of frightful oaths and wild assaults with rope and branch, he sent them skedaddling for home. He trotted right along behind, and when he reached Turners', he cornered young Turner in the barnyard and delivered himself of whatever stock of frightful oaths he still had on hand. Turner waited until Longin had quite finished. Then he said in a friendly tone, "Say, did you ever hear anything from your uncles in Siberia?"

Theodore was born very obligingly late in October, and I returned home the day before Chris's birthday. The baby lay in his bassinette, his fair skin showing clearly the pale tracery of veins beneath its delicate luster. He curled his fingers around Mary Lee's thumb, his fingers so small and seemingly boneless, like fern fronds not yet unfolded. He looked so delicate, so fragile, it was hard to believe that in a few speeding weeks and months he would be racing about, shouting joyfully, hurtling himself against anything and anyone in his path.

Mary Lee gazed at him in wonder. "He looks like Jesus," she said.

For once we were to have a serene birthday celebration. I baked Chris a cake, and listened contentedly to everyone's plans for hunting season. The guns had been oiled and polished and inspected and tested; shells had been purchased from hard-saved allowances; licenses had been bought; and there was talk that, this year, Chris was old enough to go, too, particularly if he and Longin went together. The best place to go would be where they had seen that twelve-point buck during the summer. . . . No, no, *that's* no good, get over by that big old log, you know the one, yeah, and get there before daybreak, man, yeah! before daybreak, and just *sit* there until . . .

This kind of talk went on all day long, and much of the night, when the boys should have been asleep. The night before the season opened they could hardly sleep at all, and dawn came, and POW! POW! powpowpowpowpowpowPOW! echoed from the hills. It sounded, as usual on the first day of deer season, like a battlefield. Cars crept along our roads, with strange men in bright red hats peering out. Longin's and Clifford's cows were safely in the barn, and Ellison and I took to driving the children to the school bus. The boys went hunting, day after day, and Longin, too, once in a while when he could snatch an hour from his work on the pole barn. None of them so much as saw a buck. The school-bus driver, Kitty said, drove with a rifle by her knee, but she didn't get a buck, either. And so hunting season passed, without luck, unless, of course, you count luck the way Vivian and I do, all our menfolk through another season without accident.

Winter was coming, all right. The geese flew over, headed for Mount Ascutney and points south, and the bare fields from my window were as beautiful now that the year was dying as when the grass bent before the warm summer rains. Now with the leaves gone I could see on the ridge to the north where the stone fences follow every upward thrust of the land, and with the first light snowfall, there were the lumber trails and old, forgotten wagon ruts linking sugar bush to hill pasture to ancient cellar hole, each long-forgotten trail revealed by the whiteness of the snow against the greige-beige slopes of the hill.

Longin finished roofing his pole barn, with some help from Jules. The big panels of aluminum roofing were as slippery as a greased chute. Jules straddled the ridgepole and held onto Longin's ankles, while Longin stretched out on the panels and drove home the nails.

The weather grew colder. In the mornings, when I rose to feed Theodore, in the gray light I could scarcely make out the plume of smoke coming over Bests' hill, signaling that Vivian was up and starting breakfast. As the daylight strengthened, the mist began to drift down Lull Brook valley, the ghosts of George Washington's army, we had always called such a mist in my childhood. And then it grew too cold for mist, and the valley would be, instead, a glittering magical world of hoarfrost on every dead weed stalk, every twig and branch. Then came the snow, and the stone walls on the far ridges were buried from sight.

Now the wind sounded like an express train hurtling by, and we would awaken in the morning to see new drifts in the orchard, even higher than before. The days grew shorter and shorter, and then slowly, almost imperceptibly, began to grow longer. And the cold, even as in the old proverb, grew stronger.

Mary Lee stared out disconsolately at the white world.

"Will the trees get leaves again this year?"

I said, "Oh, yes, darling. They get leaves every year."

She said reflectively, "I wonder what they will be like."

I said, "Why, all nice and green. Just as last year."

"I know," she said. "But how will they look? I wonder what kind of *shape* they will have?"

"Why, the same as last year, darling. The leaves are the same every year."

"They are?" Thoughtfully. "That's nice!"

And then tragedy struck, one wintry morning, in Turner's dooryard. Turner's father, come to visit, suffered a heart attack and died in young Turner's arms.

Mrs. Turner informed me of this, over the phone, and said her husband would like Longin to come over. And Longin went at once, and returned to say he had agreed to care for Turner's cows while Turner went to his father's funeral. "He'll be gone a couple of days," Longin said, and added that he felt very odd, because the last time he had seen Turner he had been cursing him and all his ancestors.

He went over in the evening and Turner was to show him

which cows he was milking, how to use his milking machine, which was a different type from his own, and where the grain and hay were kept. Turner's arrangements were quite complicated. He had no water in the barn, and the trough in the barnyard would get frozen over, and the ice must be broken each morning so that the cows could drink. There was an iron bar handy for this purpose. The hay was fed to the cows out in the barnyard, too, in the mornings at the same time that they got their water. In the evenings, when the cows were milked (Turner milked only once a day), each cow received a coffee-canful of grain; but, as Turner had no silage, Longin didn't have to bother with that. He did have to spread the manure every day. Turner was in the habit of spreading his manure on his fields all during the winter, an excellent practice as there was thus no manure pile by the barn. Unfortunately Turner's tractor had a bale picker attached to it, and his crawler had a leaky radiator. Longin said he would bring his own tractor over, with which to pull Turner's manure spreader.

Longin returned home to say he thought everything would go smoothly. Only possibility of a hitch, he said, would be if the milk truck didn't make it one day. Turner's milk cooler was frozen, there were several inches of ice on the top, but there was a hole in the ice for the one can of milk which Turner was then shipping to go in.

"It'll go in all right," Longin said, "because the milk is warm then. But in the morning it's frozen into the ice. Turner's rigged up quite a gadget with which to yank it out, and there's another iron bar handy, in case it's needed."

"How many cows do you have to take care of?"

"About fifteen. Eight he's milking, two dry, a steer, and four or five little calves."

"Eight Holsteins?" I said, astonished. "And only one can of milk? They must be nearly dry—why does he bother?"

"He has to ship every day," Longin explained. "Creamery has threatened to cut him off if he doesn't."

When a week had passed, and Longin still was going over and

feeding and watering Turner's cows, and then coming home and doing his own chores, and his own day's work, and then going back to do Turner's milking, and then coming home again to do his own, I began to get distinctly annoyed. "Why doesn't he come *back*?" I said. "And why should you be the only one to help him, anyway?" "I'm not the only one helping," Longin said. "Jules comes over every night to feed and water the horse."

The next morning, when Longin went to turn the cows out for water and hay, he saw that the milk can was still there, frozen into the milk cooler. The truck had been there; there were the marks of its tires in the snow. Longin checked with the Bests and it seemed that Hammond, the regular driver, had a day off, and the replacement driver hadn't known how to get the can out, he'd told Clifford. Longin started putting in long-distance calls to try and locate Turner, to tell him to get back up here and fix the cooler and straighten things out with the creamery, since he'd skipped a day's shipment. But he couldn't reach him.

Late in the afternoon Longin went back to Turner's chores once again. Something seemed to be very wrong, because it was nearly ten o'clock by the time he returned. I was in the kitchen just finishing the supper dishes, as I had put all the children to bed before tackling them.

"Well, you're late," Longin said, coming in.

"Speak for yourself," I sighed. "What the dickens took you so long?"

"I was fixing that milk cooler. I had to, couldn't put the milk can in, otherwise. If he misses another day he'll be done for, for sure."

I thought to myself I'd have poured the milk on the snow.

"I'll just grab a cup of coffee," Longin said, "and then—"

He stopped short. The phone was ringing, on and on, the long long ring that means fire.

When it stopped, Longin lifted the receiver. After a moment, he hung up, and looked at me. "Barn's afire," he said, and my heart thudded sickeningly.

"Whose?"

"Scotts'."

"The *school director?*"

"Yeah." He looked at the clock, then back at me. "My God, I haven't started milking," he said.

"Scotts' barn—why, it's just across from his hired man's house!" I said. "That'll go too!"

Longin grabbed his jacket, rammed his hat with the fur flaps onto his head, and said, "Cows can wait. They may need every man," and he got into the jeep and was gone over the hill.

I finished my work, and put on my snowboots and my heavy coat, and went out into the night. It was bitter cold, and very still. I didn't need a flashlight, there was enough light from the stars reflected by the snow for me to see where I was going. I walked to the top of the hill, and now I could see the glow in the sky, and at its base a brilliant orange that might be flames. I was shivering with a primitive fear. A barn afire . . . there might be worse kinds of fires, but I couldn't think what. Barns ought never to burn.

There was a light at Bests', so I hurried down the hill and went in. Vivian was standing at her kitchen door, looking out at the glare.

"I hope they get the cows out," she said.

"Do you suppose they can save the house?"

"Depends on the wind."

"They ought never to burn."

"No," Vivian said. "Not barns."

After a while I started for home. I wanted to make sure our house was all right. As I climbed to the top of the hill, the light from the fire was less bright. It must be dying down, I thought, it's over now, whatever had happened.

There lay our house, silent and peaceful, the lights in the kitchen window streaming out on the snow. I stopped and looked around me, at the line of hills, whose slopes were familiar now, well known, even by the strange, unearthly light of a winter's midnight, and at our fields, asleep now under the snow, waiting for spring, and I knew them, all these fields, they were a part of

[252]

me now, because I had helped to gather in their hay. And there was our barn, a dark bulk beyond the house, where the unmilked cows were waiting.

What kind of a farmer's wife am I, I thought in sudden scorn, not to know how to milk those cows? There ought to be nothing I can't do, should the need arise!

As I walked on home, I realized I had said something to myself that was extremely important. *What kind of a farmer's wife* . . . That's what I was, a farmer's wife. That's what I wanted to be, a farmer's wife. Nothing better to be, I thought.

I reached the door just as I heard the jeep coming over the hill.

"It's under control, so I came on home," Longin said.

"Did they get the cows out?"

"Yeah, just in time." He went out to the barn and began getting his gear ready.

"You better show me how to do this," I said.

He shot me a look, and grinned. "Okay, but not tonight." With a clean cloth dipped in warm water, he began to wipe down Violet's udder. "Hill too icy to get up there with the jeep," he shouted above the noise of the milker. "Everybody had to hike up from the village, they were afraid cars would get stuck and block the way of the firetruck. Truck had to go up and down with drums of water from the brook. They packed snow against the house, looks like they'll save that. Barn all gone, and all his hay, and God knows how much machinery."

"What's he going to do now?"

"I dunno. Sell his cows, I guess." On to the next cow. "Awful thing," Longin said. "Awful, a barn fire. Makes you sick to look at it."

The cows, so large and so gentle, moved obediently from pen to milking parlor and back again. Overhead the mow was full of hay, and Jenny's newest calf was under the lamp to keep her warm, a heifer calf, at last, after three disappointments. Bluebell, we had named her.

"I don't think I could stand it," I said, "if anything should happen to this barn."

[253]

"I was thinking all the way home," Longin said, "about our plan to tear down the old house and build new. I was thinking we ought not to build in the same place. Barn, milk house, garage, house—like a chain, and the wind is always from the west. Too dangerous."

So now we are like Dad, I thought. Plan the new house so that, should it catch fire—

Longin unhooked the milker and sat down to strip Iris. "How about up in the orchard?" he said. "Better view, we could live in old house while we build new one, and we would be safer there. Barn would be safer, too, if house caught on fire."

God forbid, I thought.

I said, "I think you are a genius."

"Oh yah yah," he said, and scowled.

Turner came back, and regretted the state of his milk cooler. And then, with a gesture that quite overwhelmed us, he offered Longin first chance to buy his shares of stock in the creamery, as, he said, he thought he'd quit dairying.

Longin grinned. "I'll buy your shares," he said. "And rent your farm, and buy your last cow, if I have to, so I can ship my milk to the creamery. And then," he added, "I'll give her right back to you. Okay?"

There were a number of formalities to be complied with, to make everything legal, between the two men, and with the creamery. But finally these were all attended to, and our milk house was inspected, and Longin was told to flag down the milk truck the next morning.

Longin called the creamery in New Hampshire and said he would not be bringing his milk to the village any more. And then he took a cardboard box, and, in heavy black crayon, he made a sign:

WELCOME HAMMOND!

THIS WAY!

with an arrow pointing to the left. And in the morning he went out to the mailbox and popped the box over the post.

The children had not yet left for school when we could hear the roar of the milk truck as it came hurtling down the hill from Meteses', and then it turned in at our lane, and we all lined up outside to shout a welcome. The truck flashed by the house, its big red awkward body pitching and lurching over the uneven, icy ground, and Hammond the driver leaned out and waved.

This year, as February melted into March, we had so light an attack of the Glooms of Winter Dead that it almost passed unnoticed. Every morning we rejoiced in the jaunty arrival and departure of the milk truck, which sometimes occurred before dawn, first the headlights flickering across our bedroom ceiling, then the spirited crashing of the milk cans being stacked inside the van, finally the red lights blinking past, signaling to us the opposite, *Go, go ahead with your future, go ahead with your dreams.*

The snow went early, and towards the last of March Longin and I hiked up in the orchard to pick out the exact location for our new house. The day was cold; the wind bit through our jackets and the sun wasn't much help, ducking in and out of scattered clouds.

We stood not very much higher than the roof of the old house, but now we had a much better view to the east. We could see the sweep of New Hampshire hills, two—no, three—ranges of mountains against the horizon. And we would have to get used to this new view to the north—look, we can't see that barren spot from here, and isn't that tiny blob of red way up there, isn't that old Mrs. Perry's house?

It's not impolite to call her old, I thought, even if she does mow her own lawn and chop her own kindling. After all, she's ninety-seven.

Longin was pacing off where he thought the house should be. "Kitchen wing over here," he was saying, "and there'll be room for your salad garden between here and the stone wall," and I was looking at the barns and thinking that from up here the big barn looked best of all, the white crisscross trim on the door showing and the white line under the eaves . . . how proud we were of that barn, and already we have too many cows to put in it. And the old house, so small, much too many children to put in it. Too much food for the freezers, too many children for the house, too many cows for the barn and for the farm . . . *What good problems*, I was thinking, when Longin cried, "Listen! You hear them? The geese are back!"

I looked up. There they were, a thin line strung out like a wire against the gray clouds. The wind was driving them east towards New Hampshire; their line broke before its strength and re-formed, again and again. Their crying floated faintly down to us where we stood, our hearts bursting with an exultation we could hardly explain.

Where we stood . . . Beneath us, the ground rock-hard. Over us, the reckless birds back again, always every year back and back again, and so they had been coming forever. And so they would be coming, I thought, forever and ever, in spite of all the idiocies of inventive man.

I said, "I could live to be ninety-seven here myself!"

Longin should have been born here.

"I wouldn't mind to, either," he said cautiously.